विख्यात धावक
डाकू पानसिंह
ഗാസി ബാബയെ വധിച്ച സംഘത്തെ
നയിച്ചത് മലയാളി ഐ.ജി.
AF522627
WORLD RECORD
GUINNESS BOOK OF RECORDS
का मास्टरमाइंड गाजी बाबा ढेर
दिल्ली
दो अ
था गाजी बाबा
Statesman
Jaish ■ Parliament accused to identify body: minister
shot in Srinagar...

The
nday Statesman
Ghazi Baba shot in Srinagar.
After tackling
jay Raman comes to Naxa
VIJAY RAMAN
R.K. KAISTHA
PRIME MINISTER
New Delhi
July 23, 1993
ar Shri Vijay Raman,
Congratulations on your undertaking the "Circumnavigation of the World" by car. It is indeed gratifying to know that the Guinness Book of Records have recognized your claim for the World Record for this event.
You have done us proud.
With regards.
Yours sincerely,
[P.V. Narasimha Rao]
ARGEST SELLING
CYCLE

DID I REALLY DO ALL THIS?

'Shri Vijay Raman had a distinguished police career spanning over three decades, which took him from the badlands of Chambal to the left-wing infested tribal areas and pockets of high-intensity terrorism in J&K. His first-hand experience gave him a ring-side view of India's security challenges and an insight into diverse societies, people, and aspects of human relations and their proclivities and potential. This cumulative experience turned him into an outstanding police leader, who was widely respected and admired by all those who worked with him. The book is a vivid recollection of his professional journey and makes for interesting reading.'

—**Ajit Doval,** K.C., National Security Advisor of India to Prime Minister of India

'Vijay Raman's story is a reminder that true greatness lies not in grand gestures but in the consistent, quiet courage to do what is right. I hope that his memoir will leave a lasting impact on everyone who reads it, inspiring them to find strength in their own journeys and to act with integrity and compassion.'

—**Rahul Dravid**, former India cricket captain and T20 World Cup winning coach

'I had the privilege of knowing Vijay Raman during my tenure in the Government of India. Vijay was not just a remarkable IPS officer but also a wonderful human being. Known for his unwavering principles and boundless compassion, his dedication to justice and his courageous leadership were truly inspiring. From his valiant efforts against dacoits in Chambal to his compassionate initiatives for children in conflict zones, Vijay's life was lived in dedication to making a difference. His memoirs offer a profound insight into the life of an extraordinary individual who consistently put service above the self. He will be deeply missed, but his legacy will continue to inspire.'

—**Amitabh Kant**, G20 Sherpa, and former CEO of Niti Aayog

'No book or memoir can do justice to the personality and character of Vijay Raman. I have had the distinction and honour of having worked with him and to be a brother to him. Having worked in the government for over 44 years, and having had the pleasure of having worked with some of the best, I have no hesitation in saying that Vijay is right up there with the very best. His capacity for hard work, brilliance of mind, analysing and dealing with the most difficult and complicated of situations, and above all his moral and intellectual integrity are simply unmatched. This book is merely a glimpse of this multifaceted personality, and recommended reading for all in public service.'

—**Najeeb Jung**, former vice chancellor, Jamia Millia Islamia, and former lieutenant governor of Delhi

'With his handsomeness, wit and winsome smile, Vijay Raman was a big hit from Day 1 in our batch of IPS officers. When saying his name, he'd say 'Vijay' normally, and the 'Raman' part he always said with a twirl of his tongue. Raman and I worked in many places together—the SPG, J&K, the BSF and finally the CRPF, often causing confusion owing to 'Vijay' being common in our name, which the then PM Mr Rajiv Gandhi once mentioned to me and then solved by calling him Raman. He was a dear colleague and hardcore policeman with whom I shared many happy days. Raman became Chambal's nemesis and dacoit Malkhan Singh's condition for surrender was that Raman be shifted from Bhind district. The CM himself sort of requested Raman that he join a much bigger Raipur district.'

—**K. Vijay Kumar**, former director general of CRPF and author of *Veerappan: Chasing the Brigand*

'It is a very well-crafted memoir of an extraordinary, adventurous police officer who encountered dacoits in Chambal, Naxals in Chhattisgarh, and terrorists in Kashmir. Very few know that he played a key role in the surrender of Phoolan Devi and Malkhan Singh. Eighty temples reconstructed at Bateshwar, in the Chambal ravines, then a forbidden land, are a living testimony to the help and support extended by him.'

—**K.K. Muhammed**, renowned archaeologist and Padma Shri awardee

'An amazing life story of an extraordinary man, a police officer par excellence and a mentor and guide to many who followed in his wake. Pacy and enthralling, the book will keep the reader engaged, wanting you to meet this amazing Citizen Cop.'

—**Lt Gen. Abhijit S. Pendharkar**, AVSM, YSM, General Officer Commanding, 3 Corps

DID I REALLY DO ALL THIS?

THE GENTLEMAN COP WHO DARED TO BE DIFFERENT

VIJAY RAMAN

RUPA

Published by
Rupa Publications India Pvt. Ltd 2024
7/16, Ansari Road, Daryaganj
New Delhi 110002

Sales centres:
Bengaluru Chennai
Hyderabad Jaipur Kathmandu
Kolkata Mumbai Prayagraj

P-ISBN: 978-93-6156-199-3
E-ISBN: 978-93-6156-710-0

First impression 2024

10 9 8 7 6 5 4 3 2 1

To:
My seniors
My colleagues
My juniors
My men from MP police, SPG, ITBP, J&K police,
BSF and CRPF...
who empowered me with their guidance and constant support.

And for those who come after us...
may the challenges of our times shine a light on your present!

CONTENTS

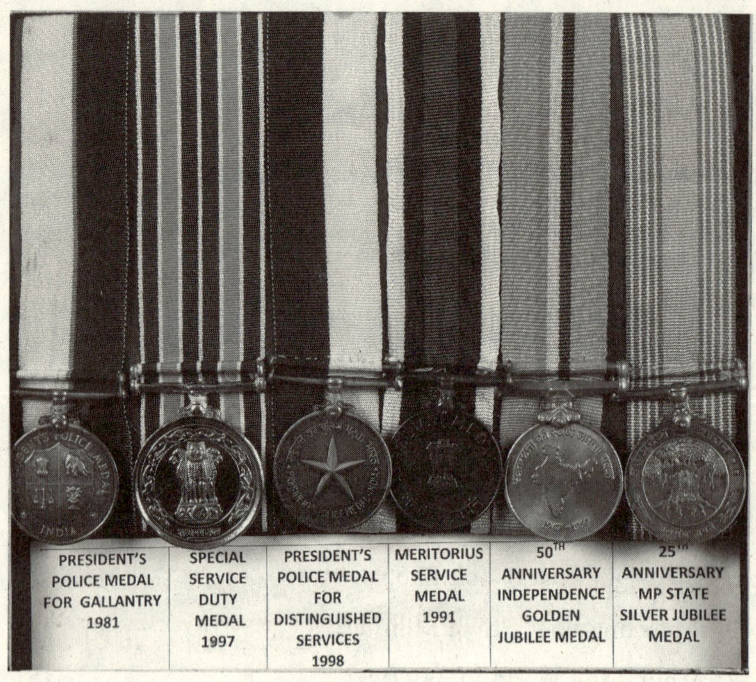
PRESIDENT'S POLICE MEDAL FOR GALLANTRY 1981
SPECIAL SERVICE DUTY MEDAL 1997
PRESIDENT'S POLICE MEDAL FOR DISTINGUISHED SERVICES 1998
MERITORIUS SERVICE MEDAL 1991
50TH ANNIVERSARY INDEPENDENCE GOLDEN JUBILEE MEDAL
25TH ANNIVERSARY MP STATE SILVER JUBILEE MEDAL

SUDDEN SHOCK

An introduction by

Veena Raman, wife of the late Vijay Raman

When my husband, the illustrious, inimitable Vijay Raman, passed away, Vikram, Divya, Shaurya and I were devastated. The cruel illness was swift and relentless; in the short space of a few months he grew weaker before our eyes, and before we were anywhere near ready to accept the loss, we had no choice but to face it.

We tried our best to console each other. Vikram said, 'We should be grateful that we had him for all these years. Papa was that proverbial cat with nine lives!'

Vikram was right. There were innumerable instances when Vijay's life was in danger, and he miraculously escaped.

As early as November 1978, when he was still in his first posting as assistant superintendent of police (ASP) in Dabra, a country-made bomb was flung at his jeep by agitating students in Gwalior. It fell and exploded nearby. Fortunately, no one was harmed.

In 1981, based in the Chambal, he had already faced dacoit encounters. The most dramatic of all these took place in October, when he led the team that wiped out Paan Singh Tomar and his gang, who had terrorized the villages in the region for years. He has described the encounter in detail in this book—bullets rained on the encounter team from all sides, caught in the crossfire between the dacoits and the police.

It was during his tenure as superintendent of police (SP) Special Branch in Bhopal in 1984 that the world's worst industrial disaster took place. On the night of 3 December 1984, when more than 40 tons of methyl isocyanate gas leaked from the Union Carbide pesticide plant over Bhopal, killing and maiming untold hundreds, Vijay drove to the railway station. Why inconvenience the driver to stay up late when he wanted to receive his parents himself? Within a few short minutes, the gas had created havoc and continued to do so, and he was shocked to see hundreds of victims. Somehow, he and his parents, so close to the scene of destruction, were spared.

Then, in 1998, as inspector-general of police (IGP) Security Jammu and Kashmir (J&K), Vijay was in Srinagar and a bomb blast took place on the route during the time he always travelled to office. That day, his driver took him on an alternative route, and they were saved.

In 2000, as IG, Border Security Force (BSF), Jammu, Vijay was responsible for erecting a much-needed part of the fence between Pakistan and India under very adverse conditions. Enemy bullets rained down from across the border throughout the operation. In this book, you will read about some daring and potentially controversial decisions he made. How very relieved and thankful we were when he came home safe from there!

Vijay was appointed IG, BSF, Kashmir, in 2003 with the secret mandate to get Ghazi Baba, the mastermind of the 2001 attack on the Indian Parliament. In an undercover exploration, along with an informer, of the site where the Ghazi Baba encounter later took place, the informer suddenly, most unexpectedly, pointed out the man himself! Vijay instinctively turned the handle to open the car door and rush out to apprehend the terrorist—only to be roughly pulled back by the informer who screamed orders to the driver to step on the accelerator and escape immediately. Later, the informer explained that Ghazi Baba never left his lair unless he was strapped with explosives, and an attack would have caused huge explosions that would have been the end of everyone in the vicinity.

One of the most stressful and dangerous situations Vijay ever faced in his risk-fraught career was as Special Director General (DG) Anti-Naxal Operations of the Central Reserve Police Force (CRPF) in 2010. In April that year, more than 70 CRPF personnel were massacred in Dantewada by Naxalites. The loss of his men weighed so heavily on him that his health declined, he neglected his meals, and even routinely forgot to take his medication. He had moved from the headquarters in Chhattisgarh to Kolkata; Vikram and I were in Delhi at the time, and it was only a few months later, when he suffered a stroke, that we understood the intensity of what he had been going through.

In 2015, four years after he retired, Vijay was handpicked to be a member of a special investigation team (SIT) investigating the Vyapam examination scam, another challenging appointment.

Vijay came close to death even in a personal adventure he undertook with a friend, circumnavigating the globe in an Indian-made car in an era when Indian manufacturing was just coming up, in the last 39 days of 1992. Through this tremendous feat, which earned them a place in the Guinness Book of World Records, he was exposed to danger of a different kind. In 39 days of driving at very high speeds in different countries, different terrains, and different political climates, they had only one accident. Yes, he was badly injured, but still found the strength to complete the challenge they had taken up and beat the record.

These are just nine examples of Vijay's miraculous nine lives. I could easily give you 19. If I spend more time thinking, remembering our many years together and my many moments of anxiety and prayer, the list could stretch to 90.

Every policeman faces bullets in the course of duty. And Vijay, throughout his career, was inviting them, daring them to try and see what they could do to him. His faith in the divine, in his own destiny, made him fearless. How very fortunate we were that, time and time again, they were deflected. 'It was a dream run,' Vikram, trying to overcome his own grief, reasoned with me and his family.

For many years I had told Vijay that he must write a book. Yes, many people have achievements—but Vijay's narrative was different. Winning without challenges is just victory, but winning after overcoming challenges is history! The range and scope of what he had done, and the consistently simple, straightforward way in which he had done it, had to be recorded for posterity.

The idea kept coming up in conversations with friends and family members. But Vijay would say, 'No. Nobody would be interested in such a book!' None of us agreed with him. And I was determined that I would one day bring the idea to fruition.

During that time, we read books by many other police officers. One thing came across clearly: his experiences were unique. Unlike others, who excelled in certain areas of policing and a few other aspects, in Vijay's case there was not just one spectacular achievement—there was a whole range of them! I feel that Vijay may be the only police officer in the country who has dealt with all the aspects of policing and has been successful at each. He was at the forefront of dealing with the changing nature of crime in the country—and also at the epicentre of many different policing challenges. His successes invariably led to major changes in the law-and-order situation in the region. In Bhind, removing the Paan Singh gang led to the surrender of a large number of dacoits who had previously considered themselves invincible, including the most notorious Malkan Singh and Phoolan Devi. Similarly, when Vijay initiated the Indo-Pak border fencing, it was a major deterrent because most of the infiltration was from Jammu and there was a marked decline once the fence came up. Ghazi Baba was seen as invincible, too, and the encounter destroyed a formidable opponent, while also sending a clear message to India's enemies.

Vijay was successful in actually making a difference, and his life and career were also intertwined with a whole spectrum of the significant events that took place in India. Even his daily life contained an extraordinary range of experiences. He grew up in a village in Kerala, and later lived in villages among the most primitive of peoples in other Indian states. But he also lived in the cities, a privileged urban Indian. He had travelled in bullock carts on rutted roads and often walked 30 km in the course of an ordinary day through ravines; but he had also jetted across the world with the prime ministers (PMs) he protected.

Equally unusual is that Vijay himself was that quintessential Indian who was intimately connected in different ways to the length and breadth of India. He grew up in Kerala, the deepest south, and later spent some of the most significant years of his career in the farthest north, in J&K. Vijay's higher education took place in Gujarat; when he retired, we came to live in Pune. The western part of India was his beloved home as an impressionable youngster, and then again in his final years. There were also important formative experiences in the east, starting with the time when, as a probationer in the Police Academy, the area he was taken to explore and understand was India's verdant Northeast. He had also spent time in Calcutta for induction training for his first job at the ordnance factory and later during his stint as Special Director General Anti-Naxal Operations of the CRPF.

With these influences of north, south, east and west, it was only fitting that Vijay should be allotted the Madhya Pradesh cadre, at the very heart of India.

Vijay was an excellent writer, and of late, I have been reading his letters to me over the years, from before we were married as well as during the tenures of separation induced by our work and careers. I can only marvel at his intellectual ability. Even at a very young age, he articulated his thoughts and feelings beautifully, and the letters reflect his tendency to introspect often, and to be constantly self-critical. Another thing that comes across is his sheer artlessness. How fortunate we are that in his field of work, steeped in the dregs of humanity, he came out unscathed, retaining that innocence and faith in humanity, and standing unwavering by the principles of human rights and democracy all through his life. I remember realizing in Bhind, soon after we were married, that my husband—who was surrounded by the most foul-mouthed people for whom obscenity was the most mundane ingredient of their daily speech—would never use any abuse stronger than 'saala'. And when Vijay said 'saala', everyone would know that he was very, very angry!

I was always extremely proud to be the wife of such an exceptional human being. But Vijay disliked being praised. At the peak of achievement, when his heroic deeds were earning him medals and he was surrounded by people singing his praises to the sky, when he knew that he was achieving success after success, he tried his best to ignore it all. And he would specifically tell me, 'See, Veena, you please don't praise me. So many people are praising me, all right. The moment you start doing it, it'll go to my head.'

So, stupidly I took him at his word.

I would, of course, boast about him to others. He was an outstanding police officer, but he was also the best husband ever, the best father ever. Even in the 1970s, when so few women had careers, he supported my ambitions. He knew that he was marrying a woman who had her own dreams, who wanted to see the world—yes, he knew that I had not yet learnt to cook!

There were many other things I admired about him. His commitment to perfection no matter how inconsequential the task. His commitment to service, to justice, to humanity. His love for reading and his wry sense of humour. His love and care for his parents and for all the members of both our families. The deep respect he drew from each person who knew him well—his family, his colleagues, his subordinates, his superiors, and even the many criminals whom he came in contact with in the course of his duties.

The saddest thing is that because he stopped me from praising him, I was never able to convey to him in words how proud I was of him and how much I admired him. It was only towards the end of his life, as he grew weaker, that we worked fast and furiously to get all that he was telling us down on paper. As the final pages of this book appeared, he said to me, with some surprise and wonder, 'Veena, did I really do all this?'

What you will read in the following pages is Vijay's story, in his words. After he became too weak to speak, and we subsequently lost him, my memories continued pouring in, and I took the liberty of including some, to fill a few gaps.

This book is a tribute to a fine police officer who brought honour to his uniform; to a wonderful person deeply loved and mourned by his family, friends, and the many whom he encountered in his professional life.

May his legacy live on.

Veena Raman
Pune, August 2024

PROLOGUE

A MOTHER-IN-LAW'S PLEA

I returned to Chambal in 1999.

In the 17 years I had been away, I had undertaken many different roles in the police force, and been through many interesting life experiences. It was good to be back in the terrain in which I had begun my career, with all those familiar sights and sounds around me.

Some things had changed, but many remained the same. I have always said that in those areas if a senior police officer doesn't see a crowd of people waiting on his lawns in the morning to petition him with their worries, he will wonder what has gone wrong with the district!

Early one morning, soon after I returned as IG Chambal, I heard a woman wailing loudly outside. '*Saheb se milna hai! Saheb se milna hai! Saheb se milna hai!*' went her repetitive refrain. My sentry was trying to turn her away. He surely knew who the woman was and what she had come to tell me. I could hear her repeating something else now, and I was not able to decipher what she was asking for. The feeling that came through was clear—she was distraught and that was making her incoherent. My ears strained to understand her words; the dialect of that region is a little different, and I was not yet re-attuned to it.

Waiting for it to come back to me, as I knew it soon would, I asked my PA, Dikshit, 'What is this about? What is she saying?'

'It's Kesariya Raju Kushwah's *saasen*,' he whispered into my ear. 'His mother-in-law!'

'Okay,' I said, 'please bring her in.'

When I left Chambal in 1982, the intense dacoit problem of the region had reduced greatly. After my encounter with Paan Singh, many of the most notorious had surrendered. Now, nearly 20 years later, there were two major gangs operating in the area. One gang leader was Ramesh Kushwah, and the other was Raju Kushwah.

I looked up as she walked into my office: a very elderly lady, bent over and hardly able to walk, entering with folded hands. Looking at me, she blurted out, '*Saheb, meri beti ko vidhwa mat banao!* (Please, sir. Please don't make my daughter a widow.)'

What was she trying to tell me?

I understood that here was someone who had seen the dacoits of the day being eliminated during my tenure in Chambal 20 years ago. Yes, I was back, this time as IG. And now there could only be a one-way ticket for her son-in-law! So, she was pleading with me. And, now that she had my attention, she leaned forward and said in a much more composed manner, 'Sir, *main aapko khabar doongi.* (I will give you information.) I will tell you wherever he is. Wherever he goes, you will know where he is! But please, sir, please promise me that you will not kill him.'

I did not have to think twice. Perhaps she had not expected that I would agree, but I did. Law enforcement doesn't always mean killing the bad guys. Quite often, information is the most useful weapon of all.

I asked her to sit and called for a cup of tea. She remained standing. Her fear and desperation for her daughter's well-being had brought her to my door. To an extent, her age may have given her the liberty to behave as she was doing. But it would have gone against every local code of behaviour for her to sit in the presence of a senior police officer!

She had already worked out the arrangement: she would call a number that only I used. And she had given herself a code name. In the months that followed, she kept us informed. We took action each time, but Raju Kushwah remained elusive.

It was an interesting operation. This was a notorious criminal. My subordinate staff would say, '*Saheb, yeh toh badmash hai! Bahut aurat baazi karta hai.* (Saheb, he is a rascal, an inveterate womanizer!)' As we kept track of him, we learnt that he had come to suspect his mother-in-law of informing against him and was inflicting all kinds of cruelty on his wife and her mother. And yet, she was resolute: 'Saheb, I know you will catch him. But please don't kill him.'

What was my duty as a police officer? Raju Kushwah was not willing to surrender. He continued terrorizing people who lived in the district. One day, she told me that he had arrived in Bhind, and was staying in a house in the heart of the town. Based on her information, the police surrounded the place, and we called for him to come out and give himself up. He was trapped, and he knew it. Instead of coming out in surrender, he climbed up to the terrace and jumped. Climbing, jumping, he shouted out continuously, '*Neta-ji, mujhe bachao! Neta-ji, mujhe bachao!* (Save me, my leader!)'

Netaji, whoever he was, could not save him, and would soon be implicated, as Raju Kushwah was apprehended and spilled out much in the interrogation.

There was a reward of ₹2 lakh for his capture. I arranged for bank fixed deposits in the name of her grandchildren.

Each and every one of us takes an oath on the Constitution when we enter service: police officers, members of legislative assembly (MLA), ministers—all of us.

We all do, but are we living up to that oath?

This is my simple question, and I can only speak for myself when I say that I have always considered it to be a sacred oath, and I have always tried to live up to it

1

THE TRANSFORMATION OF A KERALA BOY

I grew up in Peramangalam in Kerala. To call it a town would be an exaggeration; it was more of a glorified village, in the district headquarters of Thrissur, in which stood the well-known temple of Guruvayur. I grew up amid lush green fields, coconut trees, banana plantations and village ponds with kingfishers.

My father's family followed the matriarchal system. My paternal grandfather was a Namboodiri, but my grandmother was a Warrier; so we are Warriers, a community called Ambala Vasi in Malayalam—caretakers of the temples. Traditionally, the sanctum sanctorum of the temple was the preserve of the higher-caste Namboodiri, and it was the Warriers' duty to clean the temple and make preparations for the puja and offerings. There was a strict protocol of behaviour. For example, until you had had your bath in the temple pond, paid obeisance at the temple, and come out anointed with a smear of sandalwood on your forehead, you were forbidden from having even a sip of water.

My father was a Second World War veteran in the British Indian Army and, after Independence, joined the Indian Army. He was posted in different places around the country. My mother and my two brothers lived with him, while I, the eldest, was left with my grandmother in the *warriam*, our ancestral home. We were a large number of cousins and had an equally large number of people with parental authority. So, while we were under constant scrutiny by the elders, there were enough of us of the same age enjoying ourselves doing whatever we wanted most of the time.

Gathering of the Grain

One of my earliest and most defining memories is from 1961, when I was 10 years old, and my father's eldest brother, the family patriarch, came on a visit. They were seven siblings, with gaps of about four years between each, so he would have been 28 years older than my father. He lived elsewhere. Arriving at the warriam one day, he stayed overnight, receiving due deference. The next morning, he picked up his walking stick and beckoned to the family children to accompany him. Clutching our loincloths—the standard dress for village children of our age—tighter around us, we ran along behind him, marvelling at his huge beard all the way. When he stopped at a particular spot, we waited. Craning our necks, we could see some activity on the large ground—people were walking in with large sacks on their backs and leaving them there. After a while, he motioned for us to follow him again.

Till then, I had no idea what the family livelihood or source of income was. I now began to understand that this was the agricultural harvest from the fields owned by our family, and that the family patriarch had come to visit because it was time to collect the produce.

As we approached the ground, we could see bags of paddy, and a few minions were now deputed to sprinkle water around them to sanctify them. The people who had carried the sacks on their backs from the fields to this place had left them there and retreated to a distance from which they could not even be seen. After the purification, our patriarch—who had done no labour of any kind—walked forward to inspect the grain. He shouted out his displeasure at its quality, flung some coins—their wages, I assumed—and retreated so that their presence would not pollute him. Another set of people were deployed to carry the grain back to the house.

I may have been young but there was something about this purification ritual and his arrogance that I found highly distasteful. What was the purification about? Why the seclusion of the people who had done the work? I was filled with a sense of indignation at the injustices I had seen, which I felt were very wrong indeed.

These feelings never left me, and often came to the forefront in the course of my career in policing, spurring me on to continue fighting against injustice.

Many years later, the family gathers at the family warriam in Kerala

Culture Shock

I grew up studying in the Malayalam medium in the local municipal high school, deeply immersed in all the joys and discomforts of joint family life. After I completed Class 7, my father decided that I would join him, my mother and my siblings in Secunderabad, Andhra Pradesh, where he was posted. I remember that train journey well! I was crossing the Bharathappuzha River to leave Kerala for the first time in my life. My links to and love for my home state would always remain, only getting stronger over the years of absence and separation.

In Kerala, I had learnt the ABC, but there was no structured English learning. In Secunderabad, I was admitted into St Patrick's School. To help me cope with the move from the Malayalam medium of instruction to English, I was demoted by one year and admitted into Class 6. These were years of adjustment and introspection. I had to get to know my younger siblings, Durgadas and Ravi. The army lifestyle was a huge contrast to the surroundings I had grown up in. The school environment was also different from what I was used to, and there was the additional struggle of learning English to be on par with others who were familiar with the language from Class 1.

There were also many positives—being with my family, learning the ways of the city, experiencing cantonment life—and I still remember the unforgettable thrill of getting our first motorbike. What joy we three brothers experienced, riding it with our father for the first time! My brothers and I played cricket, and our dog Madhu would also be one of the fielders. We had trained him to post letters and pick up our newspaper from the front gate! Father being away in the field area, we three boys learnt to give our mother a helping hand in her chores too. I was good at making chapatis and puris; this was very unusual for our time, when it was not considered seemly for boys to do domestic chores! The joy of living at home with your own mother and father was unmatched. My father was a disciplinarian and he worked hard on me for the next two years.

Vijay with parents, brothers and beloved dog

When he was subsequently transferred to Sagar, Madhya Pradesh, I completed Class 9 and Class 10 at St Joseph's Convent there. At school, we were a class of boys and girls, but the girls outnumbered us. In our teenage fantasies, each boy had four girlfriends, and we exchanged them amongst ourselves, but it was a secret about which the girls had no idea. I made some lifelong friends there who enriched my life with fun and affection. Some of them were Ashok Pathak, Shailendra Chouksey, Guru, Masoor Ali, Vikram Mishra, Anil Madan, Fran (who later married Ashok) and Neerja. These days, people streak their hair red, blue and green as a style statement. Well, we were early trendsetters, with one genius who did that in our Chemistry class in the early 1960s! I have realized that in life, friends are an important part of building one's character, and I'm grateful that I had such good friends.

Budding scientists, enjoying their Chemistry practicals!

Teenage Boys Meet Girls' Hostel

As I was coming to the end of Class 10, my father was transferred again, this time to Vadodara, Gujarat. Due to the difference in state government educational rules, if I now joined my family at the new posting, where two years of pre-university was compulsory after Class 10, I was going to lose yet another year and would land up being two years older than my classmates! The thought was unbearable. I mustered up courage and went to see Sister Philippa, the principal of my school, without my parents' knowledge.

Sister Philippa, a Canadian nun, was a very kind and approachable lady, and very good-looking too. In fact, I used to tease her, 'Sister, perhaps you did not find a proper chap to marry. Why else would someone like you become a nun?' And she would have a good-natured laugh. She was fond of me, and I owe a lot to her influence and the values she inculcated in me in my growing years. I stayed in touch with her through the years of my career, right until she passed away in 2016.

I explained to Sister Philippa that my father had been transferred, and that if I went to the new posting with my family, I was going to lose yet another year of my life! I did not want to leave that school and join another, and asked if she could somehow help me by giving me a place to stay on the campus for one year.

She was astonished at first but, soon understanding the sincerity and validity of my plea, she agreed, subject to permission from her higher authorities. Looking back, I truly understand the extraordinary support from Sister Philippa, without which it would not have been possible for a teenage boy to be given accommodation in a convent school, and that too in the early 1970s. It was a co-educational school but with boarding arrangements only for girls.

I was provided a room close to the quarters of the reverend of the church, near the school gate. It was in an outhouse with two rooms, close to the kindergarten section. There was a bathroom with a wooden English commode system, and the person occupying the other room brought buckets of water in the morning.

> When something is important to you—take courage in both your hands and ask for it!

Having a room by the gate gave me access to postmen who brought food parcels. If the parcel was for one of the nuns, I let them pass unaccosted. But if it was for one of my classmates or any of the girls I knew, I would take the package, open it, help myself, and then deliver it. I must say that the girls were extremely sporting about the whole thing, and I got a chance to eat home-made goodies, which was a very special feeling for a homesick child! The father of one of the girls was a senior official in the railways, and this meant that parcels were coming for her nearly every day, so she was the one who suffered the most on my account! But these girls were my very good friends and they were happy to be sharing with me.

My room being close to the gate also meant that I could easily leave the school campus for late-night movies with the boys who lived in town. With all these distractions, I completed my schooling with grades I won't say I am proud of.

With Sister Philippa, a warm friendship that was retained over decades

Useless Fellow Becomes Gazetted Officer

I could now join my family in Vadodara and start thinking about what I wanted to study in college. I felt I had many options—English and History were my favourites—but in those days there was a pecking order with Science at the top. So, although I was not in the least interested in becoming a doctor or an engineer, there weren't many options. I joined the Maharaja Sayajirao University of Baroda, popularly known as MS University, and soon realized that the Madhya Pradesh (MP) board had a much lower standard. For the first time, I regretted my decision of completing my schooling there, because of which I now had to catch up with the much higher level of Mathematics and other Science subjects in Gujarat. Once again there was a cultural transition, being in the midst of groups of people who spoke only Gujarati. On the plus side, I did pick up a little of that language!

Predictably, my marks were not good in the examination, particularly in algebra, trigonometry, and calculus. I was allowed to 'keep terms', and was promoted to the second year under the provision that I pass a supplementary exam after six months.

My father was deeply disappointed with my performance. 'Useless fellow' was a phrase common in those days, and I heard quite a lot of it! He had the highest hopes for me, his eldest, and the pressure was tremendous. It was his dream that all his three sons join government service as gazetted officers. None of us actually knew what a gazetted officer was at the time, but the phrase had an unmistakably impressive ring to it.

I, meanwhile, was extremely fond of reading. My absolute favourite author at the time was Erle Stanley Gardner. His character, Perry Mason, was a lawyer, and he was helped in solving cases by his secretary, Della Street. The stories were gripping and brought the legal profession to life as an arena where logic, wit, and courtroom drama made the world a charming place indeed! My style of interacting, the way I spoke—a lot of what I did—was influenced by how Perry Mason was described as having done it. Wasn't it only natural that I should dream of being a lawyer myself?

At college, I had finally got the hang of Physics and my other subjects—but the spectre of the gazetted officer was always looming. I did very well at the National Cadet Corps (NCC), but somehow could not see myself joining the army. Many of my father's friends' children had joined; some of my school friends had been selected for the National Defence Academy (NDA). Eventually, my brothers, who were four and five years younger than me, did follow our father into the army, to his everlasting happiness.

My heart was still bent on becoming a lawyer, but I had no choice; I had to become a Class I gazetted officer! Gradually, I started trying to find out what exactly that meant. In those days, things were quite different from today, when you just have to click a button and Google gives you all kinds of details about what you want to know. I learnt that there was a Union Public Service Commission (UPSC) examination that I would have to clear. That became my focus, and I found out the range of subjects to be studied. Others, who had appeared for the exam or were preparing for it, advised that Science subjects should not be attempted unless one was an expert in every aspect of the subject.

At MS University in the final year of our BSc, we were groomed to understand that our papers would be evaluated on the quality of the answers and not on the number of questions attempted. This taught us that it was important to develop strong fundamental concepts. For example, if we were to explain Planck's Law, or Pascal's Law, or some law of thermodynamics, it had to be developed gradually, brick by brick, and with so much clarity that even a child who was listening would grasp the basics.

This gave me the habit of describing details at length, and I eventually cleared my BSc with excellent results, surprising everyone, particularly myself. This process gave me stamina and discipline, but also a tendency towards verbosity, which you, dear reader, are now the recipient of!

Despite my success, I remained diffident about attempting

Science subjects in the UPSC exam. In those days, we had no coaching classes and relied on self-study. In fact, my father believed that tuitions were only meant for 'duffers' (another popular word back then, by which disappointed fathers described sons like me).

My father was now transferred to Bhopal, and I moved into a hostel where I spent the entire day sitting in the library preparing for the UPSC exam from 10 in the morning. I had only one indulgence: to cross the road, sit on the steps of the building, and smoke one India Kings cigarette—which we considered to be the best brand back then. After that—and barring very occasional visits to the cinema and the *paanwalla*—I would return to the hostel in time for dinner and go to sleep. I was so engrossed in this routine that I could barely meet or spend time with the few good friends I had: Ashok Matoo, Jagdish Shastry, Anil Dhekne, Harshad Amin, Girish Amin, Ashok Surelia and Phadnawis. They knew my goal, and understood, supported and tolerated me.

My BSc results had given me some confidence, and I put in my first application for UPSC in 1972. I was 21 years old when I sat for the exam for the first time, in Ahmedabad. It was another big disappointment for my father when I did not clear it, but I was confident that I had plenty of time; in those days you could continue to appear for the exam until you were 26 years old.

I had also started attending evening classes at the Faculty of Law of MS University. The one who was the most disappointed with this arrangement was my professor Dr M.M. Patel, a reader in the Department of Physics who expected me to join MSc Nuclear Science under him. In those days, the achievements of Homi Bhabha and Vikram Sarabhai, and the Indian Space Research Organisation, were seen with great admiration, so there was a certain glamour associated with the field. Dr Patel was really upset with me for giving up what he felt was my natural vocation in favour of a government job that, according to him, could be done by anyone!

Sometime in 1969–70, there was police action in the campus of MS University. Student elections were coming up, and they were being fought on party lines, with candidates moving around waving the flags of various parties. When clashes took place between the student groups on the campus, the police were called and there was a lathi (baton) charge. I, too, was on the wrong side—little knowing that one day I would be wielding the lathi myself! A few of us were watching as the police pushed someone down and thrashed him. To our horror, we realized that it was Dr M.M. Patel. We rushed there and started shouting in Gujarati, 'Please stop, please stop! He is our reader.' Unfortunately, instead of '*Amharo reader chhe*', these cops heard '*Amharo leader chhe!*', and the thrashing intensified. Eventually, they gave in to our frantic pleas and stopped. Dr M.M. Patel had always been grateful to us for our intervention. And now he was disappointed with me for not taking up research in nuclear science. It was gratifying to know that, despite having failed my first-year examination, my professor saw a certain intellectual calibre in me. I was eventually able to explain to him that it was not possible for me to go against my father's wishes.

While following my father's wishes, I was also able to study Law, a subject I thoroughly enjoyed, for the UPSC. Most of the student crowd were already working and older than me, and I was a loner in class, a bookworm, constantly asking questions related to the origins and purposes of laws that my classmates found pointless but enthused my professors.

We were fortunate to have had legal luminaries as guest lecturers, and it was from their lucid explanations and high standard of language and thought that we learnt the basics of civil law and the Constitution.

I completed my Law degree with three gold medals.

One of our professors was Harshad Mehta, a well-known advocate practising criminal law in the Gujarat High Court. His lectures on criminal law, in particular the Evidence Act, would stand me in good stead in my investigations as a police officer. Here was an expert in criminal law, ridiculing the police, showing how holes could be punched in the prosecution's case. These learnings surfaced at relevant moments in later years, and I could clearly see the case from a defence lawyer's point of view—from Perry Mason's point of view!

When Harshad Mehta asked me what my plans for the future were and I told him that I was preparing for the UPSC, he was shocked, saying disdainfully, 'With these marks? What is there for you in the civil services?'

I did not have an answer to his question as I honestly had no idea what was there for me in the civil services. And when he invited me to join his practice in Ahmedabad, with an assured minimum ₹25,000 to take home each month, I had to regretfully decline. In 1972, for ₹25,000 you could buy a kilo and a quarter of gold! Anyway, here was one more person who was very upset with me. When I did eventually join the Indian Police Service (IPS), my first salary was all of ₹700 per month.

My First Appointment Letter

I filled the UPSC form once again and appeared for the exam in Bhopal. I was called for the interview, but did not qualify for the Indian Administrative Service (IAS). However, a few months later, I received an intimation that I had been selected for the Indian Ordnance Factory Service (IOFS) and was called to appear for a medical test on 9 August 1973 at Safdarjung Hospital, New Delhi. In those days, all candidates' medical examinations were conducted there. Chest, eyesight and other parameters were checked, but the only service that checked blood pressure, pulse, height and weight was the police. My father instructed me to get all my parameters checked right away so that if anything came up, we would know what remedial measures should be taken. He sent me to his medical officer, Major Ambastha, who found that my blood pressure was very high! 'Son, you will have to do something,' he warned me, suggesting that I avoid medication for now because it would become a lifelong liability. Instead, he told me to shift immediately to a completely salt-free diet. I followed his instructions, unpleasant though they were, meticulously. The day of the medical test came. I asked the intern and was relieved to hear that my blood pressure was absolutely normal. I raced down the six floors of the hospital and out onto the street, and kept running, only to stop at the first dhaba I came to, where I enjoyed my most satisfying meal ever, of paratha, *achar*, and the works!

I soon received a letter instructing me to report to Mussoorie for the Basic Foundation Course, a three-month course designed for officers of all the services at the Lal Bahadur Shastri National Academy of Administration. The Charleville Hotel, Mussoorie, was the recognized campus, but because the group was large, some of us were accommodated at The Savoy. As in any academy, most of our time was spent in academic sessions with excellent teachers—thorough professionals and great intellectuals, who made a lasting impression on us. There were a lot of outdoor activities also. It was my good fortune to trek to Kedarnath and have my first Jyotirling darshan. It was at the academy that I first heard the music of Talat Mahmood; I remember hearing an officer sing, '*Tasveer banata hoon, tasveer nahin banti*,'* as it brought a lot of emotion to the surface. Right from my school days and early college days I had been struggling, constantly trying but not achieving, so my sympathies lay squarely with the hero, who seemed to be in a similar position!

As a child I loved to sing and listen to music, but my father was very strict; no music, no songs, no dance—we could listen

*While this line, '*Tasveer banata hoon, tasveer nahin banti*,' means 'I try to paint a picture but no picture materializes', it indicates the frustration of someone attempting to create or achieve something but being unable to bring it to fruition.

to the radio only for the news. Luckily in the army cantonments, movie screenings were arranged once a month. Later in life, I understood that there is great depth of sentiment in sadness; a depth that is perhaps not there in happiness. The quality of sentiment evoked when unhappy is far more sublime than what one experiences in happiness. Even the extroverts go within and experience something wonderful.

I was one of four allotted to the IOFS and sent to Calcutta for training, after which I was posted to a factory at Chandrapur, Maharashtra, close to Nagpur, and here my life took a very interesting and fulfilling turn.

2

MY BOSS CHANGED MY LIFE

I joined the ordnance factory in the Chandrapur district in Maharashtra in 1974. It was located near a very small town called Bhandak, set in the midst of a forest close to the tiger reserve Tadoba. Accommodation was provided in a comfortable and self-contained residential colony, with its own school, hospital and recreation centre. The club, which had a swimming pool, was diagonally opposite the apartment allocated to me to share with another probationer, S.S.R. Zaidi. New to working life, we shared our official woes and remained good friends in the years to come. Another good friend I made was R.D. Mohile, a man of great qualities. The general manager (GM) was R.G. Deolaliker. He was my boss and a hard taskmaster. His wife Asha was caring and gentle. Their daughter Veena was studying in Nagpur and when she came home on vacation, she joined us in playing badminton at the club. She was a hockey player and I enjoyed hearing about her hockey achievements. It was in a friendly cricket match between the ladies and gents of the officers and their families that I was literally bowled out!

No Guts, No Veena!

About a year after I joined, I requested an appointment with the general manager's office on a personal matter. On entering, my boss (and father-in-law-to-be), who was reading some papers, looked up and, in his characteristic style, slid his spectacles to sit on top of his head and indicated that I should sit down.

'Yes, young man, what can I do for you?' he asked.

'Sir …' I began hesitantly. He waited, perhaps intrigued about what I might want to speak to him about privately. Taking a deep breath, I came out with it, the words tumbling out of my mouth. 'Sir, I have become interested in your daughter. Sir, I…I would… Sir, I wish to marry your daughter!'

He looked at me and, pouring out a cup of tea, offered it to me. By then I had learnt that he loved piping hot tea, and I had been practising swallowing my tea unbearably hot to impress him.

Taking a sip, he asked, with a mixture of surprise and amusement, 'Oh, really, young man? How interesting! Now may I ask you a very important question? What is my daughter's opinion on this matter? What does she have to say about it? Have you asked her?'

I took another deep breath and said, 'No, sir, but I will ask her, sir, but I wanted to seek your permission first!' He looked nonplussed for a moment and then, with a smile on his face, began to explain to me, 'First, I must tell you that my daughter does not want to get married. She wants to pursue her hockey career and she wants to travel around the world.

'Secondly, if you both go ahead and things work out…'—he paused, and as I listened, my surprise and admiration at his broadmindedness and openness grew apace with my respect for him—'I have heard that in your Malayali community, large dowries are paid to the groom's family. I am against dowry on principle and will not give even a penny.'

I jumped up, delighted with his positive response, and assured him that I would not expect even a pin and, in any case, I was against the practice of dowry too. Some years later, when the time came, there was no dowry; however, he did very large-heartedly host receptions in Jabalpur and Bhopal, and a grand wedding in Nagpur (though, to be honest, my preference would have been for a simple and low-key affair).

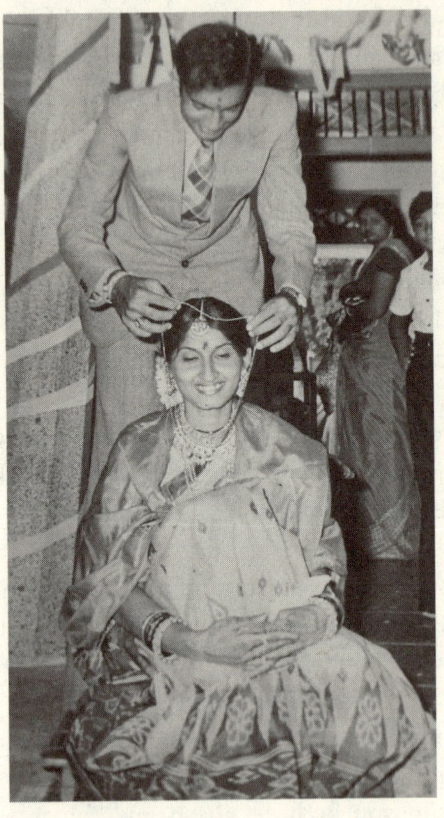

A ceremony at the wedding of Vijay and Veena

Now about the daughter, whom I had not even spoken to on the subject! I believe that Veena was impressed and floored by my guts and straightforward approach. When her father told her about my proposal, she told him that she had no clue and had not encouraged me in any way. When I approached her, she agreed to give the relationship a chance. I wooed her and finally did succeed. I always believed the saying 'You cannot choose your parents, but you can certainly choose your parents-in-law', and I had chosen mine.

Call of the Chambal

The camaraderie at work was great, but my dream of joining the IAS remained. A greater part of my reason for wanting to leave the ordnance factory post was because I found it to be an organization—not just in Chandrapur but also in Calcutta and other places I visited—with a strong hierarchy between the technical and the administrative divisions. The important posts were all held by the former. I was not an engineer and could not play an important or leadership role here; if I continued, I would always remain in an ancillary, subsidiary position. Even more intolerable was the possibility that, even if I rose in the hierarchy with merit over the years, it could always be gossiped that my father-in-law had played godfather.

I appeared for the UPSC again, setting my targets higher this time. I worked by day, and by night sat and studied. Once again, I got through and was given a date for an interview in Delhi. Candidates were entitled to first-class train travel—the most comfortable available in India in those pre-air-conditioning days! In Delhi, I would be staying with a friend of the family, another well-accepted practice. I boarded the train and it arrived at Gwalior Railway Station at about 5.00 p.m. As it pulled out a few minutes later, the compartment attendant entered. We were seeing him for the first time. He pulled down the window shutters—both the glass window as well as the metal-grilled one. I was intrigued and wondered why this was being done. We had been on the train for several hours now and nobody had come in to close our windows before this. What was going on? But I was too shy to ask him and risk being snubbed in front of the other passengers, so I went out and found him bolting all the doors securely before he sat down in the attendant's seat.

Surprised by my question, he said, 'Saheb, don't you know? This is the Chambal! This is the area where dacoits stop the train and board to loot the passengers!'

Fascinated and a little nervous, I stood outside the coupé near the attendant so that I could look out and view the ravines as the train picked up speed and began rattling past. How could I ever have known that in just a few short years, I would be posted to one of the Chambal districts, of all places, for training and subsequent career progression? And that this was where I would enjoy the most intense and lengthy portion of my career?

This time I cleared the interview and qualified for the IPS. My father-in-law-to-be was supportive. With good wishes from all at the Chandrapur ordnance estate, I left with an appointment order to go to Nagpur for an initiation course at the National Civil Defence College in November 1975. After the course, all the probationers then reconvened at the Sardar Vallabhbhai Patel National Police Academy in Hyderabad.

Police Academy

My time at the academy was a memorable one. We probationers were given training on skills and tactics required to conduct our duties. These included legal training, combat, firearm training, use of force, crisis management, de-escalation of conflicts, and many more. The day started with PT at 6.30 in the morning, and this lasted 40 minutes, followed by parade. Classes started from 9.30 a.m. and the various subjects included criminal law, police science like crime detection, forensic science and the various other things that characters like Perry Mason do. We also had classes for four hours on subjects such as psychology, sociology, photography, and others. In the afternoon, we had another dose of parade, followed by an hour of compulsory games like football, volleyball, basketball and hockey. This was followed by a horse-riding session. We also had formal dinners twice a week, with stiff-necked, ramrod-straight policemen, alternately looking pleasant, harsh, kind, cold, stupid, bored (and so on!) where our young minds interfaced with those of the stalwarts. On those days, we remained on our feet till about 11.00 p.m. The unfamiliar but welcome comfort of the air-conditioned auditorium, the dignitaries who addressed us, the after-dinner speeches, all remain clear in my mind even these many decades later.

One of the things that often goes unreported are the horrors related to equestrian skills! Approaching the horse with wariness, we were at first surrounded by a buzz of rumours. 'Feed the animal a green chilli,' a kind person whispers in your ear, 'and that will make it your friend for life!' And the ones who take this rather malicious piece of advice seriously receive a kick from the creature who has received a kick from the chilli! Then come the taunts of the syces: '*Kya Saheb, ghoda nahi chala sakte ho, jilla kaise chalaoge*! (Seriously, Saheb, you can't even control a horse, how on earth are you going to administer your district!)' The riding class and parade were a real challenge to us. I was one of the many who had never been in the vicinity of a horse until I joined the academy. One day, when it was our squad's turn for riding, I reached the stables and, to my great dismay, the horse available was one with the misleading name Good Boy. This was only our sixth riding class—and at the previous one, this horse had coolly carried another hapless batchmate back to the stables, where he proceeded to graze on the grass, impervious to commands. This was a Good Boy with a mind of his own, one who radiated defiance; even the riding instructor was mystified by him.

What choice did I have? I can only say I tried my best. At first the noble steed tried to prevent me from mounting. After a considerable struggle, I managed to get on top. Hardly had I settled into the saddle than it took off like lightning and started galloping as if it were at the Bombay races. Seeing this, the other horses got frightened and started running about in confusion. My colleagues were able to control them, but nothing would stop my horse. It was running straight ahead, then suddenly breaking its run without any warning, then suddenly setting off again, abruptly stopping to jump on its hind legs, then breaking into a gallop yet again! Those 15 gruelling minutes during which that horse tried its best to throw me off—and in which I managed to cling to it for dear life—were a torture indeed. At the end of the ordeal, more taunts came from Hanuman Singh, our riding instructor: '*Ustadji. Ghode ki galti nahin hai.* (Your highness, it is not the horse's fault)!' And the now-familiar taunt was trotted out again, '*Kya Saheb, ghoda nahi chala sakte ho, jilla kaise chalaoge*!'

It is interesting to look back and see how the painful moments have mellowed into memories that bring amusement! I also realize that even though we never rode a horse in the course of our duties, learning to ride adds a skill that instils confidence in the rider.

I also remember an unfortunate incident that took place one evening while playing football—the only game with which I could then claim some acquaintance. During the game, I got involved in a tackle in which the defender on the other side fell heavily on the ground and broke his collarbone. I felt so guilty about it that I could get no peace of mind. Finally, the doctor assured me that it was not a serious injury but a minor facture that would soon heal. However, seeing him writhe in agony brought me face to face with the limits of physical pain that one can endure. I sincerely wished to share his pain. Fortunately, he recovered soon and all was well again.

Having trainees from all around the country was also a very interesting experience. The cooks were locals, and we were naturally provided with local Andhra dishes. The police academy, previously in Mount Abu, had been moved to Hyderabad, which was much more accessible; earlier it had been Rajasthani cuisine prepared by Rajasthani cooks. The responses to the food served at mealtime varied to such an extent that it seemed like they were talking about totally different dishes!

Gradually, we all fell into our own groups, and I was very fortunate to be part of a foursome along with Jacob Punnose, Vinod Radha Raju and John V. George. I felt so blessed to have their friendship! Each one was brilliant and had a great sense of humour, and they enriched my life. Each of them carved a niche in their careers and are well-known names in police circles and in society. We were all from South India and our Hindi was not very good. Later, when I joined the MP cadre, my Hindi did improve. But at our first cultural mushaira programme at the academy, the four of us sat in the second row and listened. Urdu poets usually start their show testing the pulse of their audience, reciting couplets and modifying their offerings depending on the applause they receive. They started reciting some very mundane shayari (verses) that none of us understood. However, we had seen audience members saying 'Irshaad! Irshaad!' (something spoken or exclaimed during a performance to encourage the artiste) in the movies and wanted to show our sophistication, so we began doing so and applauding loudly. After 15 minutes of tolerating this, some of our batchmates who were Hindi–Urdu shayari connoisseurs got up and threw us out of our seats because the performers were getting the wrong signals and the poetry was heading in the wrong direction!

We performed our own cultural events too, and staged a production of the Ram Leela. I was surprised to be selected to play the lead role of Lord Rama, while my dear friend Vinod sang the *Ramcharitmanas* in his beautiful, melodious voice.

During this time, I appeared for the UPSC again and once again did not clear the interview. It was very disheartening. I had worked with single-minded determination for seven years to become an IAS officer. Everyone consoled me, but I was down in the dumps, as I felt that I had failed everyone's expectations and my own too. Then a friend said, 'Thank God IPS did not lose a good officer to IAS. IAS's loss is IPS's gain!' Eventually, I became reconciled to a new goal. I was not going to join the IAS. However, I could excel in the IPS.

In training to be a leader

Performing on stage as Rama

In those days, there were no mobiles, and letters were the only form of connection with your near and dear ones. Everyone looked forward to them, from home and from girlfriends. Veena was irregular with her letters since she was occupied with her hockey practice and tournaments; this was my constant complaint to her since I saw others receiving thick envelopes nearly every day. Yet I was proud of her, and would go around bragging and showing off to friends when she scored a hat-trick in the Senior Women's Hockey Nationals, and even more so when she was selected to represent India in international tournaments. I always appreciated women who pursued their dreams.

One of these was Jija Madhavan, the only lady probationer in our batch of 1975, and much admired for her courage in an era when women's roles in society were very different from what they are today. She was the first IPS officer of South India, and faced her mischievous and competitive male colleagues undaunted. Later, she also did very well in various fields other than policing.

'These Medals Are to Be Earned'

There was a cooperative store in the academy that stocked uniform materials, shoes, belts and other items required for police work. The products were of good quality and the store received regular orders from other states also. For probationers, it was the first place to visit when you entered the academy. Senior officers who came to attend courses at the academy after a dozen or more years of service would also purchase their needs there. A group of us was standing there, along with some probationers and senior officers, waiting to be served, when one of the probationers pointed at a medal and asked Mr Patel, who was in charge of the store, 'How much does this cost?'

Mr Patel looked at him respectfully and said, 'Sir, these medals are to be earned, not to be purchased.'

The people in the store applauded Mr Patel enthusiastically. I hoped that I would earn a medal too, one day!

One of the high points of our time at the academy was our

all-India tour, Bharat Darshan, during which we extensively toured the respective area allotted to each group. I was in the group sent to the Northeast and Sikkim sector. We left Hyderabad on the evening of 30 April 1975, in a special bogie, arriving in Calcutta only on 2 May. The next morning, we left at 6.40 for Guwahati Airport. Guwahati was about an hour's flight from Calcutta and since this was my first airborne experience, I was very excited and observed the operations with great interest, never imagining that in a few years' time I would be flying all over the world and inspecting planes thoroughly for prime ministers' visits.

Guwahati, situated on the banks of the magnificent Brahmaputra River, was beautiful and its streets and houses did not seem to be urbanized. We were taken sightseeing and treated with great respect. It was a special day, and it ended with a grand dinner with the home minister of the state. The scenic splendour of India's Northeast would always remain in my mind's eye. From Shillong, we returned to Guwahati and were then taken to Naxalbari, the place where the Naxalite movement originated.

Learning the Ropes

Kerala was my home state, and in 1975, there were only two vacancies, one for an insider and one for an outsider. The insider place went to my friend Jacob Punnose, whose rank was higher. I was placed, through an alphabetical listing also based on merit, in the Madhya Pradesh cadre. Having lived in MP did not give me any particular advantage, but it was an excellent cadre.

Similar to the Bharat Darshan of the academy, one of the traditions implemented was an MP Darshan for every new batch of IPS officers, whether insiders or outsiders, to explore and understand the state. This was initiated by the farsighted and perceptive K.F. Rustamji, who was an outstanding police officer, brave and highly competent. Rustamji was the definition of leadership for the Indian police: always considerate to the plight of the policemen in the field, a no-nonsense person with a large heart, leading by example in every challenging situation.

MP was an amalgamation of five areas, all very different from each other. One is the area around Gwalior, which is the Chambal. Then there is Mahakoshal, the region around Jabalpur, and Malwa, which is a plateau covering Indore, Ujjain, and nearby areas. Then comes the area around Bhopal, the capital, and the centre of the state. And then there is Chhattisgarh; today a different state. If you observe them closely, they are very different from each other. As far as the people are concerned—the psyche, the ethos, the methodology, the traditions, the socioeconomic conditions, the aspirations—they are poles apart. Someone who fits well into one area could be a total failure because of these differences.

A 3-ton vehicle was provided to the four of us—Heimant Sarin, M.P. George, Kalikaprasad and I—quite a ramshackle vehicle it was, with every part of its body making loud sounds, except the horn! It had no seats; we sat on its floor and, at night, rolled out our bedding and lay on the ground. Of course, it was mechanically very sound, and we also had a very good driver. This was home to the four of us for one month. Our instructions on this tour were that we would not approach any police station. We would report to the range deputy inspector-general (DIG).

With these instructions, we started on our tour. The idea was for us to get to know the people of these areas. When we arrived at a place, the police official deputed would be waiting, and he would introduce us to the people, the headman, and other seniors of the village, and they knew that a group of new probationers had come to visit them. We would stay with them as their guests, accept their hospitality, and try to understand them. This laid the ground for our understanding of the district; more about this in the pages to follow.

Mr Rustamji was a hardliner who believed that the type of problems Chambal had should not, absolutely should not, exist. But he also realized that it was not everybody's cup of tea to function in that region. You needed certain qualities, certain capabilities. He issued a brief, which every subsequent IG followed and in turn passed on to the DIGs, particularly the DIG Gwalior. At the time we were unaware of this, but they had been instructed to observe the new probationers and pick the talent they thought would be capable and appropriate to handle the Chambal situation.

At the end of this round, we returned to Bhopal, where we met the senior officer who was coordinating our movement and visits. In those days, the MP police had a lot of imported vehicles. These were vehicles belonging to the maharajas of the princely states now under MP—Indore, Gwalior, and others—and all their vehicles had been impounded and kept in the state garage. These were available for police use. He told the four of us, you must be exhausted after this one-month ordeal. Go ahead, take one of these vehicles and have a blast. Enjoy yourself, do whatever you want. You can have the vehicle for 48 hours, enjoy yourself. There was an Impala parked outside. The four of us were stunned! From our 3-tonner, here we had got this enviably beautiful and classy steed, and we enjoyed our short time with it very much.

From Bhopal, we were sent to Sagar for further training.

Letter to Veena, Sagar, February 1977

We reached Sagar around 7 p.m. on Sunday, after a tiring journey from Beena. We came by a goods train as the passenger train connection is late at night. The trip was quite interesting and afforded us the opportunity to meet a number of officers and have a better idea of life to look forward to in the districts. After this phase of the trip, I am convinced that MP is the only state where you can find so much diversity. Even today it has all the stages through which society has passed from time immemorial: the primitivity, the ignorance, the deceitfulness, the crookedness—down to the most modern sophistication. It is probably this diversity that makes the policeman's job in MP a bit more onerous and taxing than in the usual case. An officer has to change his method of work and attitude to suit the local conditions in which he is working. Success would therefore depend on the policeman's ability to adapt himself as quickly as the situation demands.

During the visit, we had occasion to meet one DIG and quite a few SPs. My, my! In what style they live! Most of them go around the districts as if they are its proprietor. The number of chaps who hang around just to talk to the SP—oh, it sent a thrill down my back!

360 Degrees

The training ended and I received my first posting, as ASP under training, to Gwalior District. This meant that the DIG in Gwalior had picked me, of the four of us, for Chambal. The others were posted elsewhere. The most sought-after place was Indore—the most cosmopolitan town of MP. Chambal was not seen as favourable—but I felt attracted by the potential challenges and was honoured to have been selected for this task.

I went to visit my DIG, Shankar Banerjee of the 1954 batch, a very genuine, good person. He advised me to get a bicycle. 'You will get accommodation, but you will have to make your own arrangements to travel,' he said, adding, 'Vijay, I hope you don't mind, but I'm the one behind your selection to Chambal.' And he explained that the rationale behind his choice was the interactions I had been seen making when we visited the Bhind-Morena area. I could not even recall what they were but apparently they were found to be pointedly purposeful! Over the years we remained in touch. I often went to meet him in Delhi. And it gave me great pleasure that he remained proud of me right till the end—and also proud of the choice he himself had made!

As an IPS officer 'in training', the theoretical training was behind us, and I was now being trained in the functional aspects of being a police officer. For this, we were made to work at every level in the police station to understand every aspect of every role of law-keeping.

It is the greatness of our Constitution that there is a provision in the criminal procedure code (CRPC) which describes the power of the SHO, the Station House Officer, or SO, who is in charge of the police station. It contains the powers to arrest, powers to search—all the police powers are vested in it. And it specifies that all the powers the DG has are extracted from this power vested in the SHO. This is really interesting, because it is a delegation of authority in reverse. This law vests the powers of the SHO on the DG; the DG has powers because he is a supervisory officer of the SHO.

It was imperative that every police officer understood threadbare the role of every individual functionary, right from the constable to the station house writer, the investigating officer and the law-and-order officer; they have to be well versed in each one's duties and only then can they command. It is a very sound system, and it really brings out the best.

In this phase, we were made to function as beat constables: we had to stand in the roll call, entirely forget IPS and the star that sat on our shoulders, and accept the duties given by the inspector who took the roll call. He was the SHO and we were probationers, so we had to accept the inspector's authority and do the work of a constable. How another person behaves depends on them; this phase was one of learning to be humble, to respect authority, and to understand that the legal power is on the chair occupied by that inspector or sub-inspector, and that you are only a constable.

Next, we had to do the head constable's job, the writer's job, and the patrolling job. Then we became the assistant sub-inspectors (ASI), and that gave us the power to investigate and to register a first information report (FIR). After that came the role of sub-inspector and then the SHO, in charge of the police station. After experiencing all these roles, we moved to a rural area where the supervisory officer is the circle non-commissioned officer (NCO), and above that was the sub-divisional officer (SDO), the subdivision of circles. This period of training in the state continues for four to five months and once completed, a regular post is allotted. Understanding the job inside-out, life became quite interesting, with new experiences every day. We had the opportunity to come across a section of society we had never been exposed to before, and met cold-blooded murderers, rapists, dacoits-turned-police-informers, petty thieves, goondas and gamblers. For the first time I visited a scene of murder and recovered incriminating articles. I began to understand that the nature of my life's work would make it difficult to lay down a specific schedule of work. Apart from the crime work, we were also exposed to police administration. I must admit that I found it appalling to see the conditions in which constables lived, with their paltry salary. The most nauseating is the contempt in which even educated people hold the police, blaming them for all the ills of society. It brought to mind Shakespeare's poignant observation in *Julius Caesar*: 'The evil that men do lives after them; the good is oft interred with their bones.' Police functioning has its seamy side, no doubt. But sadly, the drawbacks are magnified out of proportion while the achievements and the positive contribution to society are not even acknowledged. Police work is a challenge from all sides, and even as a young man right at the start of my career, I was always glad that I would be in the thick of it for years to come.

In April 1977, I was in Gwalior, attached to the Gwalior police station, about 7 km from the mess. I usually went there by bus or tempo, and used the police station vehicle for the return journey. It was the oldest police station in the city, adjacent to the Gwalior Fort. In May, I was posted at a place called Panihar, about 30 km from Gwalior towards Shivpuri. A quiet place, it had been reporting sporadic dacoit activity. To counter this menace, we continuously toured and patrolled the surrounding areas. This meant walking 30 km or more from one remote village to the next. This was a solid foundation for the work I would do in the years to come. In Panihar, we also made arrangements for the tours of the historic elections held later that year, and this took up much of my time. I remember George Fernandes visiting a village within the jurisdiction of the police station to which I was posted.

In July 1977, I was back in Gwalior doing the work of a circle inspector, with the main task of supervising investigations and inspection. A thorough inspection of a police station takes at least four days and the report runs to 50 or 60 pages. I had a language handicap, and would first make out my report in English and then sit and break my head to translate it into Hindi, a job so taxing and time-consuming that it left me totally exhausted!

The six police stations under my charge were dispersed over a large area and, having no vehicle at my disposal, I had to make long and often difficult foot journeys from one to another. The cumulative effect of all these activities over six weeks resulted in not just a thorough indoctrination into the police system of MP, but also the loss of 5 kg of body weight!

Once the training period ended and I had experienced the life of all the chaps in the ranks below me, I got my first regular posting as ASP at a place called Dabra in Gwalior District. Till this time, I had been riding around on a bicycle. When one has a kind SP, or if another senior officer is kind, they might loan you their vehicle to pick you up to go to the office, or drop you somewhere. That's not part of the training structure; it depends on the individual rapport you have with the others.

> Learn to be humble, to respect authority. Understand that legal power lies with the chair occupied by that inspector or sub-inspector, and that you are only a constable.

One of my memorable early colleagues was Mohan Menon, a fellow Malayali; we were both staying in the Gwalior police officers' mess. He was a knowledgeable sort of fellow and we had similar ideas about life. In later years, he would tease me about one of our early jeep rides together, from the mess to the residence of the SP Gwalior who had arranged an informal meeting to welcome me. Apparently, I spent the journey recording in my small black diary (meticulously, according to him) details of the route, the driver's name and address, and the city's major highlights! I do remember the informal lunch arranged for us during which our SP tried to make us comfortable by describing the difficult terrain we would be working in. Dacoities, he said, were on the rise, while there was no increase in the number of constables or sub-inspectors—which put the expectations to perform squarely on our shoulders.

I Wanted to See Her More and More

In August 1977, Veena and I got married.

I had seen her for the first time in Chandrapur, when she came to visit her parents from Nagpur where she was studying at the Nagpur Mahavidyalaya. And I wanted to see her more and more. However, her visits were infrequent. Her father would meet her when he went to Nagpur on official visits.

I was not keen to start a romance on the estate—as the campus of the ordnance factory was called—where people would notice and gossip. After all, this was my place of work, and her father was my boss!

After my meeting with her father, I did approach her and in time we decided to get married. My parents may have been making other preparations, so it took a little time to overcome those ideas and bring my father around. As for my in-laws, they were broadminded and supportive right from the first time I met her father to ask for her hand. Looking back, I realize how lucky we were to have that kind of acceptance from them. They were Maharashtrians and I was a young man from Kerala; our language, food, traditions, all were different, and in those days, inter-community marriages were not very common. But Veena's family was always warm and loving.

I was entitled to take a month's leave for my wedding but did not do so during my training period for two reasons. One was that the training would be curtailed, and this would delay my regular posting. Secondly, while I was under training, I was still riding around on a bicycle, and I felt that my in-laws may have seen me less as an IPS probationer and more as a postman! Once the training was over and I was given my posting, I would have a good job, a good position, and my own vehicle number, and I could offer a good home to my wife.

My first posting was in Dabra, a town midway between Jhansi and Gwalior, at a distance of 45 km from each. It was in Dabra that Veena and I set up our first home together. It was her first residence as the wife of a police officer.

3

WHAT THEY DON'T TEACH AT THE ACADEMY

I remember an incident that took place in Dabra, soon after I took charge in my first post as a junior officer. A crowd was protesting and we had to bring it under control. I was at a loss about what to do. As per the law, the police can use force only on the orders of a magistrate.

Seeing my dilemma, the elderly head constable said to me, 'Saheb, I'll show you the way. Just go and stand in front of the crowd.' Seeing my expression he said, 'Saheb, please don't worry. They will throw stones at you and shout slogans. Just stand there and listen. Don't worry. There will be four, five of us holding up shields. No stone will fall on you, Saheb.'

Going by his assurance, I went and stood in front of the crowd. Seeing my uniform, they began pelting stones in my direction, and some fell very close to where I was standing. After a few minutes, a pebble hit my headgear.

This was sufficient! Every supervisory officer lost control over their subordinates. The entire staff went berserk and did what they had to do. I had been hit; no longer was a lathi charge illegal.

Gradually, things were brought under control. The head constable came back to me and asked, 'Did you see what happened, Saheb? When anyone dares to even lay a finger on someone we respect and trust, we are not going to tolerate it!'

Over the years, I had similar experiences again and again. My team, my force, my men—I never saw them as subordinates, but as the people whose efforts made me the officer I became. I felt a deep affection for each and every one of the men I led, and respect for the unflinching support I always received from them in the course of duty. We always maintained faith and trust between us, and I have always been grateful for this. Without them, I could have never achieved anything.

> It is a great fallacy to imagine that only you as a senior officer can impart training. In my experience, juniors often provide training capsules that are not to be found in any manual.

Chambal 1.0

While I began my career in the dacoit-infested region of the Chambal Valley in MP, the issues I faced were of many different kinds.

Dabra had a sugar factory and one of the things we had to deal with was labour issues. There was a perennial battle between two student unions. But I always found that when we spoke to each side with logic and firmness, they listened with respect and appreciated that they had learnt something new and useful. Over time, we built up a strong relationship and also enjoyed some good games of cricket together.

I also spent a lot of time in the rural areas, and that reminds me of the first time I ever thrashed someone! It was on one of my early morning drives—while on tour, I would get up early, drive around surveying the place and then come back to camp. In those days, we had new jeeps, and this provided a certain glamour for a young man new to his uniform! That day, I was passing through a rural area, crossing a small rivulet. From a distance I saw something going on and stopped the jeep. It turned out to be a man using his footwear—a filthy juthi (a type of sandal commonly used in North India)—to fill up his milk canister from the stream. And he was going to take it and sell it as milk in the town!

I did not carry a weapon, just the regulation lathi, and that day I used it quite liberally. It was my first experience of physically assaulting somebody.

Devi Singh

When you are posted in a place like Dabra where there are dacoits, there are certain people who come to you. These are our *mukhbir*—our informers.

They come offering information that will be useful to us. Some come for the pittance of money that is sanctioned to us as anti-dacoity funds, a handout for meeting emergency expenses. But there is usually an ulterior motive. Most come with their own requirement; they want a kill: 'We will give you information that you need, information that you would find very hard to get without me, but you have to kill the man.'

As ASP Dabra, I had 10 police stations under me. One was at Pandokhar, a village between Jhansi and Gwalior, on the Uttar Pradesh (UP)–Madhya Pradesh border. A fellow from there would come to me, a very pleasant-looking chap, always smiling, always making pleasant conversation, inquiring about my health, telling me whatever was happening in the village. When I asked for information, he would say, '*Saheb, sab theek hai, sab theek hai.* (It's all good, Saheb! It's all good.)'

I would ask how he was doing, whether there was any news of the dacoits, and he'd say no Saheb, nothing, there is no movement.

One day he came with news: '*Aaj shaam ko jayenge, Saheb.* (We'll go this evening, Saheb.)'

It was December 1978—I distinctly remember the day; India was playing Pakistan in the Asian Games hockey finals in Bangkok.

One of the problems in that area, particularly for a youngster and a newcomer, is this—whom do you trust? For a young person, this is a big question. Is the informer trustworthy? Is the subordinate with whom you share the information trustworthy? I realized that it ultimately has to be your call, based on some homework you've done, your own observations, and your own intuition.

One of the dictums I have always followed is to stick to the informer's plan as much as possible. Anything else would make him suspicious. So, I asked him what we should do. He said that there was a gang of seven or eight people, Devi Singh's gang. They would be going from MP to UP to conduct a burglary at night, and since it was going to be a full moon night, it would most likely be done tonight. They would be going on bicycles—yes, in those days, dacoits were riding around on bicycles—and he would be with them. When we arrived at the ambush area, he would ring his bicycle bell and that would be the signal for us to spring into action. All we had to do was surround them, fire two shots into the air, and they would be ours: a simple, easily doable sort of plan, usually the sort that might be the most difficult to execute!

Saying a mildly regretful goodbye to the radio and the hockey commentary, I got into my vehicle and left for Pandokhar police station, which is about 60 km from Dabra, and shared my information with the sub-inspectors and inspector there. Soon the word spread, and I could see from their reaction that this was a very dangerous gang of dacoits. There was consensus that these fellows deserved the ultimate punishment.

We walked to the location, a distance of about 10 km, and took our positions before dark. There was no way I would find out the results of the hockey match there! Sure enough, a group of cyclists arrived. Someone rang a bell. That was our signal, and we surrounded them. And this was when some of the constables recognized him. '*Arre! Yeh toh Devi Singh hai!* (Oh my God, this is Devi Singh!) And there's a big price on his head!'

> Trust. Trust everyone—but suspect everyone. Let your instincts guide you on which way to move, what decisions to take. Keep both antennas up at all times.

Dying Declaration

Now the drama starts. Just imagine the type of things a young police officer has to face. It's all very easy to say no third degree, no this, no that. I'm a young officer, fresh out of the academy with just one year of service, facing a rebellious group of subordinates who want a kill. And I am still carrying the commitment to uphold the law, protect human rights, behave as the Constitution expects me to. Was it possible? Before my eyes, some of them were clearly getting ready for violence. Fortunately, there were some senior constables and sub-inspectors with us who pacified these chaps. They protested, 'They are crooks, they should be killed. Why should we let them go?' We tried to convince them that we must arrest them, take them back to the police station, and let the matter be resolved in a courtroom. But they argued that this would never work because they would bribe the authorities and get away. They must be killed now!

Somehow, after a lot of persuasion, they agreed. They requisitioned a bullock cart from the village, put me in it along with a few of the others, tied the hands of the dacoits together, and tied the rope to the bullock cart so that they could not escape. Devi Singh was a bald-headed fellow. And they thrashed him on the head with his own chappals, all along the way, to express their rage at him.

My mind was in total turmoil. What am I doing? Am I doing the right thing? And why is there so much anger against him from the lower constabulary? Is it genuine? Is this the sense of discipline that we have in the police? These were the thoughts crossing my mind on that bullock-cart ride. I was on the verge of being manhandled by my constables for having taken this stand. Luckily, there were sub-inspectors who were able to restrain them.

Back at the police station, I phoned my senior officer, the SP, a very fine officer from whom I learnt many practical aspects of policing. It was nearly midnight so I started by excusing myself for calling so late, but I was speaking from Pandokhar and had just returned from an encounter. He must have been wondering whether this kid from the south even knew the meaning of 'encounter'. With instructions to come and see him in the morning, he disconnected.

I had done exactly what my informer had asked me to do—and I had arrested seven members of a gang. We had fired only two rounds of ammunition.

We sent out the required messages to all the police stations in the district, informing them that Devi Singh was in our custody, giving information about the location, number of people arrested, and other details of the encounter. And we were astonished at the large number of requests from all around asking for them to be handed over for trial.

Here was my reward—justification for what we had done, appreciation for what we had achieved—and this (for the time being, at least) made up for all the taunts I had faced.

The next morning, I reported to my headquarters in Gwalior, met my SP, and discussed my thoughts and feelings about the encounter with him. When I told him that we had to control the level of indiscipline that we have in the force, he, being a seasoned officer, counselled me, 'These are things that we have to take in our stride. You will also learn how to go about it in the course of time!'

I was feeling quite pleased with myself for the excellent work done but my SP was more than a little amused. 'Raman, you fired only two rounds. How can you have an encounter with a dacoit when the police fire only two rounds? I'm sure even the dacoits would have fired more than that. You were just very lucky that you did not get massacred. Firing two rounds is not an encounter, Raman! Go and take his dying declaration, and let's close this matter.'

I was familiar with the belief that a person on the verge of death would not lie. And therefore, greater credibility is given to a statement made in such a situation. Little did I know that this episode would come back to haunt me, very soon.

> As a policeman, following the law is not just your duty, it is your dharma! However, there are times when, in the heat of the moment, it becomes necessary to take decisions in which strict legal procedures are not followed. *Never* for personal gain, never to the detriment of any; only, and only, for the greater good.

Letter to Veena, Dabra, August 1978

On the night of 31 August 1978, we had an encounter with the dacoit Jawan Singh and his gang near Antri village. The exchange of fire lasted 15 to 20 minutes, and all four dacoits were killed. The cries of agony of the dacoits as they fell still echo in my ears, and their bullet-ridden bodies often loom before me. The experience made me feel sick and sad; all the more because in those short minutes, my belief that Life is the greatest gift of God to Humankind was overturned. I could not restrain the tears that welled up in my eyes at the values that lay in shambles before me in that moment of alleged glory.

Letter to Veena, Gwalior, November 1978

Gwalior is limping back to normal after some student trouble. We had a close shave when a country-made bomb was thrown at our jeep. It was indeed a narrow thing, and fortunately we were not carrying firearms—if we were, we would certainly have opened fire, and there would have been certain death.

We did unleash a furious lathi charge and as usual, I was at the forefront of this operation. We arrested 68 students, out of whom 40 had injuries. We hoped that the sound thrashing we gave them would induce the required deterrence.

> Officers must change their method of work and attitude to suit the local conditions in which they are working.

My Promotion—to Fatherhood!

Veena was away with her parents in Jabalpur, where her father was GM of the ordnance factory. I was sitting on my lawn one evening when the telephone at my side rang, and I was told that the cloth shop belonging to a local MLA had caught fire. This was in that politically historical era of the late 1970s, when the Congress had been overthrown and other political parties had just started coming up. The MLA and I did not get along very well, so I thought I'd better go and pay him a visit so that he would not be able to complain that Saheb was in town but hadn't bothered to come and see him in his moment of crisis.

By midnight, I returned home and went to sleep. In the morning when I got up and was sitting on the lawn having my tea, something was niggling in the back of my mind. There was something important that I had to attend to—what was it? Yes, the MLA's shop had caught fire. Yes, there were already allegations that he had set fire to it himself for the insurance. But there was another conversation that I was unable to recall. And it was a very important one. What was it? I scratched my head and thought hard but it continued to elude me.

Reluctantly, I phoned the exchange. We would normally curse these fellows for eavesdropping on all our calls, but this time the habit turned out to be quite useful! Luckily it was the same chap; the shift had not yet changed.

'Did I get any long-distance call yesterday?' I asked.

'Yes, sir, you did, sir, from Jabalpur.'

'And what did we talk about?'

'Sir, you got good news, sir, congratulations were taking place!'

Then I remembered. Veena's father had phoned. My attention had been diverted by the calls immediately thereafter, regarding the fire. And so, it was the telephone operator from whom I now heard the good news that I had become a father, that my son was born. It was 29 March 1979. 'Mother and baby are doing fine,' as we used to convey news in those days.

The very next day, I received orders, through a teleprinter message, that I had been transferred to a place called Neemuch, as sub-divisional police officer (SDOP), equivalent to ASP.

Caught on the Wrong Foot

I had completed about 18 months as ASP Dabra and moved to my posting feeling quite pleased with my achievements. This was around the time when the Emergency had been lifted and elections were fought, and the Janata Party had come into power. I was told, 'Oh! This is the constituency of the chief minister of Madhya Pradesh. This means that you have been handpicked.' I never had any interactions with politicians, not finding theirs an attractive circle, and stayed away. But it was satisfying to know that one's work had been noticed and appreciated.

Neemuch was a reasonably nice place. It is the original headquarters of the CRPF, which was raised by the British as the Crown Representative Police Force, in Mandsaur District. After Independence, it became the Central Reserve Police Force, as it is known now. But at its inception, the force was set up to keep an eye on the princely states that were not under British rule. At the time of Independence, India had 565 princely states, referred to by the British as 'protectorates'. When any of them stepped out of line, battalions of the CRPF would be sent in to sort things out. Yes, to sort things out, not to assist! If any prince was misbehaving, the CRPF would go along and twist his arm just that little bit to bring him back to form.

Well, I left for Neemuch and took charge. Right next to the SDOP's house was the CRPF training centre. I was new, staying on my own, as Veena and our newborn son were in Jabalpur. I thought it would be a good thing to enjoy the sporting facilities there and mix with the CRPF officers, so I would go to the campus every evening to play badminton or some game, meet people, and then return home.

One day, I had just got home from my session playing games at the CRPF campus when I got a telephone call.

In 1979, having a telephone in small-town India was a privilege of very few. As a police officer, I had a connection, but there was only one phone plug in the house. It had a cord several metres long, and the telephone orderly would carry it to me, having first answered it, introducing himself and asking who the caller was. Making a call was not as simple as picking up the receiver and dialling your number. We had a manual exchange, and you had to give the number to the operator, who would then connect you.

Very early in my career, my SP, M.D. Sharma, had advised me to pick up incoming calls myself and use the telephone orderly, if at all, only to put through outgoing calls. This is because informants usually make their calls hesitantly and surreptitiously, sometimes making blank calls to check whether the officer picks up the call himself.

Accordingly, I picked up the receiver of the black instrument myself and said hello.

The voice on the other side asked if this was Vijay Raman speaking and when I confirmed that it was, he introduced himself as the IGP of Madhya Pradesh.

Oh! In those days, the IGs were the chiefs of police. I said, 'Yes sir. Good evening, sir.' It was the first time I was speaking to the boss of the police department of Madhya Pradesh!

He then asked me a simple question, 'Vijay, is everything okay on the CRPF campus?'

'Yes sir,' I replied confidently. 'I've just come back from there a few minutes ago, after a game of badminton with some officers.'

'All right,' he said. 'But could you just check once more, for my sake, and let me know?'

I made a few inquiries and found that my IG was right. Trouble was simmering; a police agitation was imminent! This was the first CRPF agitation; it happened to take place when I was in Neemuch in 1979.

The Emergency had recently been lifted. Among various changes implemented by the new government, a need was felt for having unions in the police and the paramilitary forces. Unfortunately, once unionism starts, the officers' authority gets diminished. This revolt against the officers of the CRPF—the first major situation given to me to handle—had been brought to my attention by my IGP who was sitting far away!

Surprisingly for an organization where discipline is taken very seriously, when I called him back to report on the situation, he had only two simple sentences to sum up his response: 'Vijay, didn't I catch you on the wrong foot? Be careful next time.'

'Yes, you did, sir. Thank you very much. I will, sir.' Any other senior officer could have blasted me badly for my utter lack of awareness of what was going on under my nose.

As time went by, the unease on the CRPF campus grew fiercer. Subordinate officers were indulging in physical violence against the lower staff functions.

Once again, the phone rang and a now-familiar voice asked for my position. I informed him that CRPF constabulary were being physically assaulted by their senior officers and subordinate officers. He replied, 'Listen to me, Vijay. This is your IG speaking. The CRPF people have run away from their campus and come to you. And they have come under the protection of the MP police. You are there as my representative. See that you ensure their total protection! Nobody should be allowed to touch them.'

He continued, 'Yes, there are very senior IPS officers of our cadre on deputation with the CRPF in Neemuch. They might find it easy to intimidate a young officer. Do not get overawed! And if you feel it necessary, open fire.'

For a moment, I was aghast! This was my IG, telling me in such clear terms: pick up your weapon. And if even one of our senior officers mishandles a member of the constabulary, fire!

There can be no greater professional advice so clearly spelt out, with no ambiguity. You know what your duty is, and you must do it.

Fortunately, nothing like this was necessary.

The constables were taken to the police stations and food was arranged for them from the local lodges. I went up to a DIG-rank officer and, after paying him proper respects as due, I explained to him, 'Sir, these are my orders from my IGP. I am duty-bound to obey. It will be in the best interests of the Madhya Pradesh police, and of the CRPF, if you leave this place. Please don't agitate the men by your presence.' I spoke politely but firmly. By this time, I had been issued a rifle, and seeing that I held it—though inconspicuously—while speaking to him, he knew that I meant business.

The CRPF agitation was thus defused. I reported this to my IG and he said, 'Okay, good. Try to get some sleep. I'll be arriving at midnight, don't bother to receive me. We will meet in the morning. Good night.'

When I reflect upon the past years, I recall very gratefully that I have never had to wait for a promotion, neither due to a lack of vacancies, nor due to there being no suitable post. The department always found a good post for me. And this was an early occasion that established the trend.

Within two days of this incident, after just three months in Neemuch, I was promoted and posted back to Gwalior as additional superintendent of police (additional SP). Chambal was calling me back!

Raman or Raman?

For me, it was not just a promotion but also a good posting, since I was familiar with the men, the officers, and the people of the place. I packed up and left. At the SP's office in Gwalior, I went to pay him my salutations and report that I had arrived, and he laughed in relief. It turned out that someone else had reported in my place.

'Raman Kakkad? But I had asked for Vijay Raman!' M.D. Sharma told me. 'So, I had to listen to Khurana Saheb briefing me on the value of referring to one's juniors by their first name. Not to enhance their fondness for one, but to create the right sort of camaraderie and willingness required for commitment and efficiency at the workplace!'

Vijay with his mentor, M.D. Sharma

The Price of Being Idealistic

Every day, we would receive a report called the daily situation report (DSR). It mandates all serious events such as blind murder, unidentified dead bodies, and various offences that must be supervised by either the SP or the ASP.

One day, I received a report of the discovery of an unidentified dead body. Somehow the name of the place, which fell under the police station of Pandokhar, rang a bell, and I found myself rushing anxiously towards it with a growing sense of dread. It was about 100 km from Gwalior and by the time I got there, the body, though badly mauled and with limbs dismembered, had been identified. Beside it sat a woman clutching two children tightly to herself and wailing loudly.

It was a terrible, terrible feeling to know that this was my fault. I was responsible for the death of this informer. I was the person responsible for all those who were killed by Devi Singh after his release, until he was terminated by my junior, SP Asha Gopal. It would always remain on my conscience that my actions, though purely with the intention of upholding human rights and protecting human life, had led to so much violence and misery.

These are the thoughts that often disturb sensitive police officers, making them face a type of dilemma that nobody else can help them solve.

A Land of Bandits and a Cursed River

People of my generation who grew up in India would have read news about who the dacoits were and what they did, and might even have a sense of the terrain in which the dacoits of the Chambal lived. But anyone unfamiliar with the place and time, particularly young people today, would not understand what it was like or have any sense of the obstacles and dangers that were involved in policing back then.

Chambal is a large area with a peculiar topography of dunes and ravines not seen anywhere else in India. These were formed by the force of water cutting through the land, and for an outsider, it is an area that is difficult to navigate. There are settlements and villages even in the midst of the ravines, and it is impossible to know whether they were already there when the ravine formed or whether the ravine grew around them. To get from one place to another is extremely difficult for anyone unfamiliar with the area. You can get hopelessly lost, as you might in a maze. However, once you begin understanding the geometrical pattern of the ravines, it becomes easier to know where to enter, and over time, the surroundings start becoming familiar.

Other than the terrain, the people of this region were also unique. Their culture developed almost in isolation, and while they had a lot in common with people of the neighbouring areas, some of their attributes were unique.

There was also a strong sense of justice—an interesting sense of justice, very different from what we are used to. When I studied Law, one of the things that fascinated me was understanding the causes that had given rise to a law. One of the sources of a law is the customs of the people. When a custom is predominant, the wisdom of the legislature will formulate the custom into a law that can be implemented. And some of the customs in this region are what have shaped the indigenous laws here.

First of all, people here were deeply conscious of caste, not just in terms of untouchability but also as a pecking order. While Brahmins were at the top, there were also various subgroups—Sharmas and Mishras, among others—and these had their own precise hierarchy. This applied to how they spoke and were spoken to, or where they stood or sat in a public gathering; basically every social interaction was strictly dictated by caste, marriage being the most carefully monitored! Lower castes were also kept firmly in their place. Any breach of these age-old rules was taken extremely seriously and was bound to have consequences, sometimes fatal. If a person felt aggrieved or insulted, they would hit back. But there were exceptions and unexpected alliances emerged. Notorious dacoit Maan Singh, a legend in his lifetime with a temple to his name, was from a higher caste but his gang had many dacoits from lower castes.

Secondly, women were held in the highest esteem and no misbehaviour against a woman was condoned. It may seem strange to hear that a region famous for its law-breaking dacoits could have been so particular about the safety of and respect for women, but it was so. The women were, of course, expected to behave with all propriety in order to deserve this veneration.

Next, the people in this region were very, very possessive about their land. This may well be true of everybody everywhere. But the intensity of this feeling, and the response to any infringement in this region, was extreme. Any transgression would immediately be punished, and not with a simple imprisonment, because this was not a minor offence but a serious one that deserved death.

And it was the same when the modesty of a woman was outraged.

Linked to all this was the prestige derived from the ownership of a licensed weapon. Whether a 12-bore gun or a weapon of any calibre, displaying it was as much a source of prestige as a row of ribbons and medals might have been to someone from the forces, or a car brand for a city dweller of today.

With this uncompromising, cast-iron value system, life was sometimes quite difficult! Let me tell you about a case that took place during my time in that area. One evening, two brothers returned home after working all day in their fields. They sat in front of their home, smoking hookahs, relaxing, waiting to be served dinner.

One brother said, 'I've been wondering whether I should also buy an animal, maybe a cow or a buffalo.'

He would have said this in the dialect of the region, of course.

The other replied, 'Oh really? And where do you plan to tie it?'

'Right here,' said the first brother.

'Oh really?' asked the second. 'But this is my land! You can't tie your cow here!'

The first brother jumped up and walked indignantly into the house. He brought out a short wooden post and a hammer, with which he hammered the post into the ground. This was the kind of post used to wind rope around and tie cattle to. With this, the first brother had established his right to tie his cow right there.

Furious, the second brother too jumped up and strode into the house. He went in, brought out his weapon, and shot his brother down. He simply shot him dead.

This, it was clear, was the value of land.

> Whether we like it or not, legality and morality have their own geographical boundaries!

Murder at a Wedding

Another example I'll give you took place some years later, in my post-Paan Singh years. Yes, the Paan Singh encounter is a line through my career and people saw me differently before and after! This was after; I believe by then I had some credibility with the local people.

A Dalit boy from Umri village got married. The marriage party had gone to the bride's village for the wedding rituals, and were bringing the girl to her new home. They walked in a procession with musicians playing and people dancing, and on the way, passed some Thakur homes. A group of young men sitting on the veranda watched with contempt, smoking and passing snide remarks. As the boy ceremoniously walked with his new bride into the house, a lewd comment was heard by all, 'These *chamar*s sure know how to pick their beauties!' Loud, mocking guffaws rang out.

I should mention here that use of the word 'chamar', which is the name of a caste, with the intent to insult or humiliate, is today an offence punishable under the provisions of the Scheduled Castes and Scheduled Tribes (Prevention of Atrocities) Act, 1989.

The ceremony of taking the new bride into the house continued with all its formality. But as soon as it was over, the groom picked up his gun, loaded it, and came out, walking to the house where the spoilt Thakur brats were still sitting and smoking. Taking aim, he shot and killed the boy who had made the mocking remark. In cold blood, in broad daylight. And in doing this, he was simply following the law dictated by the customs followed in this place.

For us, as you can imagine, it was a different situation altogether! The young Dalit boy was absconding, the Thakurs were up in arms, and the entire chamar community was lined up, ready for whatever was coming. We had to prevent an imminent bloodbath! It was a very tense time and for 34 days

I was roaming around searching for the missing boy, meeting the community leaders of both sides to placate them, constantly watchful, constantly alert for any sudden movement on either side. I remember walking with a few of my people in those maze-like ravines for days at a time, unable to sleep.

Ultimately, the boy surrendered and he was sentenced. You can see the consequences of what might seem like a simple insulting comment. There is an entire framework that prescribes what the punishment should be, and in a case like this, it is different from our existing laws. Who can be blamed: the people with a tradition of a certain law, or the police and the judiciary, with their own fixed sense of justice and punishment?

People ascribe the nature of the people and their customs to the water of the Chambal River! And living there, I can certainly speak for the water of Chambal River, which I have experienced in a different sense. The water was so pure and wholesome that food got digested easily. The pulses and grains grown in the region were of the best quality. The soil was very productive, and I believe the per-acre yield was comparable to Punjab. This milieu formed the background of our police system.

Now, don't forget that our police system was also manned mostly by people of the same area, having the same mentality, the same outlook, the same sense of revenge—a caste-based way of life. They accepted such incidents as absolutely normal. At the same time, as I soon found out, there was great respect for authority. I was a South Indian officer without much knowledge of the place, hardly even able to speak their language. There was a lot of curiosity on both sides, but there was also respect.

A Judicial Inquiry

In March 1980, I was promoted from additional SP Gwalior to SP Bhind. A few days before I left for my new posting, I was driving past the High Court on my way to a meeting. I saw a convict being escorted to the court by policemen and a group of lawyers was confronting them. As I watched, the altercation became intense, and in a few seconds, mayhem erupted. I got out of my jeep and as I rushed to the spot, I saw one of the lawyers picking up a large stone to hit a constable on his head. I ordered him to stop but he did not respond, so I stopped him physically. He resisted, and this led to a lathi charge. The indignant lawyers demanded a judicial inquiry into the charge. Because of the judicial inquiry, my transfer orders were cancelled.

Very few police officers face judicial inquiries in their careers. A neutral judge from outside the state was called in. The judge was not an opponent or a rival. But I had to explain everything to him—every single thing. And I was cross-examined by a battery of lawyers from the legal community of Gwalior, who were all up in arms against this police incident. I was totally X-rayed, and every single thing about me came out.

The inquiry was a great learning, somewhat like going to war but coming back unscathed.

> To be thoroughly examined, inside out, in public, may feel invasive and ravaging. But to then be cleared of all charges is a vindication like no other!

SP without a Moustache

In August 1980, cleared of all charges of the judicial inquiry, I was reposted by the government to Bhind as SP.

I went to my new posting by road and straight to my home, which is different from arriving by train where people can come and see you at the railway station to assess you. Everybody is curious: the politicians, the crooks, the overground support system of the gangs, the caste leaders—everybody. And they want to know everything! Does he enjoy alcohol? Does he eat meat? Does he have weaknesses that we can exploit? Because this is a very exploitative society.

In our home, as in the home of every SP in that area, one corner of the house was set up as a camp office, with one room for the officer to sit and an ante room for the support staff. I had a good three-bedroom house. Adjacent to the office was the garage, where people who came to see me could wait.

When they entered, they would do namaskar with great reverence. Everybody wanted to touch my feet, which was another tradition.

I always wanted to get straight to the point and find out what the problem was. But I would first ask them where they were from—not just the name of the village, but also which police station was responsible for that village. That way if anything was required, I would know whom to contact. But they would say no, sir, everything is fine, we have just come to meet you. The word they used was *darshan*, which means 'to see' but is also a word with implications of veneration.

Well, if they have only come for darshan, you dismiss them and the next person comes in, and the next—and they have all just come for darshan. But, of course, what they have come for is to make an assessment. They want to know who exactly this person is and what they can expect of him. And they may not have what you would call the most modern and scientific techniques of assessment, but they definitely have their own parameters of assessing someone based on their own needs.

I got a good sense of this because they would often sit on their haunches in a group outside to gather their thoughts after meeting me, and their conversations could be heard quite clearly through the window in my room.

'*Aa toh moda dikhtoi*! (But he looks like a kid!)'

'*Haan, iske toh muchhe bhi nahin*! (He doesn't even have a moustache!)'

They were surprised because a person in authority was expected to be broad and hefty; better still if he had a big belly, but more important were the solid dimensions! My only advantage was my height; my frame was lean. And what sort of wimpy man would not sport a moustache?

'He called us "aap"! (He spoke to us respectfully!)'

They were not used to cultured language from a person of authority. An SP of solid worth had to fit into their expectations, and I did not.

My chaps were listening too, with amusement.

'*Aa kaise daket marega*? (How is he ever going to kill any dacoits?)'

Apparently, they got a clear sense that I was not a killer! And then came another observation, quite a sensible one actually: '*Pan aane toh High Court ma vakil ko maaro hoi*! (He beat up the lawyers in the High Court in Gwalior!)'

They were impressed because I had confronted the lawyers whom they saw as people of higher authority. I don't know whether winning over a lawyer is considered equivalent to killing a dacoit. But there they were, sitting together nodding their turbaned heads, and the consensus was clear: I was not up to the mark.

Dom Moraes Visits Bhind

In his book *Answered by Flutes: Reflections from Madhya Pradesh*,* Dom Moraes has written about a journey he made through Bhind. He learnt that villagers fear the police, perceiving them to be just as bad as the dacoits, with the constabulary demanding bribes, molesting young women, beating up and torturing suspects, shooting captured dacoits on the spot, framing innocent people whom they disliked, and suborning witnesses. He qualified this by saying:

---

*Moraes, Dom, *Answered by Flutes: Reflections from Madhya Pradesh*, Asia Publishing House, 1983, pp. 187–8.

> The dacoits may be in daily fear of their lives, but so are the policemen whose duty it is to arrest or kill them. Whatever affects the psychology of a dacoit will equally affect the psychology of his enemy.
>
> Bhind has the atmosphere of a disaster area. A habit of fear has wrinkled the faces of the people to a withdrawn, faraway look. The landscape, seared by the sun, seems nonetheless frozen, lunar. To traverse it for long distances, as I did, has a surrealistic effect on the senses. The crocodiles by the Chambal open and shut their mouths as though in speech, but in this landscape, there is nothing to say. The breeze seems to reek of burnt huts and bodies. An immense silence compounded by the sounds of raped women, bewildered children, and terrified men is audible in the air. The arms of the ravine cacti, dryly stained with red flowers, have the aspect of serried crosses to which bodies were once nailed.
>
> The SP of Bhind, Mr Vijay Raman, is an intelligent and sympathetic person. After a prolonged day of dust, he sat with me over an ablative beer, and remarked a little sadly, 'Most dacoits become dehumanised. It's necessary to their profession. They have to wipe out their sensibility in order to function at all. The destruction of property, the murders of informers and villagers, are done very coldly. The sexual crimes are animal, there is physical contact but no human contact. There's no emotion involved in anything they do: no guilt and no pity, for those are fatal weaknesses. It's only when cornered, fighting for their lives, that humanity returns to them, the knowledge of a last reality.

I did feel flattered by his description of me, and the objective way in which he reported what I had told him: my understanding and sympathy for dacoits as human beings that later became influenced by the suffering they wreaked on the villagers and seeing my own men crippled and killed in encounters. I told him that when I dealt with dacoits, I had to become as dehumanized as they were, shedding all sensibility, becoming exactly what my enemy was. I did not like it, but it happened.

Recruiting Constables in Bhind

One day, Vijay was away, and I was sitting at home when the orderly came to tell me that a young man wanted to meet me. He had come with a request to be considered for recruitment as a constable. I told him to go to the place where the recruitment was being held. If he met the required criteria, he would be selected.

I sent him off and when I told Vijay about it later, I realized that he already knew. He had circumvented the process of collecting money by cutting it short. There was a physical test, followed by a written test, with a gap of a few days in between. What was the need for the gap? That was when there was the possibility of deals to be made between the aspirants and the constabulary. With the process supervised and the gap removed, results were announced within two days flat.

When the list came out, we had visits from many young men who came to thank Vijay for making the recruitment purely on merit. They explained with gratitude that they had no money to pay and would not have been selected without this intervention.

—VEENA RAMAN

The Legend of Chambal's Dacoits

I've been told that this started in the twelfth century, during the time of Prithviraj Chauhan. They were called baagis, people who had gone against the establishment. These were the people who had revolted against the system laid down by the maharajas or chieftains of their time. This area had been ruled by hereditary princes for centuries, with their own borders and their own laws. The baagis, for whatever reason, had done something that was against the laws laid down by the rulers and had no choice but to flee. Gwalior, a relatively urban area, was not as badly affected as Bhind and Morena. It is said that this could be because of the river, and also because they border with UP and Rajasthan where you have people with the same mentality.

In the initial few months, just as these people were testing me, my subordinates were also doing so. I knew that I was under a crucial test there.

Another issue was caste. What was my caste? On what basis could they slot me into the categories that were familiar to them and that dominated every interaction? 'Vijay Raman' doesn't suggest any caste. My caste is not evident from my name. But they knew my predecessor, my very well-known predecessor who later became DGP of the state, M. Natarajan. He was from Tamil Nadu, a South Indian like me. And he was a Brahmin—so they deduced that I must be a Brahmin too. And so, without any input from me, the Brahmins began to associate themselves with me. In the process, the Thakurs began to feel, 'Oh, so he is a Brahmin!' For the Dalits, it didn't make any difference.

Your Police Station—Your Dacoit

The DIG in charge of the Chambal in those days was very clear in his mind about one particular thing: that as a police force, there is a structure that assigns every citizen to a particular police station. He was firm in his belief that every dacoit leader belonged to a particular district. In that district, he belonged to a particular village, and that village came under a particular police station. So, if there was a dacoit, then there had to be a police station that owned that dacoit. And that dacoit owned the police station.

For me this meant that every single dacoit who was from Bhind was my responsibility. And Bhind had many dacoits! In fact, the dacoits of Bhind were multiplying, and quite fast. This was because Malkhan Singh, who, when I joined, had an enormous 40-member gang in the early 1980s, was from a village in my district of Bhind.

If anything related to Malkhan Singh came up, I could not get away by pointing out, 'But sir, he's in UP, not in MP!' The DIG would reply, 'What the hell? He's your absconder. He is from a police station under you. What are you doing about this? Is it not your fundamental duty to find out where he is and chase him? And make life miserable for him? He has committed a crime and has fled, formed a gang and is playing merry hell in the rural areas, or wherever he is working. And you are sitting here happily telling me, "Sir, he is in UP"? Does that mean your job is done?' This was a very important, fundamental, crucial lesson of policing in those days! None of us could sit back and say, 'Well, I've tried my best.'

Malkhan never committed any offence in Bhind District as long as I was there, during the pre-Paan Singh days. Mind you, this is very important—the pre-Paan Singh days. He would pass through my area to take shelter in a huge forest area in the district. There it was very difficult to track anyone.

And again, let me dispel any misconceptions you might have about this! In those days, no dacoits in Chambal were going around on horseback. They were all walking. The movies have depicted this incorrectly. There were no horses, and there could not have been horses, because horses meant expenditure; they meant money. Where would the fodder for a horse come from? Where could the money come from? Every source of money could be detected. At night, when a gang is surrounded, you can tell your men to be silent, but can you keep your horses silent? The horses will neigh. And horses are easy to track, by their excreta, among other things. The dacoits do not ride on horseback—they walk. They walk through the ravines. I know that Malkhan used to walk every night, often as much as 22 km! But he was not a problem for me, in the sense that he was not committing any crime in my district, or in any way making life miserable for the villagers. But he was a prime target for me because he had committed a murder, and he was an absconder. Therefore, it was my legal responsibility to catch him. In the meantime, because Malkhan was getting away with whatever he did, small gangs began to mushroom, and I had five or six such gangs on my hands.

The Shepherd Dacoits

One of these was the gang of Uday Singh Gadaria, who was of the Gadaria caste, a caste of shepherds who take cattle to the fields to graze. For us, from the point of view of the police, these are the most dangerous people! And if these people are going to be the allies of a dacoit, they will be the most valuable assets because they know the ins and outs of the area. They roam with their cattle every day and every nook and cranny of the area is familiar to them: which path is connected to which village, where the waterbodies are, where the police are to be found. Ever since childhood, they have wandered in this area and know every inch of it better than anyone else.

Another notorious gang leader of the early 1970s was Mohar Singh, very well known, who was of the Gujjar caste—also shepherds, and very familiar with the lie of the land. He was also a very slippery character on account of the knowledge of the ravines he had inherited because of his origins, which the police did not have. When he became a dacoit, he fully exploited it.

Uday Singh Gadaria had a gang of just four or five members. But the amount of tension he created for me was immeasurable. Every day there was a kidnapping, and we had another crime on our hands: a kidnapping for ransom.

In the MP State Legislative Assembly, the Opposition was making constant taunts: 'Sir, you have sent that new boy to take care of this big problem! No wonder nothing is getting done. Why can't you send someone with more experience?' These statements are on record. I would face firing and questions every day, and my time and energy were being drained by them. The questions also flustered our chief minister (CM). The home minister decided to visit and understand the situation for himself. That night, he stayed in the Bhind Circuit House, which was on the outskirts of the town. Now, this fellow, Uday Singh Gadaria, was roaming around in that area. Just as we had informers about his actions, perhaps he had his own informers about ours. And so, irrespective of the fact that the home minister was staying there, and there was considerable police bandobast (arrangements and preparations made to deal with something) in the area, this fellow and his gang stayed put there.

Now the area around the circuit house had many farms, and most of them had tube wells. A family member would be in charge of switching the pump on and off. On the night that the home minister was staying at the circuit house, this fellow went around all the tube wells, and kidnapped everybody he found. And on that one night, the night when the home minister happened to be staying at the circuit house, five people in the neighbourhood were kidnapped! In one night! You can well imagine the uproar in the town, not just from the Opposition party but citizens, activists, students—everybody. I just didn't know what was happening. Perhaps I was not getting the right type of support from the local police.

At the Receiving End

Every day when the Assembly was on, I had no choice but to answer the motions and issues raised. Everybody wanted immediate replies. I would transmit whatever I knew.

After lunch, at about 3.00 p.m., I would get into my vehicle and start driving. At first, it was just aimless. It's not that I had any particular agenda, specific people to meet, or anything like that. I did not know anyone. But I had to familiarize myself. I had joined in August 1980, and for almost all the rest of 1980, this is all I did.

As I drove around, I would enter a village. They would know from the vehicle and the accompanying policemen that SP Saheb had arrived. They would come out and the headman would invite me in, and I would sit with them on a charpoy. I was only cultivating them, observing them. Just like people were coming to see me, I was also going around to show them that I was available to them, that I was concerned about them. I would go into the village at midnight, 1.00 a.m. If I went early and they were sitting down to eat, I would eat with them: dal, roti, sabji, achar, whatever they were having. They would note that I had no issue about eating with anybody, that I never even asked. Clearly, to me, caste was irrelevant. Sometimes, my drivers and my gunman would frown saying, 'Saheb, where are you going, who are you sitting with?' I would ask them, 'Are they dacoits? Do they assist the dacoits? They're just respectable men, right? So how does it make any difference?' But they were looking at caste, something that had made no sense to me since my young days. It had never made sense to me that the upper castes shunned the temple pond where all others took a dip and prayed. When we went to offer flowers at the temple in Peramangalam, a priest would come out with a pot of water, sprinkle it around our offerings, and only then accept them. Even when offering the ceremonial sandalwood that is applied on the forehead, they would make small paste balls and throw it so that they had no contact with the worshippers. If there were five people, five paste balls would be thrown. I found it all absolutely ludicrous and that feeling never left me.

The caste situation was bad, but now we were also being afflicted by the growing power of the unions. As I mentioned earlier, it was a time when the police and paramilitary were getting unionized, and the MP police also had a union. A union meant lack of discipline, as there were people in the ranks who would challenge the authority of higher-ranking police officials. And this was naturally a major headache for all of us. At our very first meeting with the CM, we told him that this had to go, that we could not function under these conditions. It was in this situation, with a lack of discipline and disregard for authority, that a truly gruesome incident took place.

Boiling Over

The Gwalior mela is an annual event, started in olden times as a cattle fair and growing gradually, sponsored by the maharaja of Gwalior during the era when the place was a princedom. In the late 1970s and early 1980s, as Madhavrao Scindia grew in power, the mela grew with the sponsorship and encouragement of the Scindia family, the hereditary rulers of Gwalior. From just a cattle mela, it expanded to a large exhibition ground with stalls offering various products for sale. Because of government support, taxes were waived, and products were available at the lowest prices at the mela.

As the mela grew and attracted more and more visitors from all the districts of the state, the SP Gwalior would always ask for additional manpower for policing the mela. And he would request for police from surrounding districts who could spot potential mischief-makers.

At the mela in December 1980, when I was SP Bhind, 30 to 40 people had been sent from each of the five surrounding districts—

Bhind, Morena, Datia, Shivpuri and Guna. They reported to the SP Gwalior and were deployed for the mela.

Of the traders who came from Mathura, Agra, Kanpur, cities of Punjab, and other places all around the country to set up their stalls at the Gwalior mela, one of them was a sweetmeat vendor of Mathura of such high repute that while the mela was on, the officials of Gwalior, including the senior-most, would stop making mithais and desserts at home and order from him.

One day, some constables who were on duty went to his shop and demanded jalebis, gulab jamuns, and a few more things. The man was preparing their order and perhaps serving others also at the same time. The constables became impatient and started shouting. When they still didn't get what they wanted immediately, in fury, one of them picked up the boy who was helping him, and threw him into the huge kadhai of boiling oil.

It was a terrible thing that had happened. This was the attitude and shocking indiscipline displayed by the MP police that day! Just because they were made to wait a few minutes, in anger they committed a heinous crime, throwing a boy into boiling oil.

Word of the incident spread like wildfire, and there was absolute, total commotion. Curfew was declared. And this was when the government woke up. They could finally stand up and say that enough was enough. Till then, nobody had been listening. After all, even a police union would be a vote bank for the politicians. But once a serious event like this took place, nobody could deny that something had gone terribly wrong.

Come January 1981, Bhopal was full of hectic activity with back-to-back IG meetings and CM meetings, and decisions were taken. In the normal course, the process for dismissal is very time-consuming. But now a decision was taken by the government to dismiss about 135 police personnel who were on duty during that mela at Gwalior, aiming to invoke a provision in Article 311 of the Constitution that permits a government, the president, or the appointing authority to do away with the services of a government employee without inquiry.

Keeping in mind that Republic Day, 26 January, was coming up, the announcement was withheld so that the sanctity of the Republic Day arrangements, for which the police was responsible, would not be disturbed. We were informed that a decision was pending, and that dismissals would not be done as per the usual procedure of holding a departmental inquiry, among other things. However, on the night of 24 January, we were sent a list of names of the people who were going to be dismissed.

The authorities enlisted the support of the BSF to assist the local administration of the district in ensuring that no untoward incident happened. So, on the night of the 24th when I received the list, two BSF companies also entered Bhind. These companies had arrived to take over the police stations, the reserve lines, and the police. We were expected to hand over all our equipment and weapons to them.

When two companies of the BSF marched into Bhind, they were seen by the local police and by the general public. Everybody began wondering what was going on. Everyone knew that it was something serious; everyone knew that something big was about to happen.

For my part, there were arrangements to be made, and it wasn't too hard because schools had holidays and the troops could be accommodated there, while officers were put up in government rest houses. All the logistical arrangements were made. When the company commandants came to ask me, 'Orders please, sir,' I would repeat, 'Please hold on.'

My problem was that I had 18 police stations and 15 police chowkis, all armed police. And I also had 8 companies of the Special Armed Force (SAF) deployed in my district.

Whom could I disarm? I needed at least two battalions to disarm everybody.

Plus, we also had about 3,000 licensed weapon holders among

the villagers. Were they on the side of the police—the police who were revolting—or with me? It was impossible to know.

I had a very, very complex situation on hand and made my preparations. That evening, I sat down to peruse the list of people whose orders of dismissal had been prepared and sent.

Turning Point

This list contained the belt number of the policeman, his name, his rank, and the district to which he belonged. And to my great and very pleasant surprise, I found that there was nobody on that list from Bhind! Not one of the constables I had deputed to the mela that day was on that list! And this gave me courage. Why, I felt, should I hand over my police station?

Every commander knows very well that nobody likes to hand over their weapons to an outsider. It's what a defeated army does—surrendering weapons and telling another force 'you take over and do what you want'. That was something I just could not digest.

There was another aspect to the situation. Even if I did follow the orders, disarmed my boys, and handed over the police station, would everything be hunky-dory? After all, this was Bhind! A place where they first act and then think!

On thinking it over and considering every aspect of the situation—as I have always done before taking any decision—I decided not to do so. By God's grace, this was my decision. And I would report it to the collector. Before doing that, however, I spoke to my DIG. Fortunately, he was the same person who was my SP when I was ASP Dabra. We had worked with each other for about seven years and knew each other inside out.

'Sir, there is nobody from my district on the list. So where is the grievance? And why would they revolt?'

'This is a government order, Raman. And it is very serious. You could face dismissal from service under Article 311. Somebody can take it up if the procedure is not followed as laid down. If something goes wrong, your career is at risk.'

'Yes, sir, I understand.'

'But Raman, I know you will do what you think is right.'

He was not encouraging me, just expressing his trust in my abilities.

There was a BSF battalion headquartered in Bhind, and the commandant was older than me though not a senior in terms of service. I went to him and told him my decision. He tried to dissuade me, saying, 'This can land you in trouble.' I explained my reasons and left.

Next, I had to inform my collector because this was a government order, and it had come through the collector.

'I'm not going to do this.'

'Really? But why? It is a government order; you have to do it!'

I gave him my reasons. And he said, 'Fine, if that's what you say. But you will have to give it to me in writing.'

I agreed, and went back and gave it to him in writing. The die had been cast. I had no idea what was going to happen next.

Every district has an evening roll call in the police lines. Whoever is available there at the time has to assemble. Instructions are given, grievances are heard, the national anthem is sung, and they are then dispersed. As SP, one is supposed to go to this once in a while. I had never attended. But that evening, I decided to go for the roll call and informed my reserve inspector Shrotriya of my decision. When word spread that I would be attending, even those who were lazing around the house got up to come for the roll call. Most came in mufti—civil dress—as uniforms, which are a must for the morning roll call, are not required for evening roll call, which takes place at the end of the day's duties.

I can't recall the words I spoke exactly. But I'm sure any movie dialogue writer would have been proud of them! I explained to my team that I had done something nobody of their level was aware of, and that, as of this moment, I had defied a government instruction.

And what was the government instruction I had defied?

They were all well aware of what had happened at the Gwalior mela. I told them simply that because of the disaster that had taken place at the mela, 135 people were being dismissed. As I spoke, the words emerged spontaneously from my mouth. But I felt like the horses were running wild, their reins slipping out of my hands!

That was the situation, and they also knew it. I told them that I had complete faith and trust in them, and that the BSF had arrived and was in the barracks. Everybody knew that they had not come here to spend their holidays—they were here for a purpose, and this was what it was.

I told them about my decision. I was not going to ask any of them to hand over their weapons to the BSF. We were not going to hand the police lines over to the BSF. The kotwali thana would not be given to them. And I had taken this decision solely and purely because I trusted them. If any one of them now did anything that could be questioned by the authorities, I was going to lose my job.

I concluded by saying that I had only come to inform them that this was my decision. And now, I told them, my future was in their hands. Whatever they thought should be done, they should do. I had made my decision and I had told them what it was. Now it was their turn to make theirs.

I then went back to my residence.

After about 10 to 15 minutes, I heard slogans being shouted. I asked my security guard and he said there was a procession approaching. What was going on? It was about 7.00 or 7.30 p.m. by then.

What had happened was that there were three SAF companies of different battalions camping in the police lines. After the roll call, they heard the news that I had communicated. And they wanted to know—what about them? Why had their commandant not come to reassure them in the same way? They formed a procession and took to the streets. It was not a demand, more of a plea: 'What about us?'

I was sitting outside on my lawn, and sent word that some of them could come and talk to me. After a while, my orderly ushered four or five of them in. After the usual greeting formalities, they said, 'Sir, we are also MP police! Aren't we also your people?'

'What are you talking about?'

'They said you came for the roll call. And you told *your* boys something. What about us?'

Without missing a beat, I replied immediately, apologizing for what I'd done. 'I should have called you boys also. But it has been such a difficult decision for me to make, that it just slipped my mind. Yes, you should also have been there to hear my reassurance.' And I repeated to them all that I had said.

Some of the SAF were members of the police union. I told them the same thing and then repeated, 'My future is in your hands.' And they left, in the same procession, but now with a new slogan, 'SP Saheb zindabad, SP Saheb zindabad!'

The next day was the 26 January parade. I was supposed to make my announcement and take action the evening after the parade. The dismissal orders had come, and I was supposed to serve them. But since there was nobody from my district on the list, there was no action to take.

The parade went off very well. And, to my great surprise, the very day after 26 January 1981, things started changing. It was clear that something had hit the conscience of my men and officers: 'Our SP trusted us. Our SP stood by us. And he took a decision that could have been disastrous for him just because he trusted us. He put his neck under the sword because he had confidence in us. Now it is our turn!' This is the Bhind Morena mentality.

What happened next was just phenomenal. Every second day, I was having an encounter, or an arrest, or a surrender. Every second day! And this, I realized, was simply the impact of being honest and sincere with your subordinates.

Years later, I read a quote attributed to Chhatrapati Shivaji: 'If the king doesn't trust his soldier, the soldier will not trust the king.' It gave me a feeling of satisfaction to know that I had followed a principle espoused by one of the greatest leaders of all time.

Revenge on the Dead

About a month or two later, we received information about an encounter by a local deputy superintendent of police (DSP), about 30 km away from Bhind, on the bank of Sindh River. Seven dacoits were killed but no names were given; it was not one of the regular gangs.

I went to the site. As the SP, when I travelled, I had a driver, a gunman, and sometimes also took my PA, so it was mostly a group of four. In case I remembered something, or noticed something, my PA would record it. We arrived at the spot; police were standing there. There were dead bodies on the ground. We stood a little away from them, discussing how it had happened, who did what, had the dacoits been recognized, and so on.

Suddenly there was a burst of fire from an automatic weapon. A burst. All of us immediately took position; it was a reflex action arising from our training. When we looked up, we saw someone standing with his rifle over the dead body of one of the dacoits. And he had emptied all the bullets in his gun into the corpse!

The DSP and inspector chorused, 'Sir! He is your gunman.'

I took another look and realized that this was my replacement gunman; my regular gunman had gone on leave, and I had not recognized him immediately.

Now this was my responsibility. He was my gunman. I had to be the one to go and disarm him. I could not possibly tell somebody else, 'Go catch that fellow'!

I had to trust him and trust that he would trust me. I walked up to him. He was standing there, still stunned at what he had done. As I came closer, he dropped his weapon. And then he fell at my feet, sobbing. I lifted him up and asked, 'What happened? Why did you do that?'

And the words started pouring out of him in a frenzy, 'Sir, it is this fellow...' Abusive words poured out, words that my men would never ordinarily use in front of me. 'This is the guy who raped my sister!'

The point is, even after the man was dead, the atrocity he committed was not forgotten. Revenge must be taken, even on a dead body.

The Draconian Law

Our area had a lot of crime, dacoity and kidnappings in particular. Our CM was very concerned and became personally involved. He would call frequent meetings. One thing I liked about him was that he did more than just talking about it over a cup of tea with the IG or DIG. He wanted to speak to the officers in the field and would make it a point to periodically call his SPs for discussions. We could open up to him without being pulled up or told by our own seniors to not raise either this or that issue. One of the things I brought to his notice was this provision we had in the Indian Penal Code (IPC) for action against those who harbour criminals, under Sections 212 and 216 of the IPC.

It is common knowledge that gangs cannot exist without harbourers. However, the offence of harbouring a gang was a bailable one. Even if we made an arrest, the accused would walk free on bail and there would be no way we could get the required information from him. We explained to our CM that this was the weak link—that all the complaints against police inaction and incompetence hinged on our powerlessness in the face of this law. It was a law that protected the harbourer, the person without whom the dacoit could not function. Unless we pulled out all the harbourers, the dacoits were never going to get caught! We said, 'Sir, we need a new law!'

The moment we had a strong law that gave us power against the harbourers, we would bring things together. It's not that we did not know who the harbourers were—we had done at least that much policing!

Sometime in 1981, when I'd almost completed one year in the Chambal, the Anti-Dacoity Ordinance was enacted. It authorized the police to arrest harbourers and keep them in custody for up to 90 days. For a bail application to be entertained, the SP's clearance was required. Special courts were also created, which could try offences under this ordinance.

I wouldn't say that there was no downside to this law. It was a law that demonstrated the value of freedom as well as the value of privilege. It gave powers to the police that could certainly be misused. It placed a grave sense of responsibility on us. But in every such situation, there are those who will misuse and manipulate. Some did use it to commit the crime of extortion by using this law as a threat; some became wealthy through this law. Haunted by the fear of being locked up for 90 days, anyone would lose their sleep. All sorts of things would come to their mind: who would look after their family? They had to get their daughters married! It was simpler to pay up and stay out.

But that said, it must be acknowledged that it was the enactment of this ordinance, which was subsequently made into a law, that created a new regime of law and discipline in the Chambal. It enabled me to pick up Ramavtar Bhadoria, and this was key to the eventual surrender of the dreaded Daku Malkan Singh, which I will tell you about in a subsequent chapter.

4

MY ENCOUNTER WITH DACOIT PAAN SINGH TOMAR

A Call from Maharaj

'Hello, is it Mr Raman? SP Bhind?' the voice on the telephone asked. 'Maharaj is on the line for you.'

It was around 11.00 a.m. on 2 October 1982, and I was exhausted, but also filled with energy! The house was filled with people in a celebratory mood, and the congratulations were pouring in. I had arrived home at 10.00 that morning, driving straight back from Rathiyan-ka-Pura village where we had staked out all night, to be immediately engulfed by crowds of visitors—colleagues, media, local well-wishers.

That morning, the phone was ringing without stopping, and the telephone orderly was holding the instrument and its cradle, walking to wherever I was so that I could take the call. This time, the operator told me, 'Sir, call from Havana!' Puzzled, I wondered why someone was calling from such a distant place, whether the operator had ever connected a call there before, or if he even knew where it was! 'Sir, it is Maharaj,' he told me.

In Bhind in those days, there was no confusion whatsoever about who 'Maharaj' might be: he was Madhavrao Scindia, head of the royal family that had governed the region that became Gwalior State since the seventeenth century.

'Congratulations! Well done, Raman. What an achievement,' he said when he came on the line. 'Hope you and your boys are all safe.'

I thanked him and asked how he had found out, astonished that he, despite being in faraway Havana, already knew what we ourselves were only gradually beginning to come to terms with!

'I just saw it reported by the BBC!' he replied.

It slowly began to dawn on me what we had done. We had been in the thick of action for more than 14 hours, right through the night. All that time, there had been absolutely nothing on my mind except ensuring that we accomplished our mission and that my men stayed safe. Even when we made the decision to proceed—against regulations—as we had, late the previous evening, the consequences were far from our minds. But now, day had broken, a task that had seemed impossible was achieved, and we were facing something new and extraordinary. For me as a person, the Paan Singh encounter was a turning point in my career that established my credentials as a police officer and brought me the respect and affection of not just my team but also the local population.

Now, listening to Maharaj speaking of what he had heard in the international media, I understood the alternate and rather harsh reality of the situation: to the media across the world and in India too, it was a hero who had been brutally gunned down. Paan Singh had served in the Indian Army. He had won athletics medals for India. When he returned home to his village, the disparities and inequities of Indian society had given him no choice but to turn to dacoity. The media focused on these, and this gave rise to huge sympathy for Paan Singh and even contempt for the law-keepers who had gunned him and his gang down. There was no mention of the fact that, in the course of our duty, and at great risk to our own lives, we had removed a dangerous criminal and his gang from the face of this earth. However, the people of Chambal and its surroundings, who had lived in terror of the gang's burglaries and abductions, were deeply grateful for the capture.

The Background

Paan Singh was born in 1932, in Bhidosa village in Morena District, to a poor Thakur family. His father had some meagre landholdings. Financial constraints prevented him from continuing his education beyond an early stage. In 1949, he joined the army as a recruit. His latent athletic prowess soon surfaced, and he was given the training and opportunity to perform at international events where he earned medals for India. His army and sports career came to an end in 1972 when he retired as a subedar.

Meanwhile, Babu Singh—a close relative and an influential, well-to-do landlord—had usurped land belonging to Paan Singh's brother Matadin. Paan Singh made efforts to recover the land for his brother but was unsuccessful. Frustrated and vengeful, Paan Singh murdered Babu Singh and fled. It was March 1979. His brother Matadin and his nephew Balwant Singh joined him in the ravines where he was absconding. With the support and loyalty of many, in particular those of the Thakur community, Paan Singh's gang grew gradually and soon became very large. He was able to equip them with sophisticated weapons. They terrorized the districts of Bhind, Morena, Gwalior and Bharatpur, and left a trail of corpses and unspeakable deeds behind them.

The Mukhbir

On 1 October 1981, around mid-morning, M.P. Singh Chauhan, circle inspector of Gohad, came to tell me that there was a *mukhbir*, an informer, who had sent word that he wanted to meet me. As you can imagine, in the same way that the police are watching the dacoits, the dacoits are also watching police movement very carefully. And for this reason, I never met any informer at my residence. I told Chauhan to tell him to meet us outside.

For us in the police force, assumptions may be made, but our work relies on observation, data and solid policing experience. These often result in unerring instinct as well. In the dacoit-affected areas, the SP needs to be particularly aware of anything unexpected. Only when you know what is abnormal can you be more aware of the normal, of what is actually taking place on the ground.

In March 1981, Paan Singh's gang mercilessly and brutally murdered five innocent villagers of Pawa Pautha village in broad daylight, carnage they considered justified because they believed those killed were police informers responsible for the encounter during which Paan Singh lost his brother Matadin. The open conflict resulted in strife for revenge between Paan Singh's gang and the villagers. There were also, as is characteristic of the area, caste overtones. The victims were higher caste Gurjar Thakurs, and this led to Paan Singh allying himself with the Dalit (or the 'Harijan' or 'untouchable' caste as we called it in those days) community. Over the next several months, Paan Singh's gang absorbed the gang of Gopi Chamar of Rathiyan-ka-Pura village.

My informer had come to let me know that Paan Singh's gang had arrived in his village, and they were in hiding in the neighbouring village of Rathiyan-ka-Pura. There were, he said, 14 of them.

Now this was an informer I had relied on in the past but, of late, he had taken me for a ride—literally—three times. He would come with 'news', and we would set out together on a long midnight walk. Eventually, he would explain that it was getting late and we should go back. I was now quite irritated with him. When dealing with informers, my method was usually to just follow whatever they suggested. After all, they had come with special news that I had had no access to previously. And they understood the realities and constraints of the situation better than I did. I never imposed my own plans on theirs. This time, the trust had worn a little thin, but the news he brought was irresistible.

After they finished their evening meal that day, he told me, they planned to leave and begin walking along a certain route that he described to me. He gave me the name of the village where they were going to commit their dacoity that night. He suggested that I get there before dark with an armed force and wait, ready to ambush them when they arrived.

I asked if he would be able to accompany and guide us, to which he replied that he had been sent by the gang to buy mutton, and he had to buy it and return as they were expecting him back soon. However, he promised to get away and join us at the place of ambush that night. I agreed, and he left.

The Stake-out

Now, I had to decide whether I really wanted to make a midnight ambush on the advice of an unreliable informer. The risks of a night ambush are enormous. I called two senior officers, B.L. Handa and Y.S. Guraiya, and we sat in the circuit house, discussing the possibilities. Looking back, I wonder whether I should have waited for their opinions before sharing mine. When subordinates know what you have in mind, they usually only marshal arguments in favour of it. In any case, I think the decision was a good one because the risks of cross-firing in the dark are very high. Instead, we would arrive at the village earlier than the time suggested by the informer, quietly surround it, and simply ensure that no gang member escaped.

Our IG in charge of anti-dacoity operations had recently laid down strict standard operating procedures (SOPs). When planning any operation, police strength must be 10 times the known strength of the dacoits. Here the known strength was about 14 dacoits. I needed 140 police personnel, and sent out word calling for resources. The response was paltry. The neighbouring districts of Gwalior and Datia said no. Morena I did not ask because it was Paan Singh's home district, and he would have his own informers. Nobody had additional forces. After making several attempts, we realized that we were just not going to get the numbers we needed. If we violated the written rules and there was failure at any level, our necks would be on the line.

Just then, as we pondered over the dilemma, Sub-Inspector Varma, who was in charge of Bhind Kotwali, came rushing into the circuit house. He was emotionally very distraught and was weeping. Looking at him, I knew immediately what was wrong. For the past few days, he had been requesting me for two days' leave to go home to his village, Shivpuri, to see his father who was ailing. I had refused because we were in a precarious situation and there was no replacement available for him. My heart went out to him, and I put my hand on his shoulder with the deepest sympathy as he conveyed the sad news to me: his father was no more.

What could I say? As SP of the district and his boss, a South Indian somewhat culturally alien to this area, I had made my decision and it resulted in his not being able to see his father alive ever again. How could I console him? The guilt would never leave me. Sub-Inspector Varma left for Shivpuri to be with his mother, perform his duties as a son, and bid his father farewell.

The bereaved young man was barely out of the door when Guraiya jumped up, exclaiming, 'We have to do it!' It did not matter that we were too few. As per local lore, plans underway when news of a death is received are bound to be successfully executed. It did not even matter that we would be going against our orders! I was 30 years old and Guraiya, a good bit older; despite my seniority, I deferred to him as a sensible and very experienced officer. So, the devastating news was quickly converted into an energetic plan of action. We had to get to the village where the gang was, and we had to quickly surround it, in complete silence, before they left for their midnight raid. We had to do it before nightfall, making sure that we were not seen or heard despite the lack of cover in a setting where even the slightest movement could be easily detected by these habitual criminals.

We were all familiar with this village and its unusual geography. It had about 20 houses and they were laid out in an inverted U, with the base facing the national highway that linked it to Bhind, Gwalior, Etawah and Kanpur. All the families belonged to the same Dalit community, and all the houses were interlinked. If you entered any house, you could walk from one into the next, and then the next and so on, and come out at the other end of the village. One edge of the village was adjacent to Paan Singh's village Bhidosa in Morena District. There was every chance that Paan Singh would escape into Morena, where the local police would perhaps not cooperate with us.

The risks and uncertainties were many, but we had made our decision! Getting all the available officers and men ready, I left instructions for the reserve inspector to collect more men from the neighbouring districts of Gwalior and Datia, arm them, and send them as reinforcements after dark.

Within 15 minutes of making our decision, we were ready to leave, having formed ourselves into three teams, headed respectively by Handa, Guraiya and me. We climbed into jeeps and headed for Rathiyan-ka-Pura. An irrigation canal ran along the southwestern side of the village at a distance of about 700 m. The narrow-gauge railway line that linked Bhind with Gwalior in those days was about 2 km northwest of the village. About 2 km southwest was the Bhind–Gwalior main road.

It was only about 42 km from the Bhind Circuit House, and we arrived in about 50 minutes at a place where we could leave our vehicles and walk as silently and as invisibly as we could the remaining 3 km or 4 km to the village.

Between us, however, lay shallow fields of brilliant October mustard, and also of arhar—a local legume, also known as tuar in other parts of India. At the best of times, arhar fields form a fence with stalks so sharp when cut that they can even pierce a truck tyre. We walked carefully, and in good time, reached the village. Taking up our stations with stealth, we saw that everything appeared normal. Farmers were returning from their fields. People with lotas in hand were returning to the village after attending the call of nature. Smoke was wafting out of chimneys. Dogs were barking; children were playing. There was no indication that anything was amiss. Guraiya and Handa crawled towards me, and we made a quick consultation to appraise what lay ahead. We had to enter the village through its single entrance—unseen and unheard, and without any tree cover—before dark. The dacoits were right there, and we had no choice but to do a thorough clean-up job.

Crawling towards the houses that were connected to each other, I noticed for the first time that there was also a two-storey brick and concrete house, and my heart leapt. This was going to give us an advantage! In any operation of this sort that may involve the use of weapons, a high vantage point was definitely in our favour. Looking back, I recall being filled with a kind of energy I had rarely ever experienced. And this is the moment that I feel led us to the favourable outcome several hours later. I crawled towards one of the buildings, and the boys followed.

Until the early 1980s, police in India were issued ordinary weapons, usually .303 rifles that had to be loaded every time they were fired. With a focus on our dacoity operations, we had recently been issued self-loading rifles (SLRs). After one round was fired, the next would be loaded automatically—you just had to keep your finger on the trigger for a continuous burst of fire. I knew this, but Paan Singh knew it too! He had served in the Indian Army and was well aware of tactics and the advantage of vantage points. His gang had automatic weapons too. We were 30, with 30 weapons; they were 14 and we had no idea what weapons they had. We just had to wait and see what happened next.

For now, I had to get the boys up the side of the building.

None of them was as tall as I, but I called Constable Asharphilal, who was quite tall, and told him to climb onto my shoulder and from there to the top of the building. He was shocked—how could anyone expect him to put his foot, wearing shoes, on his SP's shoulder! The fact that he would be wearing his shoes while doing this was bad enough, but the shoulder is where the ranks are displayed! Seeing his dismay, I said to him, 'We are in an encounter, you must do as I say! It is an order.'

Just a few years later, when I returned to the state as additional director general (ADG), Asharphilal came to meet me. I now had the ADG rank with the Ashoka emblem and crossed swords on my shoulders. He put his hand on my shoulder and said, choking with emotion, 'Sir, this is the same shoulder on which I put my foot!' These are the kinds of feelings we in the police force often encounter in our people.

I left two of my men, Asharphilal and Jagatpal Singh, on the building with two rounds of magazines each, and orders to continuously change their position and their firing strategy. They would keep changing from controlled firing to a burst, then another, then signals—Paan Singh and his men had to believe that there were 15 or more sepoys on the building and that they were covering every inch of ground on all sides.

The rest of us then crawled through to the other side, the entrance of the village. There were 10 of us—Guraiya and I, one inspector, and seven constables.

As with most villages in the area, the first house had a raised platform where fodder and water were placed, so that the cattle didn't have to bend to the ground to get their feed. This platform would give us cover when we needed it in the course of the operation.

The families were all indoors now, having their evening meal and getting ready to sleep at night. It was completely silent. As we waited, it began to dawn on the constables that we were on the track of a dangerous criminal. They still did not know whom. And

I was keeping quiet about it—there was always that concern about who was a Thakur and who was a Brahmin and who was neither, and how these identities would suddenly rise to the surface and topple our efforts.

In five minutes, we entered. The constables kicked open the doors; these were men who, unlike me, were familiar with abuses a lot more potent than 'saala!' and they began to use them, loudly and fiercely.

Just then an elderly person came running towards us. A constable rushed to catch him, and brought him to me. I had read the term 'ashen-faced' in books; here I could see someone displaying this very attribute. In anger, in terror, he was screaming expletives, 'Why are you attacking us, you &^%$! Your father is standing behind you!'

It was with these words that we received confirmation that Paan Singh was indeed present in the village. We were supposed to be waiting in ambush later in the evening. The gang had been anticipating the ambush, but it was a trap into which we had not fallen. However, with their confidence that we would be waiting for them further up the road after dark, we had been able to enter and surround the village undetected.

A sudden volley of fire broke out, and we rushed back to the protective area. There were 10 of us taking shelter under the platform the villagers had created for the cattle feed. The dacoits were firing from inside the village.

But now firing began from outside the village as well!

This was the reserve police force that had arrived and had surrounded the village. While they were aware that their SP and some of the officers had entered the village, they had no way of knowing where we were, so their firing was controlled.

Taking shelter behind the platform, we were 10 people of different views, different backgrounds. The inspector was wailing and constantly repeating '*Marva diya*! (You'll get us killed!) Tomorrow's headlines will be about how many police have been killed! We are finished, we are finished!' It was extremely irritating to the rest of us who were focused on continuing with the operation. Finally, one of the constables couldn't stand it any longer and retorted, 'But, sir, if we are all going to die, who will read the paper tomorrow? Now shut up or my next shot will be fired on you!' Hearing this, the rest of us burst out laughing. The cheeky contravention of rank, sacrosanct in normal circumstances, added to the hilarity. We now felt all charged up to face the bullets. The firing continued.

I must say that Asharphilal and Jagatpal Singh, who had taken position on the roof of the brick building, did a brilliant job that day! They controlled their firing, locating their shots from different points in a way that made it look as if the whole rooftop was taken over by police. My team behaved with maturity right through the operation: controlled firing, no reckless moves, no shouting, no smoking. Looking back, I am filled with pride at the way they conducted themselves and the teamwork that led to our success. As per the rules, our team should have been 10 times the number of dacoits. In fact, we were probably only about double. But I can tell you this, we were as effective—more perhaps—as 10 times their number would have been.

I remember the luminous dial of my radium watch. As midnight approached, the intensity of the firing from the dacoits increased. They knew that their time was running out and the only way was for them to hit their way out. We were facing full bursts of continuous fire. Our firing was careful and controlled: we could not reveal our position and we could not waste our bullets either. Gradually, as they ran out of ammunition, their firing reduced.

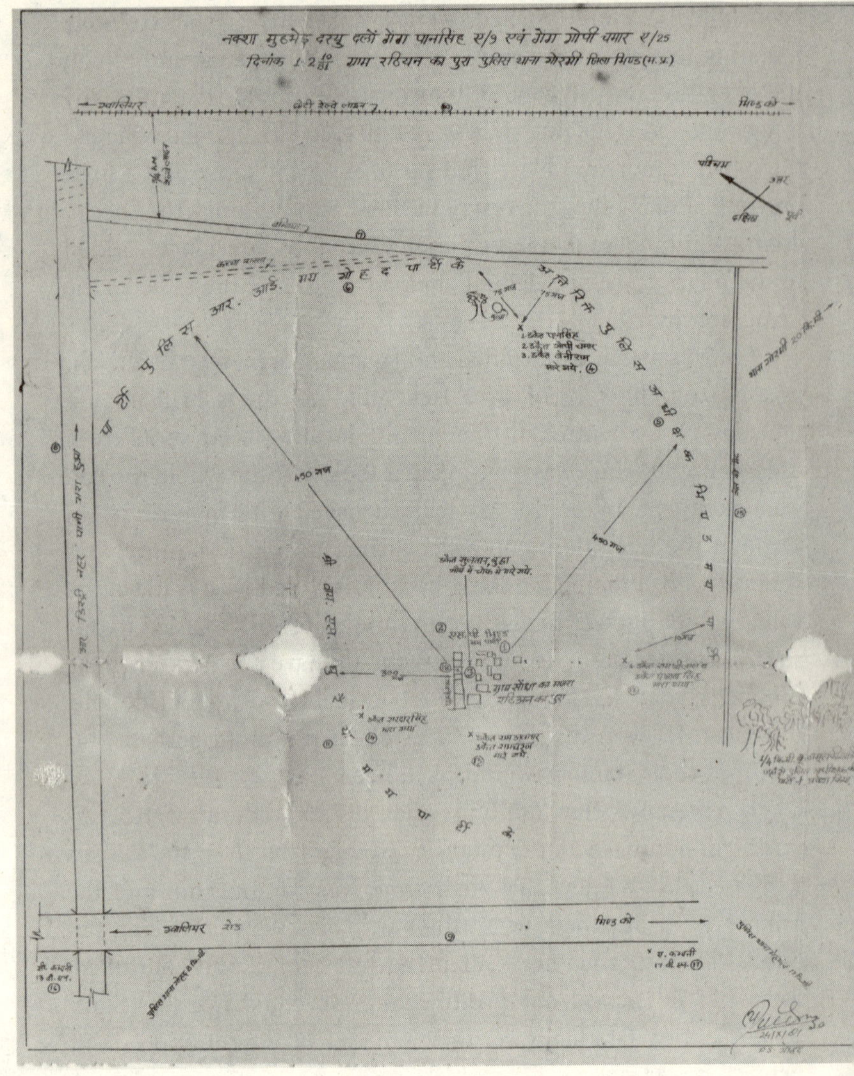

The official document showing the layout of the village and the scene of the encounter

Daylight

Finally, the first rays of dawn broke. As the sun came up, the firing stopped. I gradually left my position, walked a few steps, and turned to the right. There lay a body, fallen to the ground, clearly with no sign of life. From the unusual height I knew who it was. We had been successful in our mission! We had got Paan Singh! Identifying the corpse of a criminal is never a simple or straightforward task. There are seldom recent photographs to compare with; even rarer are people on the spot who recognize it. In this case, his features did look familiar, but that 6'4" was a dead giveaway. There were nine other corpses too.

Feeling the euphoria of a job well done, I stepped out of the village and looked around me. We had started the previous afternoon with just 30 of us, but now there were more than 300! The huge number of police personnel there was just unbelievable. It's easy to understand this increase in number of troops because when I was seeking help, nobody knew why. Once the firing started, they realized there really was an encounter, and the awareness grew that here was a chance to be part of the capture of a ferocious dacoit with a large prize on his head. In such a situation, there is the possibility of a reward; being identified as part of such an operation goes a long way in one's career. People rushed to help.

Those who had called in sick, those who were on leave in neighbouring villages—everyone had rushed to report for duty and were transported and deployed for the encounter.

It was also quite a shock to see that we were in the battle of Kurukshetra! The road was filled with buses, trucks, all kinds of vehicles—it was total chaos! In the midst of the crowd, I spotted my DIG M.D. Sharma in full battle outfit coming towards me. The moment he saw me, he called out, 'Raman!' After the stress of that long night, I was suddenly flooded with a great sense of relief. My responsibility was now transferred to a senior officer, and I could relax. My DIG put his hand in his pocket, pulled out a packet of cigarettes, and said to me with an affectionate clap on my shoulder, 'Raman, you deserve this!' That's when I realized that I had spent the entire night without smoking!

I later came to know how my DIG had turned up at the spot. He was on his way to Gwalior to meet a team of senior journalists who were investigating how the police were implementing the new anti-dacoity act enacted recently. There was great concern that such an act could be misused, and CM Arjun Singh had invited Taroon Coomar Bhaduri, N.K. Singh and others who were questioning his decision to implement it to come in person to the dacoit-infested districts of Gwalior, Bhind and Morena to check on what the police officers were doing.

My DIG had been on his way to Gwalior, and was having dinner at a circuit house, when one of the SPs informed him that Raman Saheb had called him during the day asking for reinforcements. My DIG was well versed in how things took place in these areas: such a call during the day from an SP meant that something was certainly afoot! Calculating from the time of the call, he estimated where we were likely to be. Rushing to Gwalior to put together a platoon of MP police armed with SLRs, he proceeded to the spot where I was.

There were things to be done before we left. Searching all the village houses, we realized that four gang members seemed to have escaped the cordon. It was later learnt that Balwant Singh, son of Paan Singh's brother Matadin, had escaped arrest by hiding inside one of the haystacks erected for use in winter. He remained there for three days. And it was he who survived to provide the background information for the film *Paan Singh Tomar* (2012)!

It was a terrible time for the villagers. They were terrified. They had no idea that something like this could happen; they had no idea who had informed the police and how the police had come. They were just carrying on with their lives, taking care of their children and their goods, inside their homes, getting ready to sleep that night. Once they realized what was happening, they stayed indoors with the doors shut.

Two of our boys had been injured and were rushed to hospital. We took the bodies of the gang members who were killed to the nearby town of Gohad, about 10 km from Rathiyan-ka-Pura, for the post-mortem. It was essential to have a public record that the dacoits had indeed been gunned down by the police in a genuine encounter and not killed by poisoning or any other foul means. As SP, I had expended hundreds of rounds of ammunition, and part of my duty was to account for each round for the court records.

A crowd had gathered at Gohad and was waiting for us. Prominent among them was a member of parliament (MP) from Gwalior who had come to Bhind to hold a protest on Gandhi Jayanti against one Vijay Raman, an inexperienced and incompetent fellow against whom he regularly protested in the Rajya Sabha! And now he had arrived in Gohad. But at the moment, his eager audience were not interested in him—they just wanted to see the dead bodies. The member of parliament came out and took the mike to get their attention. He loudly proclaimed that all his complaints had received a most excellent retort with this action. After wishing me every possible success in life, he now embraced me warmly and showered me with congratulations.

The CM of MP came personally to Bhind to congratulate us. When he asked me to address the jubilant crowd with a few words, I felt overcome with emotion. All I could think of was what I had said to my boys during the roll call following the Gwalior mela incident. So I spoke of that occasion, and of how grateful I was for their constant appreciation and support then and ever since. I knew that this was not a personal victory—we had all done our part and the team had been just fantastic.

A team effort

The minister congratulates the team
who accomplished a great victory

A crowd gathers, awaiting a glimpse of the corpse of the dacoit who had terrorized the region and made their lives miserable

'Please Take My Seat!'

Among the crowds waiting to congratulate me when I reached home were, to my great surprise, my newly-married younger brother Major D.D. Raman of 7th Light Cavalry and sister-in-law Viji. Taking advantage of the long weekend, they had boarded a bus at Babina, near Jhansi, the army base where he was posted. At Gwalior, they changed to a bus to Bhind. It was very crowded and there were no seats. When the bus reached Gohad, it was clear that a major incident had taken place there. People who boarded at this stop brought news into the bus that a new SP, Vijay Raman, had conducted a surprise encounter and vanquished an entire gang of dacoits!

When he said 'Oh, but that's my brother!', people started applauding and two seats were immediately vacated for them. When the bus arrived in Bhind, after dropping off the other passengers, the driver dropped them off at our doorstep saying, 'This is SP Saheb's house!'

Veena, my wife, was quite used to my being away from home till the early hours. She and Mrs Handa, the additional SP's wife, had a routine of taking an early morning walk together, then sipping on their lemon-honey drinks and wondering why they had not heard from their husbands. 'Oh, they must be sitting in some rest house eating parathas for breakfast!' was their thought at first. But as the day progressed, Veena got worried and called the control room. 'Don't you know, madam?' she was told. 'They are in an encounter! Yes, some of our police have been injured but many of the dacoits have been killed.'

Soon, she received a phone call from the wife of a superior officer showering her with congratulations because I had liquidated a gang of dacoits. Veena, who was 23 years old at the time, was bemused. 'Should I accept congratulations for my husband being a murderer?' she thought to herself. But the good wishes and felicitations were very sincere, and I think over the years she got used to being a police officer's wife.

For us, this was our daily life. But when other members of the family visited, they found some of these events fascinating. At family gatherings, Veena's sister Madhuri often spoke about the huge mela-like environment in the village with the bodies of the dacoits laid out outside the town hospital. People came from the neighbouring villages in long lines of bullock carts, hordes thronging, pointing and saying, 'Paan Singh! Paan Singh!'

Cascade

The very next day, the surrenders began. Over the next few weeks, dacoits with big gangs and small gangs, big crimes and small crimes—so many put down their weapons and surrendered themselves.

Uday Singh Gadaria, the shepherd dacoit, surrendered. There

was no fuss, no dramatics. He simply sent word to the collector, '*Mujhe aatmasamparn karna hai.* (I wish to surrender.)'

The surrender of Uday Singh Gadaria

The collector asked me, 'What do you say?'

I replied, 'I have no problem. Just because Paan Singh was killed doesn't mean I'm on a killing spree. He wants to surrender—most welcome. But there is not going to be any big media drama or anything.'

He said, 'But you must also be there.'

I said, 'Sure, I'll be there with the other staff, and we'll take care of everything.'

One of the most celebrated surrenders was that of Phoolan Devi, soon after I left Bhind. She escaped into MP and surrendered to the MP police. Phoolan Devi had killed 17 Thakurs and did not feel safe with the UP police. She found her way into MP and negotiated, offering the MP police a political triumph over the UP police. She was kept in MP; all the trials were held in MP;

all the decisions were taken in MP; the orders were passed in MP and in the end, she got a good deal in MP even though she had not committed a single offence there.

The biggest drama of all was, of course, the so-called surrender of Malkhan Singh.

5

THE TALE OF TWO SURRENDERS

My encounters with Malkhan Singh formed one of the most interesting and challenging phases of my police career, particularly in the Chambal. There are so many lessons to be learnt from this episode of Malkhan, for so many people!

Malkhan was a Mirda by caste; they are those who, like Kevats, ferry boats across the river for their livelihood. He hailed from a village called Bilao, which fell under Umri police station of Bhind District. As I indicated earlier, the caste system was prevalent in this area, with a continuous rivalry between the Brahmins, the Thakurs and the Dalits. This manifested in its most extreme form during the local elections. And, at the panchayat election in the mid-1970s, Malkhan Singh was elected as a panch.* In this particular election, there was no dispute other than caste. This gives an indication of how election rivalries can lead to grave consequences.

Malkhan Singh's election as a panch greatly annoyed the sarpanch, the head of the council. He was a man named Kailash Pandit, belonging to a Brahmin family that dominated the village.

Kailash Pandit detested everything about Malkhan Singh, and wanted him out of the way. One of the conditions he put on Malkhan was that if he ever passed in front of Kailash Pandit's house, he would have to remove his footwear and hold it on top of

*An official of the village council

his head, and only then could he cross. This was very humiliating, a pure caste-based insult, and a way for Kailash Pandit to avenge the troubling election results. What self-respecting person, regardless of their background and education, would accept this sort of a condition?

Kailash had tremendous patronage politically at the party level. As a consequence, the police machinery also supported Kailash Pandit, particularly the Brahmins in the police force, who would support him no matter what he did. Even when he made an attempt on Malkhan Singh's life, no complaint against him would be lodged. Kailash even made use of the local police personnel to fake an encounter and harass Malkhan. The situation continued and got worse and worse, and it became very difficult for Malkhan to live in the village. And so, some time in 1976, he absconded, formed a gang, roamed around in Bhind for some time, and ultimately crossed into the jungle and went into hiding.

A Dacoit's Circle of Life: Origins

Invariably, it is first a sense of injustice that drives a person in this region to take up arms and abscond.

This was certainly the case with Malkhan. He felt humiliated by the treatment that he was receiving from the authorities, who were supposed to respond to and redress the injustices he was being subjected to. It is the sense of grievance, the knowledge that the law has let him down, that turns a man into a baagi—filling him with indignation and the sense that he has to fight for justice. He goes into hiding and feels fully justified in committing whatever he needs to commit, be it a murder or a kidnapping, or whatever it is that will bring about justice as he perceives it.

In this process, more people join him because—and this is something specific to the Chambal area—a very large number of people have their own version of justice that is not in consonance with the sense of justice as laid down by the law. Like-minded people go with him, and a gang is formed.

Now here comes an interesting aspect to gang formation. To be admitted as a member, it has to be known—proof is not necessary, but it must be well known—that you have committed at least one murder and are absconding from the law. This is the kind of qualification required for entrance into the gang. If you come with a weapon, so much the better. If not, your weapon will be provided by the gang. And this depends on a particular categorization, according to which those who have committed the more severe, culpable crimes before absconding are provided the more sophisticated weapons, and the lesser beings are given lower-grade weapons.

During the period I was there, 1980–82, Malkhan's gang had around 30 to 35 members at any point in time. There would be a few who were there for support and administration, related to the gang members in some way or the other, but mostly all were hardened criminals, about 30 to 35 like-minded people roaming around the rural area with weapons, looking for opportunities to commit crime. It was indeed a very worrying situation and frequent crimes were being committed.

However, there were also some interesting things about Malkhan Singh. He was a strict disciplinarian. No bad habits were permitted in his gang: no alcoholism, no womanizing, nothing that could prove to be a weakness that an outsider could exploit, causing the downfall of the gang. Any transgression of these rules led to immediate expulsion. No proof was required, no trial would be held. The moment he was convinced that the rules had been broken, he would take action immediately. He would remove the gang member and get his weapon deposited, or sometimes simply get the member killed.

Another thing about Malkhan was that he might have been anti-Brahmin because Kailash Pandit was a Brahmin and he had become a dacoit because of him, but he did not hate the community. This was an interesting facet of Malkhan's character.

He might have hated specific Brahmins—in the villages, in the administration, or in the police station. But it was not a feeling of hatred against the community. And some of his die-hard supporters were Brahmins. The man overground who kept safe custody of all of Malkhan's ill-gotten wealth was, in fact, a Brahmin.

Going back to the evolution of the dacoit: to maintain a gang of 35 members and feed them and their dependents, you need money. And the only way for an outlaw to do this is by committing crimes.

At first, the gangs found it most convenient to commit dacoities. It was quite the fashionable thing to do. They would keep a watch on village activities and when there was a wedding coming up, or some celebration where people would assemble wearing their best ornaments, where large amounts of money were being exchanged for expenses and dowry, the target would be selected. Here the caste configuration was important, because every offence would raise that issue, and it had to be taken into account.

In the Chambal area in those days, it had become a practice for villagers to keep licensed weapons for self-defence. Having a licensed firearm was a status symbol with its own hierarchy; some were used for driving birds from the fields, then came the pachpera* from which five rounds could be fired without reloading, and the most desirable of all was the carbine.

Once villagers started owning firearms, things became less easy for the dacoits. Any act of dacoity could be met with firing from any direction. It had become a risky job! It was additionally risky because if the looted property was recovered, it became a solid piece of evidence against the gang.

---

*A type of gun, specifically an older model of a firearm commonly used in India, typically a multi-barrelled gun (often with five barrels, 'pach' indicates five). These guns were often manually loaded and fired.

It was natural that the dacoits should turn to a more profitable and far less risky crime: kidnapping. The person approached for ransom would not go to the police, being afraid that the victim could be harmed by the gang. They would stay silent and start negotiating through back-door channels. Once the victim was released, there would be no evidence—where they were, how they got there, nothing would be known. They could only tell the police that it was a gang, that they were blindfolded and made to walk on a difficult path, and sometimes they overheard snippets of conversation that revealed a few perfunctory, insubstantial details.

At the same time, these people who had suffered would raise agitations against the police and this, unfortunately, kept us away from doing our duty and focused on a show of doing it in the town, where everybody could see our presence and activities.

Vijay Raman and M.D. Sharma listen as a rescued victim of kidnapping tells his tale

A Classic Case, a Classic Capture

If you look at the list of offences committed by Malkhan Singh and his gang, it's clear that they were among those who had taken to kidnapping as their mainstay. For me, however, Malkhan was not a priority as he was not operating in Bhind District. His gang never entered Bhind—I don't know for what reason. Then, sometime in the month of September 1980, a month or so after I took charge as SP Bhind, Malkhan deputed a member of his gang, Kashiram Lohar, to Bhind town. His arch-nemesis, Kailash Pandit, had relocated to Bhind; he had been provided security and even had a gunman.

Kashiram belonged to Jalaun district in UP. The Lohars are a caste that work with metals. Kashiram was deputed by Malkhan to kill Kailash Pandit, for which he would receive a suitable reward: in return for his act, Malkhan would arrange for two of Kashiram's enemies in Jalaun to be executed by his gang.

Malkhan's brother, who would identify the target, accompanied Kashiram from the point of departure in the midst of the ravines on a motorcycle. They were dropped off in Bhind by another gang member, who then returned to the gang.

Kailash had his home in the heart of Bhind town. He had certain routines, was seen visiting various places, and if somebody was hell-bent on hitting him, it was not very difficult because his movements were quite predictable. Sure enough, that very evening, Kailash was shot. The news travelled at lightning speed, and it was presumed—quite rightly—that the perpetrator was his sworn enemy, Malkhan. The people of Bhind were stricken with terror to know that the Malkhan gang had entered their town. What was going to happen next?

Fortunately for us, they did not stay on in the town to wreak havoc but instead attempted to flee and, as they were unfamiliar with the layout of the town, we were able to capture both men.

There were no witnesses to the hit. However, the gravity of

the crime was known to all, and we took Kashiram into police remand. He admitted to being a member of Malkhan Singh's gang. The interrogation went on for days.

Interrogation is a legitimate weapon in the armoury of the police. In all the aspects of it, we stayed meticulously within the confines of the law. As the interrogation proceeded, Kashiram began blurting out many things that none of us knew. Some of these we had heard as rumours. But this was information from an active member of the gang; it was straight from the horse's mouth.

Again, coming to the character of Malkhan Singh: by the first week of October, less than three weeks after Kailash was killed, Kashiram's enemies were efficiently dispatched as per their agreement.

When Kashi heard about this, he was absolutely elated—revenge was sweet indeed! He had done Dadda's work and Dadda had paid him back without missing a beat.* In the process of his jubilation, Kashi gave us several names. And each time I led the search; locating, assembling and bringing in those named for questioning. I was also right in front in the firing line with constant questions from my superiors. Since it was work in progress, I would give generalities, not revealing anything specific.

One thing you should know, and that should be easy to understand—no dacoit gang can exist in a vacuum. It needs a support system to provide the many things that every human being requires for sustenance. Other than food and such basic requirements, the dacoit gang also needs a reliable information system that indicates who the most appropriate victim is for kidnapping or dacoity, and what the amount is at which the deal

---

*Malkhan Singh embraced the title Dadda to project an image of authority and leadership. The word conveys a sense of paternal responsibility, as well as an undertone of respect mixed with fear, suitable for a family patriarch who is both loved and revered by his family.

should close. Sitting down and analysing these things, taking the caste complications into consideration—all this is a painstaking job!

Kashi was singing like a canary—as Western crime fiction describes the act of providing information to the authorities to gain favour—and one of the most important names that came up was Ramavtar Bhadoria, a lawyer and a harbourer of the gang, who hailed from Etawah district in UP. Kashi assured us that he was a big man in town and knew everything about the gang, much more than even he, a mere villager, could know. He had joined the gang because he wanted revenge and that was it. But this fellow Bhadoria, he told us, kept Dadda's money. And Dadda kept consulting and talking to him for hours at a time. So we picked him up.

By this time, the anti-dacoity ordinance, which I mentioned earlier, had been enacted, and was being made into a law. This was ushering in a new regime of law and discipline in the Chambal; it was this that facilitated the arrest of this Ramavtar Bhadoria.

Now, I'm not going to pretend that the entire operation to do so was carried out with every stipulation of the law. I should actually have intimated to the SP Etawah the reasons for which Bhadoria was needed. Once he agreed, I should have then got a court order permitting the arrest, and so on and so forth. These things we did not do. I merely undertook a recce, got the fellow identified, and found out what time he would be available so that we did not raid the place only to find him absent. Once it was confirmed that he was there, we picked him up. Since it was only 15 km away, we were back in my jurisdiction in no time.

Kashi had told us that Bhadoria was the one who had brought him and Malkhan's brother to Bhind for the Kailash murder, and he now confirmed it. We could put him on trial in that case too, if required. But for now, we arrested him under the new act, with the support of an excellent judge, an additional district judge, who was in a position to authorize the arrest. Since bail was not possible, Kashi was removed from judicial custody to police custody, and from there to jail.

As per the law, a police officer cannot enter the jail to interrogate an accused person. However, thanks to the rapport I had with this special judge and the jailer, I was able to meet him and continue the interrogation, which, while quite intense, remained within legal limits.

Meanwhile, the entire lawyer community of the area was up in arms against me. They passed a resolution in UP. When they came to MP to protest in Bhind, I put my foot down, making it clear that so far only this one had been taken in, but I had evidence on a few more of them who were under suspicion. I think they got the message and the protests stopped.

Now Bhadoria too began singing like a canary. He gave us many details and with great precision. He was one of Malkhan's sources of investment also. Malkhan Singh was very fond of constructing temples and had asked for a Devi temple to be constructed for him in Gatti, close to where Bhadoria lived, and he was getting that done. He came out with a lot of information, which revealed that most of Malkhan's activities were restricted to UP. This was outside my jurisdiction. However, he also gave me the name of another harbourer: Virendra Singh Bhadoria.

Both these were Bhadoria by caste, and this brings up an interesting and relevant fact. The Bhadorias originated in the Bhadarwa kingdom, which is part of present-day Agra. During a conflict in the sixteenth or seventeenth century, this kingdom was attacked and was about to be seized. At the last minute, the princess of the royal family was smuggled out of the fort and taken across the Chambal to safety in a place called Ater in Bhind District. The boat that took the princess to safety was rowed by a member of the Mirda caste, to which Malkhan Singh belonged. This sealed the relationship between the Bhadorias and the Mirdas because the Bhadorias would always be grateful to the

Mirdas who had saved their queen, leading to a mama–bhanja relationship.* Hence, the chances of a Bhadoria betraying a Mirda were remote!

Virendra Singh, we learnt, was ex-army, a retired subedar. He was the source of weapons for the gang. I knew that the key to Malkhan Singh's capture lay here. How were we going to proceed with our investigation and get the results we wanted?

Interview with a Chambal Dacoit

While all this was going on, something else was happening that was going to make things very difficult for the police.

A group of three high-profile journalists, one of whom was a photojournalist, were out in the ravines, determined to bring the fierce Malkhan into the living rooms of their readers and get him to narrate his splendid story.

On one side, the police, as per their duty, were chasing the criminal and working towards getting permission to take legal action against Viren Singh Bhadoria, who was in UP. At the same time, the journalists, who had their own resources, including within the police and the underground, also stumbled upon Viren Singh. At this moment, I was still unaware of the development.

While I was not aware of it, I definitely knew that something fishy was going on.

During our interstate meetings, held sometimes in Agra and sometimes in Gwalior, I would try and bring the attention of SP Agra to the existence of this Viren Singh Bhadoria, staying in such and such village, a very strong supporter of Malkhan Singh. I

---

*The 'mama–bhanja' relationship is often culturally significant, symbolizing a special bond between a maternal uncle and his nephew. This relationship typically carries connotations of affection, guidance and familial responsibility. The maternal uncle is often seen as a mentor or protector, and the bond may be more informal and playful compared to relationships with paternal relatives.

tried explaining that the day on which we neutralized this person, the Malkhan gang would be decimated. So formidable was the support system he had created for them that they would not be able to exist without him.

And the SP, very senior to me, would enquire with waning interest, 'Oh really?' And change the topic. When I continued to pester him, he would say, 'Oh okay, yes, yes, you must do something,' and that would be the end of it. However, I continued to follow up through telephone calls as well as unscheduled urgent meetings. Finally, he told me very candidly, 'Listen, I cannot do anything about this fellow. He's politically very well connected. But if you can take him, please go ahead. I have no problem.'

I immediately latched on to the last sentence! I knew that the entire government machinery would—alongside their duties of administering law and order—be celebrating the arrival of New Year 1982. So, on the intervening night of 31 December 1981, I took two truckloads and four jeeps of policemen from Bhind and crossed into UP. One of my informers had warned me, '*Goli chal sakti hai* (Be prepared for bullets to fly),' so we were well armed and well prepared. Encircling the village, we picked up Viren Singh Bhadoria, and by four in the morning on the first of January 1982, he was in our custody.

The news spread like wildfire.

I should also tell you now that, all this while, I had been receiving love notes from Malkhan Singh. These epistles came on a letterhead grandly proclaiming him to be 'Daseu Samrat Malkhan Singh', which means 'Malkan Singh, Mighty Emperor of the Dacoits'. While couched in courteous language, they contained veiled threats if I did not stop bothering him. One of the favourites was the danger to my only son whom they would kidnap very soon! Each time I took any action against his gang, or picked up one of his loyal supporters, he would send a fresh epistle. And I, in turn, whenever I received one of his letters, would get his wife and children picked up by police jeeps in full view of the villagers. We never stopped them from bringing their own food or tried to make things difficult for them, and at the end of the day, they would be released to make their way home. This was just my way of telling Malkhan Singh, 'Seriously? Your threats mean nothing to me!'

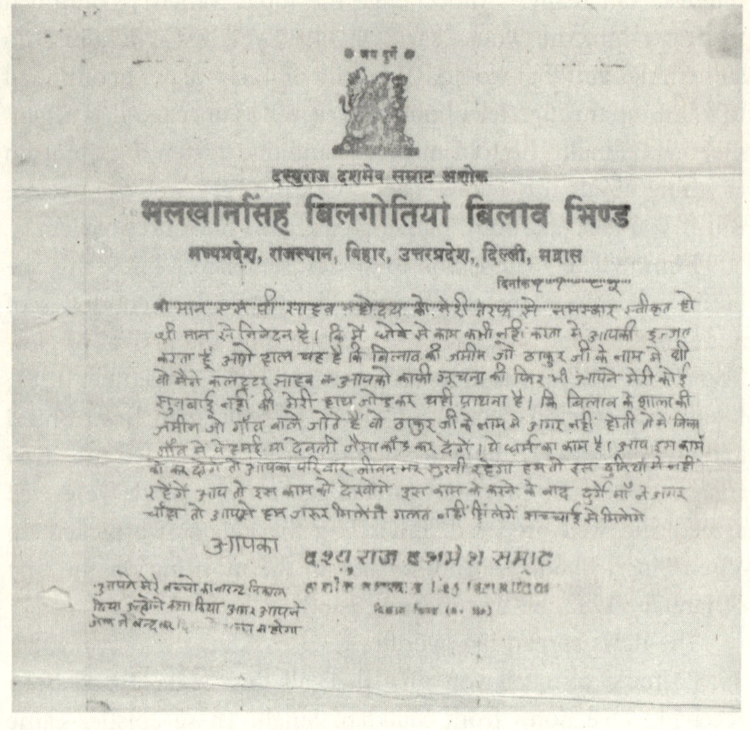

दस्युराज दशमेष सम्राट अशोक

मलखानसिंह बिलगोतिया बिलाव भिण्ड

मध्यप्रदेश, राजस्थान, बिहार, उत्तरप्रदेश, दिल्ली, मद्रास

दिनांक

श्रीमान एस पी साहब महोदय को मेरी तरफ से नमस्कार स्वीकृत हो
श्रीमान से निवेदन है। कि मैं धोखे से काम कभी नहीं करता मै आपकी इज्जत
करता हूँ और हाल यह है कि बिलाव की जमीन जो ठाकुर जी के नाम से थी
वो मैंने कलक्टर साहब व आपको काफी सूचना की फिर भी आपने मेरी कोई
सुनवाई नहीं की मेरी हाथ जोड़कर यही प्रार्थना है। कि बिलाव के शाला की
जमीन जो गाँव वाले जोते हैं वो ठाकुर जी के नाम मे अगर नहीं होती तो मै मिल
और मे बेहमई या देवली जैसा काँड कर देंगे। ये धर्म का काम है। आप इस काम
को कर देंगे तो आपका परिवार जीवन भर सुखी रहेगा हम तो इस दुनियां मे नहीं
रहेंगे आप तो इस काम को देखोगे इस काम के करने के बाद दुर्गा माँ ने अगर
चाहा तो आपसे हम जरूर मिलेंगे गलत नहीं मिलेंगे सच्चाई से मिलेंगे

आपका

दस्यु राजा दशमेश सम्राट

A New Year's love note from the man who named himself king!

All this happened again, when Viren Singh was picked up and booked under the newly refurbished anti-dacoity law. But this time, along with a letter from Malkhan Singh, I also started receiving other messages from various sources! The journalists had also been on the verge of getting to Viren Singh Bhadoria. Just as I had my agenda, my objectives, my duties to perform, they also had their passion to pursue. It was a clear conflict of interest and the pressure started coming down on me. I was getting calls from various seniors—including my DIG, whom I held in great esteem and respect. I told him, 'Sir, I will not do this. This person I will not release.'

So here, in pursuit of their passion, the journalists came across a stumbling block. They were putting pressure on me through my seniors, and I remained unrelenting. This led them to take the political path and petition the CM of MP. And in March 1982, with the Jabalpur parliamentary election coming up, there was some unease that the seat might be lost.

All this seemed to me extremely foolish. On what basis could a criminal investigation in Bhind influence an election in faraway Jabalpur? May the lord protect us from the naïveté of the enthusiastic police officer.

I continued sticking to my ground, refusing to release my prisoner. About 70 days had passed. Malkhan Singh now knew that I had come very close to catching him indeed! But the journalists who wanted to conduct an interview of a criminal in his den, which they were certainly entitled to do under the Freedom of Press Act, were pressurizing the government.

One day, orders were issued for the release of Viren Singh Bhadoria.

The Story of a Bandit King

In 1985, the book *Malkhan: The Story of a Bandit King 1981–84* by Kalyan Mukherjee, Brij Raj Singh and Prashant Panjiar was published by Lancer International. I had interacted with these journalists frequently; they had tried their best to influence me and I knew that they were working very hard to do something that was extremely important to them. So, I was interested in knowing what they had written.

Some parts of the book corroborated what I knew to be the truth, and the accuracy of their sources was admirable indeed. At the same time, I must say that I found the book to have many of the kind of small errors that even the most sincere researcher can make when trying to work in every relevant detail but making assumptions instead of checking and re-checking. For example:

> Raman was half subedar's age, and looked almost straight out of the Police Academy in Mount Abu.*

By the time I was at the academy, it was in Hyderabad, not Mount Abu!

They also wrote that they had first approached me because they knew Veena as she was in the same college as them—not true!

Some parts made me laugh:

> Raman was fond of naming suspects—he had termed the vakil as the 'Letterbox', and this time the vakil had given the subedar a name—'Elephant'. It was interesting, thought Raman.**

How could anyone have possibly known what I was thinking? In fact, these fellows claimed that they had somehow looked into my soul and knew everything that I wanted in life:

> Vijay Raman was a no-nonsense police officer with an ambition to be known and remembered as one in the line of Quinn, Patil, and other illustrious officers of the past. The Paan Singh coup had earned him well deserved kudos and whetted his appetite. A man who had longed to become a journalist was transformed into a policeman. At home with the Rolling Stones and the Pink Floyd music Raman would be at total ease in plotting out the plans for the near future. He betrayed symptoms of a workaholic, and it was this obsession that troubled Malkhan. There was nothing the bandit could do as Raman brazenly got his most trusted

---

*Mukherjee, Kalyan, Brij Raj Singh and Prashant Panjiar, *Malkhan: The Story of a Bandit King 1981–84*, Lancer International, 1985, p. 296.
**Ibid., 297.

> vakil and subedar picked up from the neighbouring state of UP under the Anti-Dacoity ordinance. The relatives and other harbourers of Malkhan were not spared either.*

These intimate and colourful descriptions made me uncomfortable, but I will admit that they were also kind enough to praise me as a cop and endorse decisions that I had taken in the line of duty.

Three Days' Notice

I had no idea at the time that Malkhan Singh's surrender was being orchestrated. What I did know was that, out of the blue one fine day in the second week of May, I received a crisp message that I had been transferred out from Bhind and was to report as SP Raipur in three days.

The normal career progression for a successful officer in Chambal is to be transferred from a smaller district like Datia, Morena or Bhind to take the position of SP Gwalior. As a Chambal expert, you spend your career in the region. However, for me, I was sent from Bhind to Raipur, which is now the capital of Chhattisgarh. My wife was very happy to be in an urban setting! For my family, this was definitely a good move. And for the first few weeks, the local newspapers were full of this. Why was Vijay Raman transferred out of Bhind? Who was trying to hide what? The media is not unfamiliar with the constant dance between the earnest civil servant and the self-serving politician. When asked for my comment, I said that I had no idea. That was the truth.

I had refused to get a criminal released on bail, and had taken a firm stand on it against all pressure. Could that have been the basis for my transfer with three days' notice? Perhaps, but I was certainly not going to conjecture or gossip.

At this point, I would be failing in my duty if I did not mention that as a police officer work is always accomplished with greater

---

*Ibid., 309.

ease when the administrative authorities are supportive. When I was in Bhind, the collectors K.M. Acharya and J.L. Ajmani who were there for a year each were very helpful, and I am grateful to them.

I duly left for Raipur three days later, leaving Veena to take care of the packing and moving. A few days after I took over, I received a phone call from her father. He had read something in the newspaper and it had given him the shock of his life. 'What is Veena doing! Tying *rakhi* to dacoits when you're not there? This girl is just impossible!' I tried to pacify him. 'Daddy, take it easy. I'm no longer the SP of Bhind. I'm in Raipur and she and Vikram will be joining me shortly. This must be the new SP's wife.'

An Outlaw with a Sense of Integrity

After my fairly uneventful two-year tenure in Raipur, I was sent to Bhopal as SP Special Branch in 1984. The following year, I was posted to Delhi in a special role and remained there for 10 years. In Delhi, my family and I lived in Sector 13, R.K. Puram, in a flat on the top floor of an eight-storey building.

One Sunday evening in 1987, we were relaxing at home, watching the Hindi film airing on Doordarshan as so many of us across India used to do. In those days, that was the ultimate entertainment highlight of the week. At around 7.00 p.m., 'Interval' would flash on the screen and families would put the final touches to their dinner preparation.

That evening, the doorbell rang when the interval came on and Vikram went to open the door. A group of villagers was standing there and one of them, a tall fellow with a huge moustache and a red tilak, was holding a gun! He asked Vikram, '*Raman Saheb hai?*'

When Vikram enquired who he was, the man replied, 'Malkhan Dadda.'

Somewhat apprehensive about letting a man with a gun enter our home, Vikram came to inform me that Malkhan Dadda was asking for me. 'Malkhan Singh?' I wondered. 'What on earth was he doing in Delhi?' But yes, it was certainly him—the photos splashed all over the media after his surrender had made him quite a poster boy.

He wanted to touch my feet, but I could see that he was being mindful of the tradition of not performing the respectful feet-touching salutation on the threshold of a house. I knew that I had to either step out to receive it or allow them to enter. On the spur of the moment, I stood aside and invited them in, offering them a seat.

Before sitting down, he performed the ritual for which he had come prepared with all the materials: after touching my feet, he offered me tilak and ₹101 as shagun.

Veena looked in and was astonished to see these rough-looking lawbreakers dressed in their best, sitting comfortably with me on the sofas where our family and friends sat!

And then, Malkhan said, 'Sir, it was not I who got you transferred.'

He repeated the sentence, adding, 'That was not the condition of my surrender.'

It occurred to me that he may have thought I was still harbouring anger against him for all those nasty letters he had written. I reassured him that I had no hard feelings whatsoever. He had followed his thoughts and instincts and played his role; I had followed my thoughts and instincts and played my role. We both had moved on.

But Malkhan had come with a purpose: he felt he owed me an explanation and carried on, telling me that it had all been arranged by the journalists who wanted to interview him, and my successor.

After Malkhan had completely unburdened himself and was ready to leave, I went to the door to see him off and he started walking down the stairs.

'Why don't you take the lift?' I asked him.

'Oh,' he replied, 'I always walk, lifts scare me.'

That was the day on which a dacoit from the ravines of Chambal came to Delhi, made enquiries to find out where I lived and, when he found out, climbed eight floors to come to my home to pay me a visit. He had honoured me with his rituals, assuring me that, despite being on opposite sides of the law, despite my holding out relentlessly against him, he had always held me in respect and continued to do so.

That was the day on which Malkhan surrendered; to me, that was the real surrender.

This incident is not covered in the book *Malkhan: The Story of a Bandit King 1981–84*.

Says Veena: 'Vijay was so annoyed with me for taking these photos. I later told him that I had only taken them so that our grandchildren would know that at a time when he should have been dancing around the trees with me, he had instead chosen to chase behind trees to catch this guy!'

A Dacoit's Circle of Life: Conclusion

As I mentioned earlier, it is usually the ordinary villager who turns dacoit; a person who has faced injustice or caste atrocity who decides to take to the ravines and make a life for himself to restore his lost dignity. The next step is materialism, and this is purely for practical reasons. To run the gang, he needs money. Over time, he moves on from dacoity to kidnapping, which is a safer and more profitable proposition.

Then comes the fourth stage, which each one approaches at a different time of life, but always after several years on the run. He realizes that he is being chased by the police all the time. He is running every day, and seldom spends even two nights in a row in the same place in any district where the police is active. This means that he gets up each morning and walks 10 to 20 km, never knowing who might betray him—a villager who feeds the gang, or someone with a previous enmity, or perhaps even a gang member himself.

A time comes when one day he stops and asks himself, 'Why am I leading this sort of life?' He sits down to calculate how much money he has gained. Things have changed in other ways too—there was a time when he was prepared to die to uphold his principles. He no longer wants to die!

Then a time comes when he does not want any further encounters, just a way to live a simple life and spend his money.

Malkhan also decided to go back to a simple life. However, things did not go the way he had foreseen.

It remained a sore point with Malkhan that the informer in the Paan Singh encounter had received a much better deal than he had. Malkhan Singh was still waiting, he told me, for what he had been promised by the government for his 'surrender'.

Daku Malkhan Singh—'Dadda', as he liked to be known—was a man of principles. He believed in tying up loose ends. And he had made considerable efforts to track me down to do so.

Family Time

Our two years in Raipur were much more relaxed than the previous years, and the years that would follow. For the first time, we had time together as a family. Vikram started school in Raipur. When we lived in Bhind, he hardly saw his father, who would not be at home when he woke up and would not yet have returned when he went to sleep. I remember going to visit friends in Gwalior, and when Vikram cried and I tried to pacify him, someone said, 'Give him to Vijay!' I replied, 'No, he'll cry even more then!' I also remember one time when my in-laws came on a visit, and we all sat down to dinner together. When I realized that Vikram was finding it peculiar, it struck me that he was used to me feeding him separately.

In Raipur, things were different. We would go on picnics. And we could even watch television. TV was new to India, and it was only available in Delhi, Bombay and Calcutta. But the communication minister was from Raipur, so Raipur received transmission too!

Vijay was always reserved and, as a police officer, was always cautious about making friends. Two of them from college, Jagdish and Ashok Mattoo, were friends for life, and now in Raipur, we made friends for the first time. Among them were the collector Najeeb Jung and his wife Ameena, and Dr Sushma and Anil Varma, and the subsequent collector Ranvir Singh and his wife Prablin. Later, we were together with Najeeb and Ameena in Bhopal when Vijay was posted there, and then again in Delhi. Vijay enjoyed badminton regularly in the evenings—never, after we left Raipur, did I see him wearing shorts! It was a relaxed, normal life that we all enjoyed. Police activities were also of a different kind.

One day, we were to go for a party. Vijay told me, get ready, we will leave at 7.00. I was quite used to getting ready and then sitting and waiting, not knowing when he would be free to leave his work and come home. But that day, he came back on time and said, 'We are not going for the party.'

'Why?' I said, quite upset. 'But my friends will be waiting.'

'No,' he replied. 'We are not going.'

I was confused and still a bit upset, so Vijay elaborated.

Raipur had a cinema and, like cinemas everywhere, it was supposed to follow fire and safety norms. But this had not been done, and the police permission was not issued. That day, the owner of the cinema had come to see him in his office, seeking permission for his cinema. In an attempt to get friendly, he told Vijay that he would be seeing him later at the party.

Vijay told him sternly that the listed procedures were not followed, and this had been explained clearly to him every time he asked for permissions. Once the procedures were followed, the permission would be issued immediately.

Apparently, the cinema owner took this to mean that Vijay was asking for a bribe. He took out a wad of notes and put it on the table between them. Vijay looked at him, looked at the money, rang his bell, and called for the sub-inspector.

When the sub-inspector entered, he instructed him to take the man away and put him behind bars.

'Now you know why we are not going to the party?' he repeated firmly. There was nothing further to be said!

Another incident I remember took place soon after we arrived in Raipur. A friend was going to Bhilai and invited me to go along in her car. On the way, we were stopped at a police checkpoint. A constable came to the window and asked for money. When we asked what for, he replied, 'Naya SP aaya hai. Dena padta hai. (We have a new SP, and he'll be expecting a cut.)' I requested his name and when he asked why I wanted to know, I explained that I had to tell my husband, who happened to be the new SP. Hearing that, he ran away very fast.

Vijay and I had a discussion about this. I felt that he should trace the people involved in this racket and put a stop to it. But he was very clear that his duty was to ensure peace and safety in the city. He had to make sure that the major crime issues were handled. Of course he punished the concerned people, but he felt that to focus just on investigating corruption would be to neglect his daily duties. 'I set a standard for them,' he said. 'I tell them very firmly that corruption will not be tolerated.'

Vijay was always particular about keeping his work-life and home-life entirely separate. But doing this also required admirable discipline, and the good side is that we were always protected from his work pressures and the grime he faced every day. At times I felt bad, like when I heard from others what he had done, sometimes at the women's club. One time, the local Rotary club invited him to speak at one of their weekly meetings about the Paan Singh encounter. The Rotary meetings were generally a male affair, but I asked if I could attend, so that I would finally get to hear all about it at first hand!

One of the inconsequential but amusing things that happened to us in Raipur was at a local village mela during Shivratri. We went to take darshan, and Vijay reached into his pocket to make an offering, only to find his wallet was missing. The SP's pocket had been picked! In the years to come, I would tease him about it—'Shall we lodge a report? Oh, we should have filed an FIR!'—it would annoy him but really, it was the funniest thing that could happen to someone who had decimated the gang of the ferocious Paan Singh.

—VEENA RAMAN

6

THE NIGHT THAT SHOOK BHOPAL

I completed two years of duty in Raipur without any extraordinary events, and then opted for a staff posting. To progress in the police force, a field posting with only field experience is not sufficient; working in a staff position is also essential. Field experience is objective-oriented: you are sent to the field with an objective to achieve. In a staff posting, on the other hand, you need the ability to undertake policy formulation, as well as the ability to handle the legal issues connected with the work. For a successful organization, both are equally important.

Accordingly, I was posted to Bhopal as assistant inspector general (AIG) Special Branch. It is the rank equivalent to SP in the Intelligence Branch, which in some states is called the Crime Investigation Department (CID), and in MP, the Special Branch or SB. This put me in charge of security in the state—all security installations and VIP security. My first major assignment was to take care of the prime minister's security over a two-day visit in the first week of December 1984. He was to enter MP through Morena, travel to various places, come to Gwalior, and stay overnight in Sagar.

It had been just a few weeks since the tragic assassination of Indira Gandhi on 31 October 1984. Rajiv Gandhi had taken over as PM and elections were announced. We had received the schedule. I had joined duty just a few days ago, and started making arrangements for the tour including laying the carcade, earmarking officers, ensuring security at the public meetings, and so on, with the approval of the IG.

On 2 December 1984, Veena and I were invited to have dinner with our dear relatives Prabhakarettan and Rajamchechi at their home. It so happened that one of the other guests, also from Kerala, was an officer in Union Carbide, and we chatted for a while. After dinner, we went home and I called the Government Railway Police (GRP) station to check whether the train on which my parents were coming from Kerala, scheduled to arrive at 2.30 a.m., was on time. There was no information yet. After tossing and turning and remaining sleepless for a while, I called again. Why had nobody called me with the train arrival timing yet? The person who picked up the phone spoke courteously and explained that he was unable to leave the building to go to the railway platform and enquire. In Bhopal, the GRP station was in an independent building between the platform and the parking area. The boy explained to me that there had been a gas leak and it was dangerous to go outside. 'What kind of gas?' I asked.

'I don't know,' he replied. 'It is something strong and dangerous. People are saying it's chlorine! I cannot leave this building.' Chlorine? This young man, a constable, had probably just about completed his schooling. He told me that he was trying to ask the railway staff and nobody was picking up the phone. I understood his dilemma—there was nothing he could do. I told him to call and let me know as soon as he got some information and hung up.

It was now past midnight. Wondering what to do next, I suddenly remembered that the Union Carbide plant was situated very close to the Bhopal Railway Station. I took out the visiting card the dinner guest had given me earlier that evening and phoned him. Apologizing for disturbing his sleep, I described to him the information I had received from the GRP station. And his answer chilled me to the bone.

'Sir,' he said, 'if what you're telling me is true, if there has been a gas leak, you will have to evacuate the town immediately.' I told him that I had to get to the railway station and asked what the antidote was. 'Water,' he replied. 'Be prepared with a bucket of water and a towel soaked in it. Repeatedly press the wet towel on the face of anyone who has been affected, particularly the nose and eyes, at frequent intervals.'

I immediately phoned the CM and apprised him of what I had learnt; the Special Branch had the freedom to use a private line in any emergency or critical situation, and the CM would always attend to such calls no matter what time of the day or night it was. I explained that I had found out because my parents were arriving in Bhopal shortly and my enquiries about their train arrival had led me to this information. Since there was no further information on which we could act, he thanked me and asked that I keep him informed.

Now, I had to make sure that my parents were safe. They were in the Jayanti Janata, on their way to Bhopal from Ernakulam. Their train must have stopped at Itarsi by now, the big junction where the north–south and east–west train routes meet.

I had sent my driver home that evening, never imagining that anything like this could happen! The train was due at an odd hour, and I had wanted to go myself to receive my parents. All I had to do was drive to the station, park, put them and their bags in the vehicle, and bring them home. I had not wanted to put the driver through a night of broken sleep, so I was on my own. I got into my jeep with a bucket of water and a towel, and started driving towards the Bhopal Railway Station. As I approached, I saw a crowd of people walking towards me. As a policeman, one is used to seeing crowds. But this was more than an ordinary crowd! It was a huge and growing mass of people. They were rushing in my direction, and they were absolutely terrified and frantic. When I turned into the narrow road housing the Sultaniya Zanana Hospital, the situation became unbearable. People started banging on the bonnet of my jeep and one of them came to my side and asked, '*Saheb, aap maut ki aur kyun jaa rahe ho*? (Saheb, why are you driving towards your death?)' He forced me to stop and asked me to put the gear in neutral and pushed the jeep back almost half a kilometre.

What was I to do now? My anxiety about my parents rising, I decided to drive out to Habibganj, one of Bhopal's suburban railway stations that was quite close to my residence. The train did not halt there but would have to pass through. I parked the jeep, walked on to the platform, entered the station master's office, and asked if the Jayanti Janata has arrived. 'No, sir,' he replied. 'It is late.' I introduced myself, realizing that he had no reason to believe what I was saying since I had joined this new assignment just a few days ago, and had no proof of who I was except an identity card! But he saw my jeep and the wireless set in it, which told him I was indeed a policeman. I urged him not to let any train pass through under any circumstances.

'Why?' he asked anxiously. 'What is the problem, sir?' He explained that he knew something was wrong and was very worried because he had been trying to call the Bhopal station on the railway line phone but there was no response. This corroborated what my constable had reported, and drove home the seriousness of the situation in my mind with renewed urgency.

'I don't know yet,' I replied. 'But something serious is going on, so please don't let the train pass.' I gave him my phone number, but since I was unlikely to be at the desk, I also requested him to reach me through the police control room whenever he had anything to report.

It was now about 6.30 a.m. Reassured that my parents were safe, I left for the state control room in the police headquarters. There, my worst fears were confirmed: a gas leak had taken place at the Union Carbide factory and people had fled. By all accounts, they were still fleeing.

'Any news from the hospitals?' I asked. But—and even at that late stage—there wasn't any. I knew of two hospitals in Bhopal and, despite the reassurance from my state control room, felt it would be safer for me to take a round of them to check for myself. Sure enough, there was nothing untoward to be seen in the hospitals. Yes, a few small groups of people affected by inhaling the gas had come to seek treatment. But even in the main Gandhi Medical College Hamidia Hospital, there was no indication as yet of the magnitude of the problem. I realized that I might find a better pulse of the situation at the railway station. I could go and meet the constable who had first alerted me that something was wrong.

This time, driving towards the station, there were no crowds. I wondered where they had gone. In fact, it was completely deserted and, closer to the railway station, it felt like a ghost town. I entered the GRP station and there was no activity. All was silence. Then I saw the boy sitting on a chair near the table. His arms were splayed out on either side of him, and his rifle was resting on one of his knees. He was dead.

What a shock! There was nobody else in the place. Perhaps I would find answers at the railway station.

Nothing could have prepared me for what was to come next. I walked across the parking lot and entered the main entrance onto Platform 1. The entire platform, a huge expanse, was filled with dead bodies. They were lying helter-skelter, as they had fallen, and I could see many corpses with intestines spilling out of the anal area. I did not allow the dreadful sight to affect me—it was my duty to find someone here who could tell me what had happened. I walked around to try and locate a person who was still alive, but could not.

By the time I returned to the police control room, it was nearly 9.00 a.m., and now the figures were coming in from the hospitals. Every few minutes, a new report came in of the casualties in the gas leak. The numbers were rising, and the feeling was horrible. We had to settle down in the police headquarters and address the grim reality of counting dead bodies.

What had happened was also becoming clearer in our minds.

Winter had set in and the air was foggy, preventing the leaking gas from escaping into the atmosphere. The air being breathed was getting more and more polluted by the poison in the gas—methyl isocyanate (MIC), a pesticide.

Inhaling the gas created a physical urge to rush desperately towards water. As they ran, people panted, struggled for breath, and inhaled even more than they would have if they had not ran! That image of people running for their lives, and the very act of running taking them closer to death, is one that will never leave me. There were people who ran 40 km that night. They too died. We know this because bodies were found in Raisen, 40 km from Bhopal.

Another tragic occurrence was that some of those who ran away to save their lives, tried to come back to save their belongings from burglars. In many such cases, these people too died. Bhopal's Lal Parade Ground, about 3 km from the gas leak, was also strewn with bodies that fell there from sheer exhaustion, never to rise again.

At around noon, I again visited the station. And there I began to understand the puzzle of the dead bodies on the platform. In the early hours, a train had come in. As soon as it stopped, the windows were opened. All of us who grew up travelling on long-distance trains know how this works! You want to know where you are, you want to check the time, and you want to have that chai–kaapi that will come round with loud announcements soon. But that fateful day, the windows opened and the gas entered the compartments. People rushed towards water. How many taps did the compartments have? And how many actually had water coming out of them? People rushed out of their compartments, onto the platform where the gas was at its densest, and there they met their fate. When the engine driver realized that something was terribly wrong—perhaps because he heard a station official who staggered out to shriek, 'Why did you stop here! Didn't you see the signal?'—he dimly realized that he was responsible for some sort of catastrophe, started the engine and kept going, leaving many of his passengers behind!

The corpses on the platform were unknown people. While we may have been able to guess which train left them behind, how could we know who they were, where they came from? Very few carried identification documents in those days. It was the known deaths and cases of maiming that would be compensated; those were the ones who were counted.

One silver lining in this ghastly tragedy: an NCC winter camp was being held in the proximity of the factory; providentially, nothing untoward happened to the youngsters, as the wind blew the gas away from them.

'IPS Officers Are Supposed to Know Everything!'

While we were monitoring these ghastly tragic events at the police headquarters, it occurred to me that the PM's visit, which was to have been my first major duty assignment, was very likely to be held sooner than planned. After all, Rajiv Gandhi was an up-and-coming world leader, a leader with a conscience. A terrible national disaster like this would surely be a priority over his election tour! When I alerted my IG to this possibility, however, he preferred to focus on continuing the arrangements as per the previous schedule. And so, when the PM, who was in Bengaluru on 3 December 1984, decided to rush to our afflicted area for a personal visit, we had to make arrangements on the spot. I had not yet been issued a car. I had not had the time to train my men to form the defence ring around him. But most important of all, and now with no time to prepare—what about the PM's police escort officer?

'You do it, Raman,' the IG said in an offhand way.

I tried to explain that I might have handled PMs' and presidents' visits in the past, doing general bandobast and public meetings, but had no experience in this crucial post in the PM's security entourage!

The role of the escort officer is crucial, as he is the fulcrum on which the mechanism of proximate security functions.

The IGP responded that I could very well do it, having functioned as SP of two districts and killed dacoits! I began to mutter to myself that killing dacoits is quite different from protecting dignitaries from killers. But he had a checkmate move up his sleeve: 'Raman! You are an IPS officer. And IPS officers are supposed to know everything!'

This is one of those loaded taunts to which there really is no civil response.

I started by requisitioning the IG's Ambassador car. After all, I needed something of utmost reliability, for the good of the people. He would just have to make do with some other vehicle. There was a lot to be done and my team and I made sure that it was all done in time. Fortunately, there had been no discussions or egoistical demands from anyone—this was a situation of grave tragedy—and the plan was very simple. The PM would get into the car and the carcade would travel with him the 10 or 12 km to Hamidia Hospital, where he would meet and talk to the doctors and officials on duty. Since the elections were imminent, there would be no media interaction.

As soon as I had assembled vehicles for the carcade and the essential personnel, I decided to do a dry run. The scenes at the hospital were heartrending, with people weeping over dead loved ones, and they were absolutely inconsolable. At a distance from the hospital was a group of highly agitated people seeking revenge and the death of the owners of the factory whom they held responsible for the tragedy. It was into this atmosphere of two extreme and contrasting emotions that we would be bringing the recently-bereaved Rajiv Gandhi, now shouldering an enormous responsibility, for a visit the next day.

At the appointed hour of 3.00 p.m., we stood at attention on the tarmac, along with the Madhya Pradesh CM, waiting for our PM to arrive.

The PM stepped out, dressed in his trademark white kurta-pyjama, with matching sports footwear and a fawn-coloured shawl wrapped around him in a style that many others also sport these days, from Amitabh Bachchan to various dignitaries.

As was always the case back then, the carcade consisted of sturdy Ambassador cars. The vehicles travelled in a secure formation and the escort officer—in this case, yours truly—was in control of the carcade.

As we left the airport area and drove on to the road, I issued an urgent order on the wireless set for the pilot to stop. All the security detail members, in particular the joint director, were taken aback. Everyone stopped as ordered. I got out of my car and walked the 15 feet to where the PM's car had stopped and opened the PM's door. Lifting a part of the shawl that had got stuck between the body and the door of the car, I placed it carefully inside the car. He gave me a warm smile and I smiled back, saying, 'Can't have the PM opening his car door while it's moving!' before closing the door. I then turned to the personal security officer (PSO) and reprimanded him in an uncharacteristically stern manner for not ensuring that the car doors were locked from the inside.

Later, I wondered if I had done right by scolding the PSO, a professional travelling with the PM's security team, whom I had met for the first time. Usually, a person in that position is a favourite of the person whose security he heads; over the years I've noticed that all heads have their favourites in such positions. Maybe I was in trouble!

The PM's tour was conducted with efficiency and ended soon, as he had to return to Bengaluru and resume his election tour. The Rajiv Gandhi that we bid goodbye to that afternoon was a man unable to mask the anguish within him, overwhelmed as he was by the enormity of the tragedy.

The flight took off and the CM, still standing on the tarmac, sent a message for me to meet him. We discussed the visit and he gave me some further instructions. Before we parted, I asked whether any offence had been taken at my harsh words to the PSO. 'Of course not!' Arjun Singh assured me. 'The PM was full of praise for you! Raman, these are the type of security officers we need, people who are focused more on doing their job well than on simply pleasing the PM.'

'Major Arrests' Shortly Released

The senior management of Union Carbide came to Bhopal and were arrested, and the world knows what happened. As a police officer with a Law degree, I concede that it would have been difficult to pin criminal culpability on them. The charge of criminal negligence against them could not have been sustained either, even vicariously. The Central Bureau of Investigation (CBI) later took over the case.

Sadly, as history records, the release orders had massive repercussions.

May the souls of those lost in this tragedy rest in peace and may the survivors recover their health and zest for life. We can only pray.

Recognition

It was a grim time for Bhopal and for India, facing the aftermath of the gas tragedy, the world's worst industrial disaster. For me there was a small silver lining—I received the President's Police Medal for gallantry. It was given to me on 26 January 1985. I had never expected anything like this, having only done my duty to the best of my abilities. For my family, it was a day of happiness and pride. Being recognized was a very pleasant feeling, and it brought back to my mind all the struggles and frustrations I had experienced; I felt satisfied with the manner in which I had handled the situation under very difficult conditions. I had stuck my neck out and exposed myself to the threat of action under Article 311 of the Constitution—if it had happened, I would have been the youngest to ever be punished in this manner. But receiving the award was an achievement that enhanced my confidence and gave me the feeling that I was capable of facing any kind of situation!

Receiving the President's Police Medal for gallantry on 26 January 1985, for liquidating dacoit Paan Singh and his gang

With some members of the team that vanquished Paan Singh and his gang

The SPG Is Born

Soon after the PM's visit—in fact, we later learnt that the idea germinated on the flight back from Bhopal to Bengaluru between the PM, Joint Director Dr S. Subramaniam and the parliamentary secretary Arun Singh—we received an announcement that a Special Protection Group (SPG) was to be instituted within the police for the PM's security.

After the assassination of Prime Minister Indira Gandhi on 31 October 1984 by two of her police security personnel, the security of the PM was immediately given to the Indian Army. However, Arun Singh was insistent that no security of a democratically elected prime minister should be provided by the army! It must have a civilian face and not a military face. This led to the creation of a new force, the SPG. For Rajiv Gandhi, a man whose mother was killed by her own bodyguards, to agree to this gives a sense of his own democratic values and high thinking.

Once the SPG was instituted, Arun Singh and Dr Subramaniam had the responsibility of scouting for talent to select its officers. My IG (who in a huff had pointed out to me that being an IPS officer, I was supposed to know 'everything') told me that I was on the shortlist. A few months before this, the MP government had declined my posting as SP Gurdaspur, Punjab. It was the peak of the Khalistan movement, and I believe it was K.S. Dhillon, IGP, who had recommended me. He was an excellent senior officer whom I had worked under as ASP Gwalior, and I admired him a lot.

National and state elections were held simultaneously; Rajiv Gandhi and Arjun Singh both came back to power. Exhausted after the election tour, as well as the intense events of the past two months, they decided to take a rejuvenating break in Kanha, a national wildlife sanctuary in MP. And my IG, Mr Mukherjee, called and informed me that I was in charge of the security arrangements there.

That is how I came to enter the next phase of my career as assistant director (AD) of a new unit called the SPG, the Prime Minister's Special Protection Group.

7

PROTECTING FOUR PRIME MINISTERS

From 1985 till 1995, I had the good fortune of working with four PMs of India as a member of their security, a mid-career tenure that I found very satisfying. It was a tremendous opportunity to be exposed to heads of state, to understand how the Government of India works, how the Prime Minister's Office (PMO) works. I travelled a lot during that period, across India as well as to many foreign countries, and learnt a lot, arranging security for the PM when he travelled to international forums such as the Commonwealth Heads of Government Meeting (CHOGM), the World Economic Forum and United Nations meetings, amongst others.

After Prime Minister Indira Gandhi was assassinated by her own security personnel while she was walking from her residence 1 Safdarjung Road to her residential office at No. 1 Akbar Road, following Operation Blue Star—the storming of the Golden Temple in Amritsar—those premises were converted into a memorial to her. A new home was being built for the new prime minister, Rajiv Gandhi. No. 7 Racecourse Road (now Lok Kalyan Marg) was being refurbished as the PM's residential office, where he would meet visitors and hold meetings, and the adjoining bungalow No. 5 as his residence. As the new building came up, a lot of security inputs had to be incorporated. The SPG was a new organization, a new work area, and we were starting from scratch. For me, too, I was in a new job that carried a lot of responsibility, at a young age. I had to first understand the important components of the PM's residence. Apart from the PM's small family—his wife and two children—there were the various services' staff who managed the residence, and various office personnel and political functionaries who frequented it. In addition, there were guests of the PM who were frequent visitors—both state guests as well as personal guests. Naturally, each of these had to be handled with a different security protocol and access control.

In terms of the people selected to work in the PM's residence, there were two aspects: first, they had to be highly proficient in the functions and responsibilities that would be assigned to them. Whether it was civil work, electricals, the kitchen, the garden, the housekeeping—all had to be the very best available to serve in the residence of the leader of India! Second was the security clearance, now critical, in view of the security breach that had enabled the tragic assassination. Along with putting the physical security in place, the person's antecedents and affiliations also had to be scrutinized and verified.

VIPs: A Short Aside

During my tenure with the SPG, I dealt with VIPs on a daily basis and the only response was to be respectful and concerned about their safety. However, some incidents remain in my mind.

Some superstars were fussy and arrogant but there were also some who were very down-to-earth, and among them were Jaya and Amitabh Bachchan. They never expected special favours and always went through the security process without any fuss.

I also remember the dignified way in which our PM's family members conducted themselves. In those days, his children Rahul and Priyanka were in school. I remember how one day Rahul was eating ice cream at India Gate. All of a sudden, his classmate, a boy with a turban who was clearly a Sikh, came up to greet him. It was a reflex action for us to immediately cordon Rahul off for his safety. It's sad to think of children growing up in this manner. It was tough for these children.

Life in the SPG

Since the SPG was new, the induction and on-the-job training were being done. The rigorous training was a continuous process, and you could say that an individual in the SPG would be in training every second! This included about an hour and a half in the training area every morning doing physical exercises and various drills and firings. There were sessions on building physical fitness, firing capability, use of firearms, and driving. Driving was an essential component of SPG training where we were taught to use a vehicle as a weapon, both for attack as well as for defence.

There were physical barriers around the residence to protect it from attack by a heavily armed or armoured vehicle barging in. The gates and physical structures inside the boundary walls had to be planned to withstand this sort of attack. No attack did take place, but we remained constantly alert, and intelligence reports were acted on immediately. It being a house under construction, every aspect had to incorporate security: lights and CCTV cameras had to be placed in a certain way, every space and barrier had to be planned appropriately, and every eventuality had to be considered and prepared for.

It was during this time that we developed the safari suit as the ideal dress for security personnel to wear, primarily because it easily concealed weapons that may need to be carried in the course of duty. Today, the safari suit is worn even by private security officers; it was we at the SPG who introduced it.

For me, it was not just an honour to work with the PM but also a real pleasure. Rajiv Gandhi was a stickler for good work. There could never be any compromise whatsoever on standards. If you had been picked for a particular job, you had to do your very best, and your performance had to be perfect.

In addition to being motivated to always do one's best, one of the most striking things about Rajiv Gandhi was his personal charisma and good looks. During my stint with the SPG, I had the occasion to be present in gatherings of world dignitaries, and quite often also to meet and interact with them. But there was nobody to match Rajiv Gandhi! I remember one instance when he was invited to give a lecture in Boston, USA. I was standing at the entrance to the building with our host, John Kenneth Galbraith, a very respected and influential economist, who had served as ambassador to India in the early 1960s. J.K. Galbraith was about 6 ft 7 inches tall and I, at a little over 6 ft, was feeling like a dwarf as we waited for the arrival of PM Rajiv Gandhi. J.K. Galbraith said to me, 'Mr Raman, your prime minister is a very, very handsome man! Perhaps the most handsome head of government today in the world. The only person who could have matched him was our own John F. Kennedy.' What a testimonial!

Rajiv Gandhi was extremely popular. I had the good fortune of travelling with him as a member of his security staff wherever he went, not just internationally, but all over India as well. He was particularly popular in the Northeast and also in the South: in Kerala, Tamil Nadu, Karnataka and Andhra. It was amazing to see the kind of crowds he would attract! People would be waiting in droves even if he was coming at midnight. The excitement and joy is impossible to describe, you had to be there to see it. I don't think any film star or cricket superhero of today could match Rajiv Gandhi's charisma and magnetic personality.

One time, we were on a road journey through Kerala. Apart from my regular duties, I found that I was also needed for something else quite unexpected, and that was my language skills! The then CM, Mr K. Karunakaran, was unfortunately rather hard of hearing. When people in the crowd spoke in Malayalam to the PM, he would look at me for the translation.

Kerala—and I say this as a simple fact and not as a boastful Malayali!—had excellent crowd-control measures. This was not just because the Kerala police were efficient, but also because the people of Kerala were responsible. If you drew a line and told them not to cross it, they would not cross it. Whether it was barricaded or not did not matter. They knew that that was the line they were not to cross, and they would not cross it.

It was that sort of disciplined crowd through which we were passing, and I noticed a group of young girls standing and giggling, looking at the PM, delighted at the opportunity of being able to see him in person. Then the PM also noticed the group of girls. Seeing that, there was an uproar from the girls. 'What are they saying?' he asked, seeing that they had started jumping up and down and repeating a phrase in great glee. I translated it for him: 'He saw us! He saw us!' What a thrill they got! It was this type of response Rajiv Gandhi drew from the people of India.

22—28 SEPTEMBER 1985 □ AN ANANDA BAZAR PUBLICATION □ RS 4.00

Reportage on Punjab Elections

SUNDAY

An old Girijan woman greets the Prime Minister during his Kerala tour

Rajiv Gandhi's Discovery of India

A report on the Prime Minister's visits to the tribal areas

On tour with Rajiv Gandhi in Kerala

Photos of His First Trip Abroad

Vijay's first international flight was in 1985 to New York for a United Nations conference, along with Rajiv Gandhi. I was so excited! Vijay never wanted to push his way into anything or draw attention to himself by asking for photos to be taken. In those days, a camera was a big deal—unlike today when everyone can take photos from their phone! At my insistence, he took our camera, but later gave it to one of his colleagues and delegated him to take photos of the trip. But when the photos were printed, I was disappointed to see that they were all of air hostesses and glamorous-looking women! And there were only four with Vijay...standing in front of Manhattan high-rise buildings.

—VEENA RAMAN

Best of the Best

India's PM has three parliamentary secretaries, MPs without a portfolio, appointed to assist the prime minister in their work. In Rajiv Gandhi's time, they were Arun Singh from Uttarakhand, Ahmed Patel from Gujarat, and Oscar Fernandez from Karnataka. Them being, respectively, Hindu, Muslim and Christian, we referred to them as 'Amar, Akbar, Anthony'! They were absolutely excellent people to work with, very helpful, very well educated, and completely down-to-earth. Despite their proximity to the PM—and unusually for Indians—they never, never threw their weight around.

My office was on 7 Racecourse Road, in one of the outhouses of the main building. Arun Singh conducted a weekly meeting there every Saturday at 10.00 a.m. to assign tasks from the PMO. Key personnel from every service department were expected to attend: the head mali, the junior engineer PWD who looked after the water supply, the junior engineer electricity, and so on. I represented the security, so anything that he wanted to convey to the security establishment would be through me; similarly, the heads of other departments would take instructions for their team. It was a short meeting of just 10 or 15 minutes, depending upon the issues raised, and the decisions were prompt and immediate. If there was any matter that required the PM's opinion or assent, Arun Singh never picked up the phone to call. Instead, he would walk across the lawn, through the connecting gate to the next house, raise the issue with the PM, and come back with the answer in 10 minutes. This is how we got decisions from the PM. It may sound different from what one normally expects from the Indian government, but this is the way I experienced it.

I can give you an example of this instant decision-making that affected me personally: the accommodation of the newly appointed SPG personnel. We had all been selected from good positions in the states of our cadre. And we had been assured that housing would be provided on priority. This was a motivating factor to accept the new position. The main reason police personnel hesitate to go on deputation is because they have to release the housing given to them, and are never sure of getting accommodation on par with one's standard of living at the other end. Sometimes, one had to make do with 'temporary' accommodation for extraordinary lengths of time. But here, we had been assured that we would get accommodation as per our ranks within three months. Having joined in June, I should have been granted my accommodation by September—but was not. It was okay by me; I had a roof over my head and was managing just fine. But on one of those Saturday meetings, after all the others had left, Arun Singh asked me, 'Vijay, I hope you chaps have been allotted your accommodation?'

That was one of the nice things about Arun Singh—everything was on a first-name basis. There was no pomposity. And this query came out of genuine concern. When I told him that we had not, his annoyance was visible, and he immediately spoke to the concerned officer and demanded prompt action.

In less than one hour, my phone started ringing with information about vacant houses and enquiries about which one I would like to select. This is where the problem lay. Vacant houses, suitable houses within our entitlement, were available. It was sheer lethargy that they had not been provided. And it had taken an ultimatum to get things moving.

Whenever I hear or read about the deficiencies of that particular administration, I can only describe what I saw personally. What I saw included swift and sensible decision-making, and strict accountability. Rajiv Gandhi was addressing a slow and complacent bureaucracy and he was making every effort to improve things. He was a very hands-on person.

Arun Singh was not the only person who worked systematically and with utmost efficiency. Our PM had handpicked an absolutely wonderful team: Montek Singh Ahluwalia, G.K. Arora,

Sam Pitroda—and so many others who were the foremost names in their fields of expertise. They brought the most advanced thinking as well as technical gadgetry in their areas to the table. There was a high energy and ambition to get things done. But there were also light-hearted and fun-filled moments that happen when people with a great sense of humour get together! I remember the constant banter between Rajiv Gandhi, Mani Shankar Iyer, Arun Singh and some of the other creative wits he had around him. We would all be in splits.

'Can This Be Done?'

One of the most interesting things about working with PM Rajiv Gandhi was a daily task he gave me, to enquire and find out about some or the other new improvement or initiative he wished to implement. Every day, before he got into the car, he would hand me a magazine, the copy of an article, or something he had noted. He used to read a lot and had access to a lot of information from which he would pick out relevant items that could be considered in our security set-up.

Jawaharlal Nehru, India's first PM, is often quoted as having said that we as Indians need to develop a scientific temperament. I can tell you that I was a witness to his grandson practising it! Everything he thought about and planned was scientific. Everything was objective and logically reasoned.

I received this type of input from him every day, along with the request, 'Please go through this. If it can be done, please go ahead. And if it cannot be done, please get back to me.' This is what the PM was saying to me, an IPS officer with only 10 years of service, and I took it very seriously. Once the PM left for his office in South Block, I would immediately address the issue he had given me and that I had to report back to him. While passing on the message, I never said, 'The PM wants this.' Never. He had only asked me to find out if it was possible—and that is exactly what I asked: 'Is this possible?' If they came back with an answer that I found lacking, I would ask again, providing my view on the subject.

Most of the time, I would collate all the inputs received and find that it could not be done. When the PM returned for lunch at 1.30 p.m., I would be standing at the porch again to receive him. He would look enquiringly at me and I would meekly inform him, 'Sir, that cannot be done.' Sometimes he would ask the reason, and I would explain it to him. Then he would sometimes ask the concerned person to speak to him with details.

There were very few occasions when I was able to tell the PM that yes, it could be done, that this was the timeline, that these were the resources required.

Today, when I sit back and reflect on the controversies of that time, I cannot help but wonder whether similar enquiries made to other heads of his staff were passed on not as questions—'Can this be done?', which is what the PM actually asked—but as orders—'The PM wants this done, so do it.'

Darshan

Another routine at the PM's residence was the daily public darshan, where groups of people came to visit him with their grievances. The PM was available from 9.00 till 9.45 for this every morning, and people would arrive by about 8.30 a.m. for the security formalities. The groups came as per the appointment time given—except for groups from Amethi, the PM's constituency. Groups from Amethi who wanted to meet the PM were welcome without an appointment, and they would be given priority access.

The PM would come out of his residence, No. 5 Racecourse Road, and walk through the connecting gate into No. 7, towards his residential office. Before he walked to the office for the darshan, there would be a group of his own staff waiting with queries, the senior-most personnel of each department—a crowd of about eight or 10 of us. If any of us needed his attention on any matter, we had to speak up right then. We had just a few seconds as he walked from one lawn to the next because once he reached the other side where the groups were waiting for him, he would be lost to us for the day!

Our VCR!

We were exposed to world cuisine and handicrafts when Vijay travelled and bought local things home. There were camel skin lamps from Pakistan, spices from Turkey, and malai ghilori from Lucknow, among other things. But my most favourite story is of the time he was returning home from official duty abroad and I asked him to buy us a VCR.

In the 1980s, VCRs were high technology, and it was an unimaginable luxury, a real thrill, to be able to view a movie on TV at home! But a VCR was very expensive in India due to our foreign exchange restrictions, and people would buy them abroad and carry them back. Vijay agreed, and did so. Before the flight, he sent me a message to come to the airport with money to pay the duty.

I had a friend who was with the Customs department, who arranged for me to wait inside the arrival hall (security restrictions only became what they are today after the 2001 attack on the Twin Towers in New York).

Vijay, with our VCR, went to the red channel to declare that he was carrying a dutiable item.

Some of his subordinates, who had also purchased VCRs and assumed that the boss had made impeccable arrangements to get through, followed him.

I was watching when the kind Customs official asked Vijay, 'Which model are you carrying?'

Vijay took out the papers and read out the model number.

The Customs guy asked, 'It is an old model, isn't it?'

'No,' Vijay replied, 'this is the latest model!'

No further questions. Vijay waited expressionlessly until the documentation was complete, paid the full duty, and then walked to where I was waiting.

I felt so sorry for his subordinates!

Gaddafi's Security Force

When Vijay travelled for work, he had the opportunity to see the heads of state of various global governments closely, including Nelson Mandela, Margaret Thatcher, the Libyan revolutionary Gaddafi, and many others.

One of the most interesting incidents Vijay narrated to us was when he went to the Bahamas for the CHOGM. Protocol was for all escort teams to walk with their heads of state to a certain point in the conference venue, after which the local police took over, escorting them to their designated seats.

The local police were escorting Gaddafi to his seat when they somehow fell into an altercation with Gaddafi's security force, who refused to follow protocol and stop at the designated spot. Gaddafi was known for his cadre of about 30 fierce women, known as his Amazonian guard, for his protection. They were believed to have taken oaths of virginity and were dressed in camouflage, with nail polish, coiffed hair and heavy mascara.

One of these Amazonian women jumped, like a cat, on one of the local security guards and bit his ear! What a shock—they were prepared for guns, but a biting woman? No! Gaddafi's Amazonian guard proceeded to escort him to his designated seat, while the local police moved to the back of the room where police personnel from other countries were standing. Vijay noticed that he was standing next to the man who had been bitten, saw that his ear was bleeding, and enquired, 'Hope that's not too painful?' The man laughed and said, 'I'm not worried about the pain! But how am I going to explain to my wife that a woman bit my ear? That's going to be more dangerous than the bite!'

The Rickshaw-wala

Vikram and I were in Vadodara for a special Satyanarayan Pooja at my parents' place. Vijay was very busy in the SPG and joined us later, arriving from Delhi by train. He took an autorickshaw to the house, and when the driver overcharged him, Vijay was upset. He said, 'I have lived in this place and know the distances. I have come for an auspicious function, so I will not argue with you. But don't cheat passengers in future. Ill-gotten money does not make you rich.'

The next day, he was to return to Delhi by air. On reaching the airport, he paced up and down, as was his habit, waiting for a friend. Suddenly he heard someone calling out, 'Saheb! Saheb!' He turned around and asked, 'Yes, what do you want?'

The man handed over ₹50. 'I don't think I dropped any money,' Vijay looked at him, puzzled.

The man said, 'Saheb, I am the rickshaw-wala you hired yesterday. I am sorry I overcharged you, please forgive me!'

Pleasantly surprised, Vijay told him, 'No, you keep it. You realized that you did something wrong and won't do it again. That is good enough for me!'

—VEENA RAMAN

A Man with a Mission

We toured through the villages and towns of India along with Rajiv Gandhi, driving all day with periodic halts where meetings had been arranged, and quite often stopping for dinner only at midnight. The next morning, we would start early and keep going. Often, against our advice, he would want to travel in an open vehicle. Who could ever have imagined that this longing to always be in contact with his people would cost him his life?

When one thinks about Rajiv Gandhi as a person who never wanted to enter politics, it is truly amazing that he took up his position so sincerely and made such a huge effort to connect with every part of India. He travelled to every state—most on multiple occasions, even though his tenure was so short.

Glimpses into a PM's Life

My responsibility grew over the years, but the focus of the job remained the same. At the same time, each PM was very different from the others, and it was a very interesting phase for me.

Rajiv Gandhi's election loss in 1989 gave way to a new leader, Vishwanath Pratap Singh, who was from an erstwhile royal family and had served as the finance minister, the defence minister and the agriculture minister of India. He was a senior and experienced politician who, to us at the SPG, came across clearly as a person who looked at everyone and everything with suspicion. We found this an unhealthy way to work!

When V.P. Singh stepped down after a vote of no confidence, he was replaced by Chandra Shekhar. Chandra Shekhar was sometimes seen as a rough, rustic sort of person, as he was from a farmer's family and had never held any official government position. But having been in regular contact with him through the seven months of his prime ministership, I found him to be a person with a lot of wisdom—a fine person, very humble and very kind. We at the SPG saw this in many ways, one of them being his response to our night-shift team, whose shift started at 8.30 p.m. and continued till 7.30 in the morning.

One unusual but admirable thing about Chandra Shekhar was that he never bothered to move into the official PM's residence at Racecourse Road. He remained in his home at 3 South Avenue Road, which was allotted to him as a member of parliament. He would come to No. 7 Racecourse Road, the residential office of the PM, but never used the residence. This shows you how practical he was—he never expected to remain PM for long—so why bother to disturb his household?

It was November when he came to power and the Delhi nights were getting cooler. One evening, he was sitting on his lawn, chit-chatting with people of his party, when he noticed a vehicle being parked outside his gate and something being unloaded from it. He asked the SPG boys and they told him that it was their chai, brought to them from our canteen, which was close by. Surprised, he immediately called for someone from his kitchen and instructed that the present arrangement be discontinued. Why should tea be brought from outside? The SPG was there to look after the PM. So, the PM must look after the SPG too. From now onwards, he said, tea must be provided from the PM's kitchen to the SPG boys whenever they wanted.

It was a very humane reaction and this feeling of reciprocity continued. For many years, long after he relinquished his role as India's PM, the SPG officers would be invited to Chandra Shekhar's Bhondsi farmhouse for a meal in the first week of every New Year. And at that event, there would be none of the formality of lining up to shake his hand or anything of that sort! He would circulate, meet each one of us, shake hands, and exchange heartfelt words.

One of the things we all remember about Chandra Shekhar is that whenever he was invited to a lunch or dinner function, he would ensure that the accompanying security persons were served their meal before him. This was something he never failed to arrange for because he knew that once he had finished his meal, he would leave, and the security personnel would go hungry unless he ensured that they were fed first.

Another thing about Chandra Shekhar was his great sense of humour, and we all enjoyed that a lot. It was quite different from Rajiv Gandhi's sense of humour. I remember one time we were testing a car that had recently been made bulletproof. In those days, we had only the Ambassador car. Bulletproofing basically meant replacing the windshield and glasses with bulletproof glass, and inserting bulletproof metal into the body of the car, the doors and the boot covering the fuel tank. These things were generally imported, or the cars were sent to vendors in another country, the changes made, and then they were brought back. But as the need for personal security kept increasing, an indigenous solution was sought, and some private agencies began dealing in these items.

Our government has always been focused on self-reliance and developing India as a great manufacturing nation. One day my director, Trinath Mishra of the UP cadre, suggested trying out a local workshop. We gave them a car, and it was done up to our specifications and delivered to us to test. We found everything working fine, but before approving it, we decided to request the PM to do a test drive. We explained to Chandra Shekhar that we had used our own Indian resources to fit out this new car and if approved, we would be able to continue making it in India instead of importing the required parts. He agreed to do so and set out in the car on his next weekend trip to his Bhondsi farmhouse. The PSO sat next to the driver, Trinath Mishra sat in the rear seat next to the PM, and I travelled in the car following them.

It was a drive of around 40 to 50 minutes, with all the traffic arrangements laid out. Once we got there and alighted, we went to the PM to hear his remarks on the drive. And he said, 'Trinath-ji, if you are going to take your PM in this type of car, we don't need any terrorist to kill him! The car is good enough to do that!!'

We were all rather shocked at this statement and only

realized after a while that he had been making a joke of a very uncomfortable situation. The driver had inadvertently turned on the heating! The car had become like an oven. Chandra Shekhar must have assumed that he was test-driving a special car and had to go through the experience to give feedback. But the response from our PM, who had made light of an adverse situation—'Yes, seat your PM in such a car and he will die automatically!'—was one we would always remember.

One of the finest PMs India has had was P.V. Narasimha Rao, and I am honoured and privileged to have had the opportunity to work under him. It is unfortunate that he did not have a longer tenure, as he did wonders for India even in the short time he was in power.

Mr Rao was a diabetic and had undergone a bypass surgery. For him, daily physical exercise was mandatory. On the recommendation of his personal physician, he would walk at 6.00 every morning from his residence at 9 Motilal Nehru Marg to Rashtrapati Bhavan. When he became PM, we extended the residence from No. 5 and No. 7 to 9 Racecourse Road to accommodate his family, and created a large walking track for him, about 1.6 km, so that two rounds would take care of his doctor's requirements. On the first day, I decided to accompany him on his walk to take note of his observations about the track and see if there was anything we could do to improve it. We walked together and I thoroughly enjoyed the conversation. I continued to accompany him on the following days too. Mr Rao was an erudite person with great depth of knowledge and he would talk about many things—history, political science, diplomacy, religion. It was a free flow and I found it very enriching. Those daily 45 minutes were like an education for me! Our PM kept me engrossed and seemed to enjoy the walks too. His son-in-law, K.R. Nandan, IPS Andhra Pradesh cadre, was my batchmate at the academy, and our PM was aware of this. Maybe that could have softened his attitude towards me.

I have always been grateful for the opportunity to work closely with PM Narasimha Rao, a highly educated and mature person, and to learn from him. I sometimes sit back and reflect on how fortunate we in India have been to have had Dr Sarvepalli Radhakrishnan as our president, and P.V. Narasimha Rao as our PM. They were philosopher statesmen, fitting Plato's ideal. It was P.V. Narasimha Rao who changed India dramatically by putting us on the track of fast economic growth, and this is something future generations must never forget.

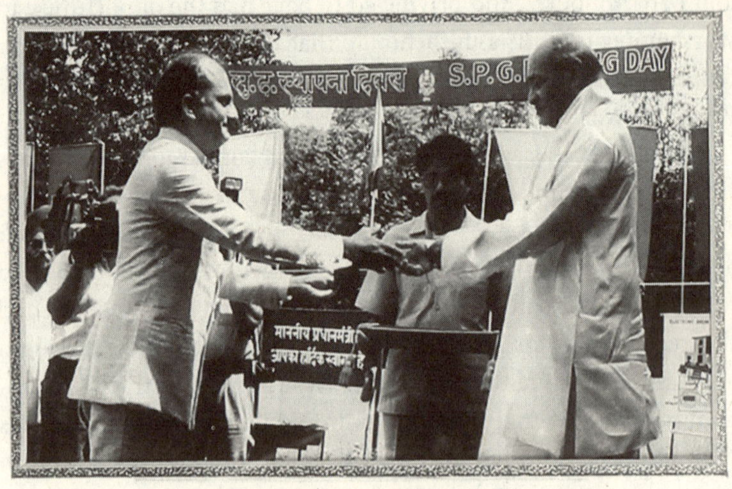

Receiving the award for meritorious service from Prime Minister P.V. Narasimha Rao

8

AROUND THE WORLD IN 39 DAYS

Driving six continents: The fastest drive taking in the six continents, with total distance of more than an equator's length (40,075 km 24,901 miles), is one of 39 days 7 hr 55 min by Navin Kapila, Man Bahadur and Vijay Raman driving a Contessa Classic. They left New Delhi, India, on 22 Nov 1992 and returned to the same place on 31 Dec 1992.

—Our entry in the Guinness Book of World Records

WORLD RECORD

GUINNESS BOOK OF RECORDS

VIJAY RAMAN, MAN BAHADUR
& NEVIN KAPILA
FASTEST SIX CONTINENTS DRIVE BY CAR
39 DAYS 7 HOURS 55 MINUTES
STARTING AND FINISHING IN NEW DEHLI
22 NOVEMBER - 31 DECEMBER 1992

PETER MATTHEWS NORRIS McWHIRTER

The certificate received from the Guinness Book of World Records

One of the most spectacular events that took place during my years with the SPG was something that happened off duty. It was in 1992, when Narasimha Rao was the PM of India. We had an officer by the name of Vijendra Kapila, on deputation with us in the SPG from the Sashastra Seema Bal (SSB).

Vijendra was a master of motor vehicle speed, and he was deputed to train us on this special skill of offence and defence. Our training ground was close to Delhi, a dilapidated runway of 1.6 km, and this is where we practised under Vijendra's hard whip! He was a DSP rank officer when he came on deputation, and all of us were senior to him—but that was completely irrelevant because, on the track, he was a hard taskmaster and did a really great job. I'm not one of those people who are crazy about driving, but I have always enjoyed using the controls, the anticipation, and other aspects, and it was great learning how to use high speed, take a swift U-turn, and other such skills. While the training was very focused and impersonal, over time we did become friends and got to know Vijendra's younger brother Navin also. One day, Navin walked into my office casually for a chat. I was surprised, because most visitors came by appointment, but called for a cup of tea. We talked about various things, and he happened to mention that he had recently scored a podium finish in the Himalayan Car Rally. Without thinking, I said to him, 'Navin, it's good to know that your driving skills have been acknowledged at the national level. Now it's time for you to do something that the whole world will recognize!' It was an absolutely casual remark. He finished his tea and left, and I forgot about it completely. Once in a while I asked Vijendra how Navin was doing, but we had no further contact until several months later when Navin sought me out once again.

'You know what you said to me that day?' he asked.

'No!' I replied, perplexed.

It turned out that my offhand remark had got him thinking. He had explored various options and decided to attempt getting his name in the Guinness Book of World Records.

He had found out that the current record for circumnavigating the globe by road was held by the British Army, whose team had done so about two years previously, in 40 days.

'We can easily beat their record!' Navin said in excitement. 'And that too in an Indian-made vehicle!'

What an idea!

It took a while for him to convince me, and he did so by explaining the conditions of the circumnavigation. First, we would have to cover a distance of 40,075 km, which was the length of the equator. We had to touch all five continents and drive a minimum distance of 2,000 km on each one. Next, we could select our own route, our own starting point, and there would be no gun fired to send us off unless we fired it ourselves, as the time of starting would also be up to us. The clock would stop only after we returned to the same point. Finally, we would have to follow an east–west or west–east route; it was not permissible to travel north–south or south–north to cover the requisite distance.

As I got drawn into Navin's plan and his enthusiasm began rubbing off on me, he also explained that we would be a crew of two drivers and could have one navigator. They would have to be the same right through the journey until we returned to the point where we had flagged off—surely, surely, in less than 40 days!

In our excitement, we began thinking about the countries we would like to visit on this wonderful dream drive that now seemed well within our grasp. Because we were not only going to break the record, but have the most exciting adventures too!

But Where to Start?

Navin and I both felt more attracted to driving through the countries of Africa and Latin America, which Indian travellers in those days did not have much exposure to. However, this was not practical. After several hours spent scouring atlases—as there was no Google Maps in those days—we decided to pick our home city, Delhi, as the starting and ending point.

We realized, with growing excitement, that we could drive from Delhi and across the Wagah border to Lahore, drive through Pakistan and parts of Afghanistan, and enter Iran. Then, driving through Turkey, we would carry on through Europe, crossing the Channel to arrive in England.

The thought of this journey was delightful. However, before we could start making the arrangements to embark on it, an officer in the Indian embassy, posted in Islamabad, was beaten up for alleged acts of misdemeanour. It was a diplomatic incident, and Madhavrao Scindia discouraged us from taking this route.

Looking at the maps again, we realized that, as is typical of most of us Indians, we were looking westwards. Why not east? If we started our journey in Australia, we would cut our teeth on a fast drive in a foreign country where traffic drove on the left, as we were used to, and it would have many familiar road signs. And we would not have to swerve to avoid cyclists!

Selecting the Vehicle

Our first choice was the Tata Sierra, which had just entered the market. We found an acquaintance who had the vehicle and did some test driving on it. It was a pleasure to drive! But could we cover 1,500 km per day on this car? Unless we could, we were not going to break the record. Giving ourselves a driving time of 12 hours per day, this meant that we would need to travel at a speed of about 130 to 135 km per hour. However, to our great disappointment we learnt that the Sierra's maximum speed capability was 135. Could we drive it every day for over 40,075 km at its highest possible speed? Of course not. We did not need to be auto engineers to know that this was simply impossible—if we tried to do so, on the second or third day, the engine was sure to crash.

By this time, we had got really excited about the Sierra! Tata was an Indian company with an international name. People anywhere in the world would look at it and know where we were from, and that meant a lot. We went to Pune and met the officials of Tata Motors. Even the chairman was aware of what we were doing and was thrilled about it. They tried their best to increase the speed but despite all their efforts, were unable to.

Meanwhile, sponsors were pouring in with funds for this project. Unsurprisingly, most of the sponsors were insurance companies. Pressure was rising—we had to make a decision and get started soon.

A new luxury car had entered the market, Contessa, from Hindustan Motors, modelled on Vauxhall, but fully made in India. It was being used by the wealthy and famous and was clearly a great vehicle, comfortable as well as good to look at. We borrowed a trial car from a friend and did some test driving. It was heartening to see that it had a speed capability of 180 kmph. We at the PM security were familiar with the engine this car used. It was built with technology considered outdated in other countries. This meant that service and repairs on the route were uncertain—a minor risk that we decided to take.

One of the Guinness conditions was that the vehicle should be owned by one of the contestants, so Navin Kapila purchased one for himself. The government willingly waived the excise duty charges, and this made the rate quite reasonable. Our only modification was to remove the rear seat and replace it with a single bucket seat, to create more room for our luggage and for spares. We carried a spare windshield, just in case; to find this particular windshield in Europe or the United States (US) was most unlikely. Apart from the seat, Navin's car was like any other Contessa on the roads—an 1,800 cc 56 kW Isuzu Powertrain, with power disc brakes and hydraulically dampened coil spring suspensions. There was no air conditioning; we consciously planned our trip for low comfort as we wanted to focus on covering the maximum possible distance at the highest possible speed, with nothing whatsoever to distract us or make us sleepy! The Contessa was ceremoniously handed over to us by the great Indian cricketer Nawab Mansoor Ali Khan Pataudi.

Now that we had decided on our car, it was time to think about which aircraft could carry it across the oceans. To circumnavigate the globe, we had to plan how our vehicle would be airlifted, travelling as cargo when possible on the same aircraft we travelled in. The aircraft that could accommodate a vehicle did not operate daily on each of the air routes, and this would limit our choice of day and might even delay us.

We had decided to start in Australia, so our first airlift would be Bombay to Sydney, and after we completed our drive around Australia, we would fly Sydney to Los Angeles. The next jump was Miami to Caracas, followed by New York to London and, finally, Riyadh to Delhi.

Change of Plans

By this time, we had decided that Navin would drive and I would navigate. All my experience with looking at maps had made me the route expert! It is difficult to explain to anyone from a generation who finds their way from street to streeet around the world with Google Maps, what it was like for us. The atlases were all quite old and outdated. To get current maps, especially in places where borders had changed, we had to put in requests to the embassies of those countries. Road maps of actual current roads were so rare and precious! I would sit in my office every day in the PM's residence after office hours, until late at night, studying these. Though computers were very new in those days and, in fact, most government offices did not have any, we at the PMO did, and this was very useful. My chaps would wonder what I was up to! In fact, at this point, even my family were not really aware of what I was planning;

it was only after the dreams started materializing and decisions had to be made that I took them into confidence.

Navin was an expert driver, accustomed to driving in rallies, and he was quite capable of driving comfortably at a speed of even 150 kmph. We needed a second driver and Navin brought someone on board who was confident about driving at 100 kmph. Based on this, we planned our route and calculated that our journey would take 31 days. I must admit that even those who knew Navin's background as a successful rally driver were sceptical.

For the international licence, our driving ability would be tested, and we also needed to pass a medical test. Keeping in mind that we would be driving at high speed on the right side of the road in many countries, our vision and reflexes were also tested. Unfortunately, our second driver was disqualified as he needed a high-power lens due to his poor eyesight.

This was a real setback as our sponsors were looking forward to making publicity announcements! The obstacle, and possible delay, was also very embarrassing for me as a member of the SPG. Eventually, Navin convinced me to take on the role of second driver—I was familiar with the route, and he also had faith in my driving skills.

It was at this time that I consulted my family, and both Vikram and Veena supported me totally. They were absolutely confident and, in fact, pushed me to go ahead! They were well aware that there was so much that could go wrong: we would encounter hostile terrains, varied climatic conditions from freezing Europe to scorching Australia, unfamiliar languages and traffic conditions, and different and often unpredictable customs regulations. All of this would be magnified by the fact that we would always be in a tearing hurry. I greatly appreciated their unconditional love and support for me in this adventure!

While it was decided that I would be the second driver as well as the navigator, we still needed someone who would take care of mechanical problems that the car might face. For this role, Hindustan Motors provided us with Man Bahadur, a skilled mechanic from their organization. As per the Guinness rule, the third person could not drive the car; he was not entitled to even sit at the steering wheel.

Paperwork

That decision made, we continued planning while simultaneously starting the process of getting the political permissions to travel, which was—then even more than now—lengthy, cumbersome and often quite demeaning to Indians. We also needed a Carnet licence* to clear customs without paying duties and import taxes on our car when we crossed international borders, since we would be bringing it back to India with us. Then there was the international driving licence, which would allow us to drive in all the countries.

Every visa application requires a purpose of travel, and ours was to break the Guinness record! We had a lot of help from Ramu Damodaran, Indian Foreign Service officer and personal secretary (PS) to PM Narasimha Rao, who guided us through the processes, and we received almost all the visas we needed in time. We had also applied for visas of some of the South American countries that we had not planned to drive through, as we felt safer having them in case of last-minute changes en route. Safer? Yes, because the administration stamped our passports but also gave us a list of names and contact numbers. We had official permission—as well as the unofficial requirement of clearance from the drug-lord millionaires of that era!

The limited number of flights was also a constraint. The first airlift was from Bombay to Sydney, but this entailed a layover

---

*A travel document used by tourists to import private road vehicles across international borders, free of duty

in Bangkok. Both flights did not operate every day of the week, and this limited our options. We had to plan our flights very carefully. The reservations had to be made in advance too, as cargo is the most revenue-earning component of any airline and can't be booked and not used.

The risk of missing the connection and losing a whole week was frightening indeed as that would send our dreams of beating the record crashing down!

With the basic groundwork done, Navin flew to London to discuss our plans with the Guinness officials. The route plan was finalized, and they had identified people all over the world who would sign the logbook to testify the journey. For our own records too, we decided to follow a strict bureaucratic process of filling a logbook at every fuel stop, with the signature of the pump owner. Each page of the log would include place, time, mileage, amount of fuel filled and other relevant details. It would have three carbon copies. For young people who don't know what a carbon copy is—Google will tell you!

Flag-off

Many Indians of those days (and I believe quite a few even today) would have chosen an astrologically propitious date and time to set out on such an ambitious mission. However, we picked a Sunday because that was most convenient. All our documents were in order. I was the only one of us with a government job and had been issued leave as well as permission to travel. My colleagues—and, in fact, everyone who knew me—were very excited about the whole thing!

It was 22 November 1992 when we were flagged off from India Gate at New Delhi by the Speaker of the Lok Sabha, Shivraj Patil, amidst a cheering group of friends and well-wishers. Our journey started in the morning with a slight drizzle, and the first log entry was made as we filled fuel.

In 1992, Indian roads were only just being built to what they are today. Still, I must say that Delhi–Jaipur was not bad at all. As we entered Rajasthan, however, we followed a signboard that had probably swung around in the wind, sending us off in the wrong direction as sometimes seen in the movies! We had lost time, and arrived in Jaisalmer—a slightly circuitous route, planned to comply with the distance requirement—a little behind schedule. Our logbook was to be signed at the police station but, to our amazement, no one was willing to tell us where it was! It was very frustrating, and when we eventually did find it, we learnt that a major shoot-out had taken place that day between the police and a terror gang, and the locals must have been petrified. Clearly, our adventures had begun!

We were to refuel at Barmer, but it was still very early in the morning and the pumps didn't open till 10.00 a.m. Luckily, we located the pump owner's home and convinced him to open early! On we rushed to Barmer and then Ahmedabad, maintaining a good speed of 160 kmph. However, the Vadodara–Mumbai highway is a commuter belt with a lot of slow-moving cargo vehicles occupying the fast lane as well, and we were down to 40–50 kmph.

Leaving at noon, we arrived in Bombay the next morning after a run of 23 hours, having completed 2,300 km—comfortably more than the mandatory 2,000—in our own continent, Asia. Navin and I had taken turns at the wheel, with the other snoozing on and off in the passenger seat and Man Bahadur sitting quietly at the back all the while!

While we rested at the Centaur Hotel, a Hindustan Motors service team was busy servicing and sterilizing the car to comply with Australia's strict quarantine requirements for the Air India flight to Sydney via Delhi and Bangkok. Despite the captain's annoyance at the delay, the crew was very helpful and went out of their way to load the car into the plane, even when the pallet broke and the car had to be re-palletized. We were thankful that

Air India, one of our sponsors, had made special arrangements to fly the car along with the team in a passenger aircraft. Using a cargo plane for the car would have put our precarious time schedule off gear, apart from the practical difficulties of coordinating the flight timings of the two planes.

Touching down around midnight in Bangkok, we went through the aircraft changeover and arrived on schedule in Sydney on Tuesday afternoon. After a long rest on the flight to Sydney, we were ready to take on the challenges that the varied Australian terrain would throw at us. But we were unprepared for an encounter at the airport itself!

A Beautiful Country that Whizzed Past

Our car was emblazoned with logos of our sponsors and we, too, were dressed in clothes that were difficult to miss! The Australian customs officer was astonished. He just could not believe that Indians—he clearly did not have a very high opinion of us—could be planning such a feat. Our papers were all in order so there was nothing to hold us back, but he kept making us repeat our plans, the route we were following, and the record we aimed to beat, listening with increasing incredulity. A distance of 40,075 kilometres? In this vehicle? The three of you? And you plan to be back here in Sydney next Tuesday after covering all of Australia? We nodded patiently to every question. Finally, he challenged us—$100, he said, $100 that you can't do this! We, with a much larger stake in our minds, agreed good-naturedly and carried on.

We were racing through Australia, but unfortunately, I am unable to regale you with long descriptions of that extraordinarily beautiful continent! As Veena always relates, when friends who know her love of travel would ask why she didn't insist on being taken along, she would simply say, 'If I was there, he never would have broken that record!'

We were pleasantly surprised by the beautiful coastal drive from Sydney to Melbourne, but pushed on to Port Augusta to log in a very fast stretch. The one from Ceduna to Perth was probably the fastest of the trip, where we averaged about 145 kmph. We were doing great and catching up on the time that we had lost while getting the clearance at Sydney. However, in the process, we also landed up with a speeding ticket! Continuing to drive fast, we passed urban pockets, and it was a really exhilarating ride.

When we left Perth for Darwin, we were cautioned that we must carry everything we would need for the journey as nothing could be purchased on the way, as there were only a few fuel stations. We were also told that we must report to every police station on the route. What?! At first it seemed like there was some kind of restriction on us—what had we done? But the authorities reassured us, explaining that this was only out of concern. If we did not reach the next stop at a reasonable time, the rescue helicopters—which remained always on the alert in those remote areas—would be sent out to find us. Slightly subdued at the thought—but not for long!—we raced off again.

We were driving through very tough conditions, with temperatures hovering over 40°C and very sandy terrains. The car was being pushed to continuous high speeds, as the pressure was mounting. From Geraldton we called home to our anxious families—from telephone booths, relics of that bygone era before mobile phones! In my short conversation with Veena—'I am fine, how are you and Vikram?'—I asked what the cricket score was, but she suggested that we talk about cricket later and insisted on first hearing about our adventures!

Horn Not OK Please

One of the biggest impediments to a fast drive in Australia are their 'road trains', which frequent the highways at low speed and can be a nightmare to overtake. A road train is a trucking vehicle with two or more trailers, which carries freight across the continent. And as they travel in packs, it means overtaking something that could easily be 100 m long. We soon learnt the signals drivers give each other during this intricate process. Loud and insistent honking, which some drivers in India continue to do unaware that it only displays their ill manners and lack of maturity, would never motivate any driver anywhere in the world to give way! Here, we learnt the courtesy of horn signals used to inform the other driver that you wished to overtake and the response given to indicate that you may do so. After whizzing past successfully, there is another set of notes from the horn that says 'thank you!' and yet another for 'you're welcome!' from the driver of the other vehicle—a communication that creates goodwill and camaraderie on the journey. This prepared us for a similar situation in the US, where, of course, the additional challenge was that we would be doing it on the 'wrong' side of the road!

In Australia, the most exotic—and dangerous—road companions are the kangaroos, who leap before they look. It was not at all uncommon for one to jump out onto the road, sometimes in front of the vehicle, or sometimes even right on top of it, which could damage it beyond repair. In India, we are quite used to sharing the road with cattle of all kinds—even bison, wild boars, camels and other creatures. However, we do not drive at 140 kmph in India! The Australian highways are strewn with dead wild animals.

We had a kangaroo encounter too—two of them suddenly appeared on the road in front of us. Navin slammed the brakes and managed to stop short, but the tail of one hit our headlight and broke it. The other kangaroo wasn't so lucky and got crushed under a speeding truck.

Through the changing terrain, our last lap in Australia was from Daly Waters to Sydney, and we travelled nonstop for 36 hours, covering about 3,500 km. Since we had to make it to Sydney in time for the Los Angeles flight—as all airplanes did not carry the car as cargo along with passengers—Navin had no option but to drive at over 100 kmph on winding roads through the mountains. He recalls this as one of the toughest stretches he has ever travelled. In all, our drive through Australia was very pleasant. Best of all—the authorities never had to undertake a search operation to find us!

We reached Sydney Airport and completed all the formalities on time—and saw to our amusement that the customs official who had greeted us on arrival had somehow made sure that he was on duty to also see us off! He was shaking his head in disbelief as we approached—or perhaps it was awe?—and he congratulated us and paid up the $100 we had won. Walking into a duty-free shop, we purchased a gift with the money and went back to give it to him with a smile and a salute: 'Never underestimate us Indians ever again!'

A Good Night's Sleep

In those eight days driving across Australia, we had covered 10,000 km. On two of those days, we had actually covered 1,800 km in a 24-hour span. You may wonder where we slept on that journey, and my answer would be, 'In those bucket seats, of course!'

There was just one thing we kept in mind, and that was a cautionary remark made by Madhavrao Scindia, who knew we would want to be on the move every moment of the day or night: 'Avoid driving between 3.00 and 5.00 in the morning. Whether you are in a hotel or in the car, just relax during that time and do not drive.' That was the only concession we gave ourselves; in that timeslot during which we may have been at our most vulnerable, we parked on the side of the road or pulled into a service facility area, pushed the seats back, and relaxed. Sometimes, we got out and walked for a short while, sometimes we just snoozed for those two hours. And other than those two hours, we were on the go all throughout. In fact, the protocol we followed was to stop the car only to refuel and, while doing so, also replenish food stocks and other necessities, and attend to the call of nature. In the entire period—which turned out to be 39 days and not 31 as hoped, just narrowly beating the previous record—we checked into hotels on just 10 occasions for a night's rest.

Cruise Control

The flight from Sydney to Los Angeles offered a much-needed rest for the team. On board the flight, it was a pleasant surprise when the pilot announced our presence. This was followed by cheers and clapping, and a toast for our success from all on board—such a great feeling to be acknowledged and appreciated!

The Air India representative at Los Angeles got us an early clearance and we drove out of the airport surprisingly soon. But it was 4.30 p.m. and there was nothing we could do about the LA rush-hour traffic! Now came the real test: driving for the first time on the 'wrong' side of the road. Everything was inverted! We had practised for this on Rajpath (now Kartavya Marg) late at night in Delhi with kind support from the traffic cops on duty: how to orient ourselves, how to overtake, and all at extra-high speed.

It is a straight drive from Los Angeles to Miami, via Texas. Racing down the American freeways towards Phoenix, somehow Bahadur goaded us into a speeding match with a Toyota Lexus and a Nissan, which were in the region of 170 kmph. The other two car drivers eventually acknowledged the might of our Indian car and waved cheery goodbyes as we passed them!

By the time we reached Miami, we had made up for lost time and raced ahead of schedule. As we waited at Miami Airport, we were relieved to learn that the coup that took place in Venezuela had been neutralized and our scheduled airlift to Caracas could take place. However, our Carnet was not valid. We could leave the US—but would not be allowed to re-enter as we were scheduled to do after two days! Once again, it was Ramu Damodaran to the rescue, resolving the issue with the intervention of the PMO, and reaching out to the Indian ambassador in Caracas, who assured us that we would be safe and looked after.

That was not the only shock of the day; the foreign exchange restrictions had also resulted in the withdrawal of our 'miscellaneous charges order', which meant that we would have to pay cash for our expenses. Both spelt doom for our expedition. However, with the support of the PMO and Air India, they were resolved. It was a short flight from Miami to Caracas and we were happy to see Indian Embassy representatives waiting at the airport to receive us.

Setting out immediately to cover our route of 2,000+ km in 24 hours flat, Navin raced along, and I was a little worried about him getting distracted by the many pretty girls on the road! Soon we were cruising towards the beautiful sea coast, and it started feeling like a day trip, with not too many miles to log and, finally, some time to spare enjoying the waterfront. We parked on the beach to take photographs, without realizing that the tide was rising. What a shock to see our car getting submerged! We laugh about it today but there was panic as we extricated it from troubled waters with great difficulty. That evening was the first after many days on which we checked into a hotel for a night of rest.

A narrow escape from the rising tide!

Mobile Irrigation

In those days, Air India was not well connected in Latin America, and this meant heading back to Miami and driving on to New York. We had done barely 20 km when Bahadur, sitting in the rear seat, spoke up, 'Sir, *bahut zor se lagi hai!* (I'm bursting!)'

Oops. An overfull bladder. This was not good news.

'Why couldn't you go at the airport?' chided Navin. 'No, too busy browsing the duty-free shops, weren't you? Too bad, I am not going to stop, just do it in the car, ok?'

But Bahadur kept whining and, eventually, Navin had mercy and stopped the car. Bahadur flung open the door, tumbled out and ran into the fields to relieve himself.

Now that we had stopped, the two of us got out too, to stretch our legs. Within seconds, we heard sirens approaching. We quickly opened the bonnet and made a show of checking the engine. Two cops on motorcycles pulled up. 'Yes, gentlemen, is there any problem?' one of them asked. '*Arre bhai, yeh police ka mamla hai*! (Oh dear, a police matter!)' Navin muttered, and quickly introduced me to them as a senior police officer from India.

I explained to the Miami Police Department cops that we had just landed from Caracas and were on our way to New York to catch the flight to London to continue our drive to beat the Guinness record. Wishing us good luck in our quest, he presented me a sheriff badge.

Meanwhile, Bahadur had completed his assignment and quietly sneaked into the back seat. We closed the bonnet and got back into the car, ready to take off. Navin was driving and I was on the other side. One of the cops approached and I lowered my window. He said to me, quite solemnly, 'Sir, in the United States, use of mobile irrigation systems in public is illegal.'

Use of mobile irrigation systems in public is illegal!

What a very elegant warning, in those few words, informing us that they knew exactly what Bahadur was visiting the fields for.

But also that, as a member of the same brotherhood, a pleasant message would be more than sufficient as a rebuke and warning!

We began driving north from Miami, aiming to log 2,500 km and arrive in New York in under 20 hours. Speeding towards Atlanta via Jacksonville, we found the city of Atlanta being spruced up for the Olympics. However, we were dependent on maps collected from the embassies, and driving fast, we must have overshot an exit. Hopelessly lost, we were running behind schedule and finally managed to find our way onto the highway. Somewhere near Nashville, I got out of the car and walked up to a man to ask for directions, a rare opportunity as, unlike in India, not a soul was to be seen for miles together. This man had other things on his mind; he pulled out a gun, put it on my temple, and asked me to get out of his sight. In Delhi, I had a gun of my own, issued to me by the Government of India, and I knew better than to argue with a person with a gun. Contrast this encounter with the delectable aroma of *poha* that met us at the Patel Motel we stopped at for breakfast the next morning!

From Nashville onwards it was smooth sailing, until we were hit by a snowstorm and the temperature dropped to -7°C. We could certainly not afford the luxury of stopping. As the snowfall increased, the wipers, unable to brush aside the falling solid matter, stopped working. Inside, we were shivering too: as I mentioned, we didn't have air conditioning, which obviously meant we didn't have a heater either. Stopping at an urban area, we went into a shop, bought candles, and lit them along the windscreen to warm it. This was the only innovation that was possible, and we sustained it until we arrived in New York. The airport had been snowbound due to a blizzard, but flight operations started just in time for us to catch our flight to London.

With the larger part of the journey behind us, the record was well within our reach. We had encountered problems on our adventurous journey, but we were running more or less on schedule. By the time we reached London, there was a feeling of excitement and celebration. The London office of the General Insurance Corporation, one of the sponsors of this round-the-world trip, hosted a banquet to honour our team. To be honest, the United Kingdom was not high on our list of places to drive through—after all, it was a British record we were challenging!—and the only reason we did so was to visit the Guinness office in London. We were given a warm and encouraging welcome there and reassured that we were on track with all the boxes ticked. It was also in London that we had the luxury of one of our 10 hotel nights on the trip. We then got back into the car and carried on south as fast as we could.

A Mosque Attacked, a Route Abandoned

Driving on to the ferry at Dover, we crossed the English Channel and arrived in Calais, France, driving through to Spain, one of the most beautiful countries we saw, although I must admit that all we got was the view that flashed past as we sped along! We crossed the border into Morocco after completing 2,000 km in Europe, on schedule, on Day 25 of our 31-day target. Our first impression was one of beautiful landscapes and friendly people. When we stopped to fill fuel, people asked, 'Oh, you are from India! How is Momtaz? And how is Shammi Kapoor?' They wanted to know if they would be able to meet them and other Indian film stars, whom they admired greatly, when they visited. I must say that it was unexpected to have these pleasant interactions with the ordinary citizens of Morocco, particularly because at the state level the relationship between India and Morocco was not very warm.

Crossing Morocco, we entered Algeria and at the border post, showed our documents. One look at the Indian passports, and the officers showed unmistakable hostility. This was a first for us—all through the journey, even in the countries where Indians often faced racism, we were received at the borders with friendliness.

'Why are you here?' came the angry question, followed by an even angrier statement: 'You have destroyed our mosque!'

At that time, we had no idea what they were talking about. But it was the second week of December 1992, and on the 6th of that month, the Babri Masjid had been attacked and demolished. Since we had been living in our own world, moving fast, following the plan, not exchanging news on current affairs on international phone calls with our families, we had no idea. And we were now at the Morocco–Algeria border, spending two nights at sub-zero temperatures, being viewed with hatred and suspicion and humiliated with abuses. Our documents were immaculate, so they were not within their rights to turn us out or try to repatriate us. However, in view of the political situation, they informed us that we would be allowed to drive through Algeria only if we agreed to report at every police station we passed.

Navin and I conferred. Could we afford to stop at a police station each day to get papers signed? Even finding a police station at each place we passed was going to slow us down. With this kind of restriction, there was no way we could break any record! We also had to keep in mind that from Algeria, our route took us through Tunisia and Libya—which were even more Islam-oriented. Even Egypt and Jordan were deeply disappointed with India; how would they treat us when we knocked at their doors?

It was a difficult decision to make, particularly because we had been looking forward to driving fast on the excellent petrodollar-funded roads in these countries, just under 6,000 km, all the way to Riyadh. And from Riyadh, Air India would fly us home!

We were on Day 27, and had kept precisely to the timetable, intending to complete the journey in 31 days. It was now clear that we had to seek an alternative route, and this was possible because we had completed the 2,000 km due in Africa in Morocco itself. Now, on the border of Algeria and Morocco, we made a phone call to Guinness, informing them that we had no choice but to change our route.

In fact, Guinness had warned us against this route in the first place, and they now reminded us of that! We were confident that we would be fine in those countries and, resenting what we took to be their patronizing suggestion, had declined. Who could have ever imagined that something like this would happen in India? But they had turned out to be right.

Having made our choice, we now turned around, gritted our teeth, and kept going. Fast! Sadly, we had another major setback when the Spanish customs refused to clear us and we lost two precious days, pleading with the Algerian border police to sign our exit papers, as they had orders to prevent our exit. It was a moment of relief when they did, but now we had to reschedule the rest of our trip, this time from inside a fast-moving car: visas would have to be obtained and route plans chalked out. With renewed commitment we went onwards to Paris, and then Brussels, Rotterdam and on to Berlin. The mercury had dipped to -9°C, and we were travelling through snow. When the German police advised us not to travel without snow tyres, Navin, well experienced in driving around Shimla, coolly informed them that these were Indian snow tyres. I must say that both Bahadur and I were very impressed with the way he handled the car in the snow.

Driving along the German Autobahn where, as you may know, there are no speed restrictions, Navin took the wheel and, at one point, said to me very excitedly, 'Look, sir! We have touched 180!' The Contessa could not exceed that; when he pressed harder, it came down to zero. We had a small celebration sharing a chocolate, but our joy and thrill were short-lived.

Ours was a right-hand drive and so it was I who, sitting in the passenger's seat on the left-hand side, was the first to see something very embarrassing indeed! In the midst of all the excitement, there was a motorbike—yes, a two-wheeler!—quietly overtaking us, the rider looking expressionlessly ahead, oblivious to our dismay. Our car was fitted with equipment that could display the speed of the vehicle overtaking us; primarily to protect us from being charged for speeding. Well, I can assure you that the pride of all our achievements was very soon deflated with this 240-kmph motorbike!

Just beyond Stuttgart, we were stopped by the traffic police and asked to wait as the road was closed; a truck had turned turtle. There was a communication problem. The police did not understand English and we didn't understand German. Navin, as assertive as always, got out and shouted, 'Rally! Rally!' Understanding our dilemma, the cops immediately went out of the way to clear enough space to somehow let us through.

Arriving in Frankfurt, we had completed another 2,000 km in Europe, and boarded the Air India flight back to India. We had lost time and now needed a new strategy to tackle the Indian road conditions and traffic. We were still 4,000 km short of our target, and decided to drive south to Kanyakumari and then back to Delhi. We had informed Guinness and they approved the new route.

Crashing Back to Reality

While we were all extremely happy to be back on home turf, there was an undeniable handicap: would the Indian roads support our ambition? Could we cover 4,000 km in less than a week? Without wasting time worrying about it, we rushed straight from Bombay down the NH4 via Bengaluru to Mangaluru and along the west coast to Thiruvananthapuram where my parents were living at the time. They were delighted to see us, and after a refreshing bath and breakfast, we drove on to Kanyakumari, and from there to Madurai, Hyderabad and then Nagpur, from where we planned to head straight back to Delhi.

About halfway between Hyderabad and Nagpur, our sturdy Contessa fell victim to its first tyre puncture of the entire journey. We had travelled around the world and not had a single flat tyre—but now, back in India, after covering nearly 38,000 km, it had happened in the hilly terrain of Hinganghat. Arriving at Nagpur in the late afternoon, we refuelled and drove through Jabalpur, heading towards Sagar, the town where I had completed my schooling. The plan was to head from Sagar to Jhansi and on to Delhi.

Driving along the Jabalpur Road, we came to an intersection of two national highways and drove towards Sagar. It was getting dark; I was exhausted and must have lost my concentration for a few seconds, and the vehicle crashed into the hilly side of the road. Fortunately, we did not hurtle down the ghat on the other side! But the vehicle was badly damaged. Luckily, Navin and Man Bahadur were unharmed. I, however, had glass splinters in my head and other injuries, and was in shock. We tried waving down trucks to help us, and as we waited, it was a time of despair; there was no way we could get the car fixed and drive on fast enough to beat the record.

Eventually, a truck driver stopped for us. We were in MP, my home state, and I requested the driver to take us to the closest police station. He did so, getting off to inform the police personnel inside that one of their seniors was in the truck and badly injured. What followed in the next several hours were among my most moving and memorable moments as a police officer of the MP cadre.

By then, it was about 2.00 a.m. on that wintry December night on the road to Sagar. The elderly thanedar came towards the truck, and I started explaining that he wouldn't know me, but my name was Vijay Raman and I... 'Sir,' he responded, '*MP mein aapko kaun nahin janta!* (Sir, there is no one in MP who doesn't know you!) Please don't worry. I am here to help you.' He assisted me in climbing out and led me to the rest house adjoining the police station. Opening the door, he quickly cleaned up the room and, gently helping me to lie on the bed, brought in a constable to sit by me while he raced out to get a doctor.

The doctor administered first aid and gave me an injection. I was now less disoriented and realized that our team was very close to breaking the Guinness record—and just as close to losing it! There was not a minute to be lost! We had already covered 42,000 km, which was more than the required distance. All we had to do was get back to our starting point on time. In fact, even if the vehicle was loaded on a truck and we reached Delhi on time along with it—the record was ours. I told the sub-inspector to arrange for the car to be brought to us.

Next morning, still groggy from the sedatives and painkillers I'd been given, I learnt that various senior police officers had paid me visits, including the DIG and SP Sagar. They had made arrangements to take me to Sagar and were waiting for me to wake up. The car had been brought from the accident site and a police report was filed as per protocol.

I had lived in Sagar as a teenager and been to school there for two years, but had never done any policing there. And it had now been nearly 10 years since I was out of the state cadre. And yet, from the sub-inspector in a remote police station who had instantly responded and swung into action on hearing my name, to various others who were very solicitous—all had made it clear that I was their very own. The district SP Sanjay Choudhary sent his vehicle to take Navin and me to the district headquarters. Another small vehicle was towing the damaged car, and Man Bahadur sat in that. Seeing the damaged car, people started to gather around us; in India, there is no incident big or small that will not draw a crowd! Soon, a small gathering became a crowd pushing against each other to find out what was going on.

In the midst of all this, somebody recognized me—Arvind Patil, two years junior to me in school, and now the MLA of Sagar. The crowd was holding us back and the badly damaged car with all its colourful sponsor stickers was not making much progress. People were trying to peer into our car to see who had got injured and what the extent of injuries was. It being winter, the sub-inspector had given me headgear to protect me from the cold, so my head was covered; not only that, but also my face was partially bandaged. Despite that, and despite all the many years since our last meeting, Arvind Patil recognized me and gave me a warm welcome.

He inquired about the trip, and I explained to him that we had to rush to Delhi immediately. We could not waste even a single minute!

What a stroke of luck it was, bumping into Arvind. He owned a Contessa car! Arvind was not just an MLA but also a wealthy local businessman and he took us to the only workshop in Sagar that could handle a Contessa. He informed the man there that he would have to fix our car and give it to us by evening. 'Impossible!' the man said, shocked that he could even imagine such a thing. Getting spare parts from Bhopal and maybe even Delhi, considering the condition of the car, was going to take time! But Arvind told him that he was bringing his Contessa, and he could take out and replace anything from it that our car needed. 'This evening!' he asserted, and we left.

The car was indeed delivered to us by evening, but then better sense prevailed, and we decided to stay on in Sagar for the night, hosted by the SP to dinner, with accommodation at the police officers' mess. The next morning, we got into the car and set off again. It was completely roadworthy—the engine, steering, everything was fine—though the body work remained dented and scratched. Also, the left-hand-side door could not be closed. We tied it with a rope so that it wouldn't fly open as we drove along.

Driving through Madhya Pradesh, we crossed Chambal and entered Agra on the way to Delhi. All of us were intimately familiar with this road! It was 11.15 p.m. on 31 December 1992 when we arrived at India Gate, our starting point, to a huge, rousing welcome. Our family members, my SPG colleagues, friends and sponsors were waiting, and champagne was popped. Sukh Ram, then the communications minister of the Himachal Pradesh government, and a very dear friend of the Kapila family, was also there to receive us. It was 39 days, 7 hours and 55 minutes since we set out, and we had broken the British world record by a few hours. The Guinness representative was also present at the finish line at India Gate to authenticate the record, and gave us an interim certificate confirming that we had indeed broken the record. It was the most memorable day of my life; I had never even imagined in the wildest of my dreams that I would accomplish such a stupendous feat! I felt so grateful to have had these partners on this adventure; we had each pulled our weight, contributing in different ways and, working superbly in tandem, we had been successful.

However, very sad news was also awaiting our return. Navin's father had passed away while we were on our drive. The family had protected him from knowing about it; there was nothing he could have done from so far away. Now we had come home victorious, but our celebrations were muted.

Later, it was a pleasure to receive the original certificates in our name, with the names of the other two as team members. We also received letters of congratulations from various senior dignitaries and officials appreciating our efforts.

These were all very gratifying but, most of all, we felt very grateful that we had returned home safe and sound with just one mishap, and only a few difficult days on the way. We received international recognition—and it had all started with just a casual remark.

The team that broke the record!

PRIME MINISTER

New Delhi
July 23, 1993

Dear Shri Vijay Raman,

Congratulations on your undertaking the "Circumnavigation of the World" by car. It is indeed gratifying to know that the Guinness Book of Records have recognized your claim for the World Record for this event. You have done us proud.

With regards,

Yours sincerely,

P.V. Narasimha Rao

[P.V. Narasimha Rao]

Shri Vijay Raman, IPS
Deputy Director
Special Protection Group
9, Race Course Road
New Delhi 110 011.

PM P.V. Narasimha Rao congratulates Vijay on his achievement

9

PLAYING GOALKEEPER IN J&K

I have been very lucky to have had many different kinds of opportunities. God has played a great role in taking me to various places.

I completed my tenure with the SPG in 1995 and then, due to my son's education, I needed to remain in Delhi for another year or so. When the position of a Delhi-based DIG for the Indo-Tibetan Border Police (ITBP) came up, I was selected for it. I joined as DIG ITBP Delhi in June 1995. One of the people I particularly remember from that phase is Diwakar Prasad, for his support in the ITBP.

About a year later, PM Narasimha Rao took a very bold decision. Till then, the government of J&K had been under President's rule. There was discomfort about this essentially undemocratic situation in various quarters, and PM Narasimha Rao decided to change that. Elections were held.

Security was a major threat: the militants would not have wanted election results that cost them their credibility and legitimacy! They became more active and would even threaten those who were planning to contest the elections. If a candidate files his nomination and the candidate gets killed, as per law the election is countermanded. The government was able to keep things under control, the elections went through, and Dr Farooq Abdullah became the leader and CM-designate.

Despite so many varying opinions about this gentleman, the fact remains that this was the election result. He was one person who, at the time, would shout his loyalty to India from the rooftops even in the heart of Srinagar. Naturally, Dr Abdullah was a very highly threatened person. And as the leader of this extremely troubled state, it was essential for his security to be strengthened.

Until Indira Gandhi's assassination, personal security was never given that type of importance in India, and it was clear that it was essential here. Most of our leaders assumed that they were very popular and nothing would happen to them, and this had been proven untrue time and again.

A Brief History of the Police

The Indian government has largely only been reactive in creating police organizations. In 1947, our only central police organizations were a legacy of colonial rule: the Intelligence Bureau, Assam Rifles and CRPF.

The India–China War created the understanding that our borders with China needed policing, and this led to the creation of the ITBP in 1962. The 1965 war with Pakistan resulted in the formation of the BSF. Massive investments in, and the creation of, a large number of public sector undertakings led to the establishment of the Central Industrial Security Force (CISF) in the late 1960s. The assassination of PM Indira Gandhi in 1984 led to the creation of the SPG in 1985. The crash of the Air India flight Kanishka by sabotage led to the creation of the National Security Guards (NSG). The 2008 attack on Mumbai led to the creation of the National Investigation Agency (NIA).

Getting a Head Start

The new government of J&K was looking for someone with an SPG background to take care of Farooq Abdullah's personal security, using the best technology and the most evolved SOPs.

Once again as luck would have it, or as God ordained, I

was available, and I was in Delhi, posted as DIG ITBP. If I had returned to my cadre, there would have been a third entity whose clearance was required. But I was already on deputation, so it was only the Government of India and the state government of J&K that had to agree. I was approached by a senior intelligence officer, later a dear friend, to see if I would be willing to go to J&K. I had no second thoughts and agreed instantly. It was a two-year deputation to set up an organization for the CM's security in J&K.

When I met Dr Farooq Abdullah, he was very candid about his discomfort with having a personal security set-up. I understood his feelings well because it was something new and was bound to create some amount of resentment, and even a trust barrier between him and the electorate. When he suggested that it would be easier for him if he increased the scope of my responsibility, I agreed at once. He then explained that my job would be IGP Security, which would include not just the CM's protection but also taking charge of security for all those people of J&K who could be the targets of militancy and were required to be provided security by the government: the governor, the secretariat, all the ministers and MLAs, and all the vital establishments. I was fine with this but did explain to him that while all would be covered, the priority would be the CM, even if I had to choose between the governor and the CM.

Dr Abdullah announced to his team that a security specialist had been recruited for the personal security of anyone who was under threat. Being an outsider, this person would have no personal biases. And this is how a new post was created, and I landed up as IGP Security, promoted as IGP overnight ahead of all my batchmates. The CID branch of the J&K police was now bifurcated into Intelligence and Security—as had also been done when the SPG was formed. A new DGP had been appointed, Gurbachan Jagat from the Punjab cadre, also on deputation.

I moved to Jammu and took up accommodation in the police officers' mess there. It was March 1997, and the government had not yet moved to Srinagar, the summer capital. I spent my time getting acquainted with the new job—it was important for my subordinates to know me and for me to know them. Although the police are the same all over India, every state has its own nuances. There are always special needs and there are always special methods of handling them.

There was already some security infrastructure in place, and I tried to enhance it by replicating as much as possible what had prevailed in the SPG. Right from the terms of recruitment of the men and officers—their antecedent verifications, their weapons, their training, their recommendation, their incentives—the infrastructure was replicated as far as possible and my recommendations were accepted by the state government, with the gap in funds happily covered by the Government of India.

Some of my important security sites were the Vaishno Devi Temple, the two commercial airports in Srinagar and Jammu, and a large number of vital installations. Security had to be reinforced in all these but, of course, the first priority was the CM.

Other than the ministers, we also had about 25 MLAs, and even the candidates who had lost the elections were provided security. In all, I had close to 1,000 protected persons. Each one had to be provided with a bulletproof vehicle—in those days these were mostly Gypsies—and an armed driver. The extent of resources was huge and it was really very necessary. We had to show that we meant business; we had conducted the elections successfully and subsequently, all the candidates remained safe.

One day I had a visitor. His card said Altaf Mohamed, DC (name changed), so I admonished my staff for making him wait and asked for him to be ushered in immediately. I stood up and shook hands with the middle-aged gentleman who entered and requested him to be seated. We exchanged pleasantries: '*Janaab, aap kaise hain* (Sir, how are you), how is the situation in the district,' etc. Then I asked, 'How can I help you?' He requested that his petrol quota be increased. Puzzled, I asked, 'Why would you, as district collector, need petrol from my department?'

It turned out that I had misunderstood DC to mean district collector. He was a DC—a 'defeated candidate'! I stifled my guffaw, pacified him, and showed him out politely, enjoying a good laugh with Veena when I later told her about it.

I soon realized that the security we were providing was an incentive to contest the elections. A vehicle, a driver and a gunman were provided, and so was fuel at government cost—who would want to forego that? This meant that we had all sorts of people to protect. There were people who were militants who surrendered, entered the mainstream, stood for election, and even won! After a few months, I scrutinized the monthly security-related expenditure (SRE), and was shocked to see that, apart from the pay and allowances of the personnel involved, it amounted to a massive ₹35 lakh per month! This was funded by the Government of India and not the state government. And this was the figure without considering the pay and allowances of the personnel. Looking closer, I realized that a major component of this ₹35 lakh per month was our cost of fuel. I approached Dr Abdullah with the suggestion that we implement changes to cut the fuel cost. Not the cost of the ministers' carcades—each carcade had three or four vehicles—that was fine, it was a necessary cost. But why were we paying for the fuel of candidates who had lost the elections? And what about those MLAs who travelled outside their constituencies? Why should the government pay for their movement outside the area of duty and for their personal work? Why not fix a quota for the MLAs, which would be available for their travel within their constituencies? And similarly, a quota for the defeated candidates as well.

At first Dr Abdullah was reluctant. What politician would like to implement an unpopular decision? By now, there were so many who had started taking these things as their right! Very grudgingly, he agreed to try it out. As expected, there was a lot of resistance.

I was faced with a barrage of personal requests. But none of them were my responsibility. My mandate was to make sure that they were safe, and that I was doing wholeheartedly. But the demands they brought were sometimes quite outrageous. Once, I saw a requisition that would dent our budget by a few lakhs. Making inquiries, I found that it had been made by a minister for a bathtub. He wanted a bathtub in his bathroom.

What did security have to do with his bathtub?

He was, at that time, living in his own home and we had a security force covering it totally—barbed wire, lighting, people—all paid for by the government. Now he wanted a bathtub. Perhaps these were things they had got used to and did not expect to be questioned about. When I put it up to the SP, he replied, '*Janaab*'—Janaab is a much-used word there, a very polite and respectful way of addressing someone—'Janaab, but this is quite justified!'

'Really?' I asked him. 'There are so many ways of having a bath! Why should anyone expect the government to pay for their bathtub? This gentleman has been a minister for years. If he wants a bathtub, let him buy one for himself.'

Yes, security was essential in J&K but it was badly misused. People with police protection would come to know that a new vehicle had been received by the security branch, and immediately there would be a rush at us—'Sir! I want this car! Give me this car! I must have it!'

Why? Why should any new vehicle received for security purposes be immediately allotted to a minister? It was a situation where favours were being handed out, and that had got to stop.

When checks are enforced, restrictions do arise. But I never compromised on the actual security. Yes, the PSOs would be well trained; I would check in and ensure that they remained physically fit, medically fit. I took care to ensure that all the vehicles remained roadworthy and maintenance was done as required. There was no problem on those counts. But the extra facilities and perks were routinely denied.

The Darbar Move

One of the interesting things about the administration of J&K was a great event that took place twice a year, and that was the Darbar Move. This is a phrase that comes down from the time when J&K was a princely kingdom and the 'Darbar' was moved from Jammu to Srinagar in summer, and back in winter. Representatives of every department remained in the other capital to take care of urgent matters but the main office moved. Packing everything and moving everything was an absolutely gigantic effort! Clearly, the decades of doing this brought a great degree of expertise. Because, when things were unpacked at the end of the move and the office resumed in the other place, not a file or paper was missing—every single thing was in place!

All of us are familiar with this experience: whenever you really need a particular paper, you just can't find it. Why is it lost? Where has it gone? The person you are questioning looks at you with his head hanging down; there is no explanation. But never when the Darbar moved! Everything moved in place.

For the security team, the Darbar move was tremendous. When security personnel moved, residences had to be earmarked for them. Officials moving from Jammu to Srinagar would stay in hotels, and security had to be provided for them there. Security had to be provided to them as they travelled between the hotel and the office. It was a huge job. Sometimes when I sit back today and reflect, I don't know how we went through all this with such a lean subordinate staff.

I had joined in March. Traditionally, the Darbar Move is in April–May. It is generally believed that Jammu Division is safe, whereas in Srinagar every district is bad. Whether it is Anantnag or Baramulla—all places are infested with terrorists. I realized that the big challenge was going to be Srinagar. And since there was not much going on in Jammu, I decided to visit Srinagar before the Darbar moved, to get a feel of the place and know what I was in for. I was accommodated in the circuit house, as the police mess was not in a good condition. Everything was fine.

One problem I had faced in J&K was the language. In Jammu, Hindi is spoken widely; not so in Srinagar. But again, my experience has shown me repeatedly that when subordinates know that you're a sincere person, straightforward and with integrity, they will always stand up for you. I have spoken about my Bhind experience. I experienced the same thing here too: unquestioning loyalty from the J&K police.

Unquestionable Loyalty

When we moved into Srinagar with the Darbar, I was accommodated in a tourist hut of J&K Tourism, called the Pari Mahal huts, close to Chashme Shahi, the royal springs. It was a very nice arrangement. The water of Chashme Shahi is abundant and said to be so good that, according to one rumour, Jawaharlal Nehru (whose family was originally from Kashmir) used to source his daily water consumption in Delhi all the way from there. Well, to be honest, I can't vouch personally for the water of J&K because it did not agree with my constitution, and I almost fell ill drinking it. Be that as it may, the Pari Mahal huts were beautifully located, overlooking the Dal Lake with the Shankaracharya hill on the other side. Now, from there to go to my office, I had to pass through Gupkar Road, a kind of civil lines where all the town's dignitaries lived. The CM and various ministers lived there, the army headquarters were on one side, and senior IAS and other officials all lived here. Access was restricted, as this was a secure route, with police patrolling and security measures.

The police headquarters (PHQ), secretariat and other government buildings were in the heart of the town. There was another parallel road that skirted the Dal Lake—a beautiful drive, one that I always preferred to take. This gave me the opportunity to keep track of tourist movement in the city. If the women were wearing saris and a bindi—it meant that they felt it was safe. There was a lot of BSF deployment on that road. They had their offices and headquarters there but had also occupied some of the hotels and buildings. It's not that every building had a militant sitting with a rifle cocked and ready to shoot. But I wanted to get a sense of how the local people and the tourists were faring. So, this was the route I took—my driver had standing instructions to use it, and we travelled daily on it with my gunman, the wireless operator who travelled with me, and the escort.

One day, I had to go for a meeting and, reviewing some papers in the car, did not realize that the driver had taken us on the other route. When I asked him why, he seemed evasive, nothing convincing. Then he disclosed that he had received a message when I was in another meeting. There had been a bomb blast on the route I always preferred to take. He told me what the message said, describing all the damage done and the number of people killed and injured.

When I came down after the meeting, my vehicle was waiting for me. The first thing I did was to apologize to my driver for blasting him. By this time, the news had spread and everyone knew about the vicious explosion.

My security staff had been assigned to me—I had not selected them myself. I had no connection with J&K and did not know anybody here before I arrived. I had come in at a senior position and they had picked the boys they thought were appropriate. I never cross-checked their background, their religion—nothing.

The point I'm making here is that they may have been aware that something was going to happen. And they had not told me, perhaps not wanting to be questioned. But being aware, they took due precautions. This was just one example of the sharp efficiency of the J&K police. When people say that they are unreliable—I disagree completely. Yes, they have made mistakes, but there is no state police that does not have its own share. Their loyalty is unquestionable, and they will support their seniors to the hilt.

By God's grace, none of the targets were ever hit during my tenure. As I mentioned earlier, there were some surrendered militants who joined mainstream politics, contested elections, and became MLAs. They had retained their old contacts and continued to meet people who were not very desirable. However, except for one solitary instance of a bomb blast in the MLA hostel in Srinagar where some members of the public were killed or injured, my tenure as goalkeeper was free of any other mishap; none of my protected persons or installations were attacked.

A display of arms and ammunition confiscated by BSF

> When subordinates know that you're a sincere person, straightforward and with integrity, they will never let you down.

The Students' Viewpoint

The Regional Engineering College in Srinagar was established to cater to the technical education needs of students belonging to the states of Punjab, Haryana and Himachal Pradesh, besides J&K.

Sometime in November 1997, my DGP received a complaint that students from the other three states were not getting adequate representation in the college, and that almost all students were from the Kashmir region, with a sprinkling of them from the Jammu region. The DGP wished to ascertain the facts and, as he did not want policemen in uniform to enter the campus, asked me to visit and find out. I was hesitant and pointed out that this was not a police job, and should be done by the civil administration. He, however, cajoled me into doing it, and I fixed an appointment with the college principal.

While going through the records with the principal and his staff, I soon realized that the complaints made were substantially accurate and reported this to my DGP. Before I left, however, the principal of the college, a pleasant man with charming manners, showed me around the campus. At the men's hostel, he introduced me to three boys. I had tea with them in the canteen and found them to be bright young men who excelled in their studies—inquisitive and enthusiastic. They told me that they would be going to either Bengaluru or Hyderabad for their postgraduate education.

I gave the boys my number and asked them to feel free to contact me any time. They kept in touch regularly and often invited me to their hostel, which had an excellent view of the Dal Lake. One day, out of the blue, one of the boys told me that it would be better if I did not visit them on Fridays. The other boys agreed. Taken aback, I asked why. Another one of them replied, saying that when they visited the mosque for Friday prayers, mullahs visiting from outside Srinagar made hate speeches designed to incite anger and feelings of revolt in their listeners. They, too, were affected by these speeches and did not wish to meet me when under the influence of such feelings. I understood their plight. In any case, the time to move to Jammu for the winter was approaching and as their final semester was coming to a close, I knew from then onwards the chances of meeting them again were slim. I bid them goodbye and wished them all the best for the future.

When I returned to Srinagar in May 2003, I remembered these boys. A BSF battalion under my charge was functioning from the campus premises and I requested the commandant to try and locate them. Soon, he reported that one of them was indeed in Srinagar and was a lecturer in the college. I went to visit him and realized that, it being the first time he was seeing me in uniform and in a position of authority, he felt overawed. I did my best to make him comfortable and we began to chat. He told me that after completing their graduation, all three of them got admission in three different institutes in Bengaluru. It was a good stint, he told me—however, they had also faced instances that gave them a new perspective. 'Do you plan to settle down in Bengaluru?' they were asked. 'And if you get a job, will you buy a home? Do you know that none of us can buy property in J&K? Is that fair?'

The young man candidly admitted that he was shocked to learn about this distorted state of affairs. 'I agreed that this was really not fair!' he said to me.

Here was a young man who, just four years ago, had told me that he did not wish to see me after Friday prayers because the sermons he heard inflamed his sentiments. Now, after his brief brush with reality in Bengaluru, he had veered around to the view that the whole constitutional arrangement was lopsided and unfair.

A Temple Resuscitated

In Delhi, some years before I was posted to J&K, my friend and collegemate Ashok Mattoo had introduced me to Hriday Nath Kaw, a Kashmiri pandit who lived in Delhi. Mr Kaw is a person with psychic powers, an astrologer and face reader with whom I interacted a few times. At our first meeting, he asked me a few basic questions and I realized that he knew me, my background and my personality very well. He had a certain awareness about people and things that was beyond the ordinary. So, although I had never asked him for guidance or been initiated by him into any group or anything like that, I started referring to him as Guru-ji. Ashok must have informed him that I was being posted to J&K, because at our next meeting he told me about a place called Omoh, just as you enter the valley from Jammu, close to the calm and deep-blue Verinag spring, source of the Jhelum River, a most picturesque place with a lovely garden. Mr Kaw knew that I was a Shiv bhakt; he was aware of it before I told him. He told me to go to the temple in Omoh. 'Enter it,' he said, 'and close the door. Pour water on the Shivling. Close your eyes. And you will have a darshan of Lord Shiva.' Having said this, he mused regretfully on the fate of the shrine. Perhaps the militants had razed it?

The thought remained in my mind, and I found out that it was not far from the Nehru Tunnel, which connects the valley with Jammu. When it was time for us to return to the winter capital, I made enquiries and found out that there was an ITBP battalion located at Omoh, with the task of guarding the tunnel. They knew me and when they confirmed that there was indeed a temple there, I told them I wanted to visit it. When they went to check the place, however, they called to inform me that there was no Shivling in the temple. This reminded me of what Guru-ji had said: perhaps it was destroyed by militants.

I decided to go anyway, out of respect for Mr Kaw's wishes.

The ITBP officers received me at Verinag, where the headquarters were, and from there we drove the 3 km to Omoh village. As we drove along the road, we came across a group of people a little lower on the hillside, digging up something.

On the other side of the road was a structure. It was a Shivalaya, the kind of which there are many in the valley, but there was no trace inside of any shrine.

Now, one of the things about the ITBP is that every unit has one Brahmin soldier who is made responsible for conducting all the poojas, and this one did too. The base of the Shivling was there; they had cleaned it up and put ordinary stones on top to replicate a Shivling, and they were doing the pooja. They invited me to participate and I did, pouring some water and so on. Now in the Shiv pooja, water flows down to the base towards the north, which is usually to your right. Here, the water was flowing in the opposite direction, towards the left. Anyway, the pooja continued and the panditji was in the midst of chanting mantras when suddenly loud voices interrupted, 'Sir, *mil gaya, mil gaya!* (We found it!)'

The commandant and I stepped out and saw that the boys who were digging on the other side of the road had found the Shivling, which was buried underground. They rescued it with a feeling of victory, and it now lay before us, covered with mud.

People in the village were curious about the digging taking place and now, when the troops had unearthed something that was clearly a special object, they gathered around with curiosity. One of them stepped out from the crowd and introduced himself as a teacher of the local village school. He pointed to the bottom of the hill, to a barracks-like building, below the spot where the Shivling was unearthed. And he told us that this had once been a very popular shrine, which the villagers had great faith in. To them, the Shivalaya was Pir Baba. They took care of the premises and their wishes were granted there. Then, one fine day, the militants came. They marched through shouting slogans and helping themselves to whatever they wanted. And they entered the Pir Baba's shrine, pulled out the Shivling, and flung it down the hill.

The next day, the children were kicking it, and throwing dirt and heaping all sorts of indignities on it. 'I couldn't bear the sight of it,' the teacher told us. 'But what could I do? I got some of my friends together and we pulled it aside and buried it. And today, I heard that there was a senior officer coming to the temple, so I showed them where they would find it.'

It was a great event for all of us that something had been recovered, and I told the commandant to keep it in the unit's temple. I then carried on to Jammu, arriving late in the evening.

When the Darbar moves, all of us get a week off and I decided to go and visit Mr Kaw and tell him what had happened. I also had a mild concern about having taken actions outside my purview; I was an outsider from another cadre; I was a Hindu in a Muslim-dominated area; I had made decisions that might displease the government.

I asked Guru-ji what I should do. His immediate emotional response was, 'Bring it here! I will spend my life worshipping it.' But in the next breath he continued, 'No, it should not be removed from there.'

'But what should I do?' I asked him.

'You don't worry,' he replied. 'By the time you get home, it will all be sorted out.'

Sure enough, I reached home and was told that ITBP had called to speak to me. I called back and was informed that the villagers had come in a group to the unit. They had requested that the Shivling be returned to its proper place in the temple, where they would make sure it was looked after with all due process. And it was reinstated with ceremonies conducted by a pandit from an ITBP unit.

It was an excellent ending to the episode—but for me, there was still something pending. I had only seen the Shivling in the horizontal form, not vertically as it should be. And what about the vision my Guru-ji had promised me?

Fortunately for me, K.R. Narayanan, the then president, was to come to Srinagar for a convocation at the university. So as IGP Security, I had to go there again along with my friend K.S. Bains, who had retired as DGP in Rajasthan, as we had the joint responsibility of tying up security arrangements for the president.

I told him that after the visit was over, on the way back to Jammu from Srinagar, I would like to visit this place, and he decided to accompany me. At about 7.30 that December morning, the two of us, along with the ITBP people, arrived in Omoh. There we met Mr Moinuddin, caretaker of the temple.

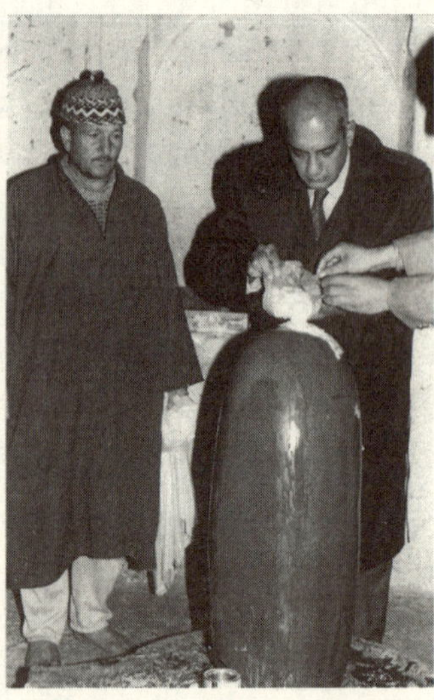

Paying respects at the Shivling in Omoh

We had carried the Gangajal, honey, milk, and other things required for a Shiva pooja. The photographers stood at the entrance of the Shivalaya and we stood behind it so that the water would flow to our right. We continued following the pujari's instructions. Later, when the photographs were developed and sent to us, I showed them to Guru-ji. He pointed out an Om that had naturally formed with white flowers and said, 'This is the darshan Lord Shiva has given you.' It was one of the divine blessings granted to me during my stint as IGP Security in J&K.

I remained in J&K from March 1997 to March 1999 as IGP Security. Though MP is my parent cadre, J&K became my foster cadre, and it has been gratifying that the J&K State Police have always treated me as one of their own.

The Privilege of Receiving Information

I had started my tenure in 1997 and the Omoh temple episode took place in 1998. Subsequently, when the biannual Darbar move took place, I visited and also took visitors to see it. Verinag is a beautiful, picturesque place and the temple is close by. I opened a police chowki in the village so that the place remained protected, and arrangements to stay were made for the personnel. The security personnel had also grown attached to me. As winter approached and the date of the Darbar move came closer, they knew that my tenure was ending and I might not return to Srinagar in the summer. Many people came to visit and bid me farewell. And many of them would casually mention that of late, a lot of infiltration was taking place over the border. It was a general remark, nothing specific. I heard this from various people and over a fairly long period. I would tell them to go and report it through the proper channels, as this did not come under the purview of Security.

Since they were not willing to talk to anyone else about it, it began to weigh on me.

As a last resort, some time at the end of 1998 or early 1999, I recorded a note and sent it to my DG, Gurbachan Jagat, who later became chairman, UPSC, and governor, Manipur. He must have got the information verified through his own means and sent it on to the relevant ministry.

In March 1999, I was repatriated back to my cadre and posted as IG Chambal in Gwalior.

That was when the newspapers started reporting on the Kargil War. Now, we are all aware of what happened in Kargil, so I will not go into that. After everything was over, K.S. Subramanian, a security specialist and analyst, was appointed as a one-man fact-finding committee to collect information. And one day, the IG Chambal—yours truly, that is—received a call from the office of Mr Subramanian, saying that he wished to meet me on a confidential basis. He would fly to Gwalior in a special aircraft and I would secretly meet him for half an hour or 45 minutes in the airport lounge, since he did not wish to even enter the city.

Mr Subramanian had just one question for me: How had I come by the information I had passed on to the DGP? How had I, who was only responsible for protecting people and installations, come by it?

I told him that people were coming and telling me. They were not coming and doing so for any reason except that they were under my purview as protected persons. It was very clear that what was happening in Kargil was known to many. There was no intelligence required, no sources had to be cultivated; it was general knowledge. There was infiltration from Pakistan, people were crossing over and entering through Kargil.

> As a police officer, all you have to do is meet people and listen to them. Information will be made available to you. It is as simple as that.

10

MY THIRD INNINGS AT CHAMBAL

There was a time in Indian cricket, before the advent of the Gavaskars, Vengsarkars and Vishwanaths in the late 1960s and early 1970s, and later with the arrivals of the Tendulkars, Dravids, Gangulys and Laxmans, when it was almost customary for the Indian team to make a paltry score in the first innings of a test match and run up a big score in the second innings—consistently, both at home and abroad. A wag wryly commented, 'In test matches, India should play their second innings first so as to make matches less one-sided and last the distance!'

Similarly, of my three stints in the Chambal, it would be in my favour to highlight this phase over the earlier stints as assistant SP and additional SP in Gwalior District, and SP Bhind from 1977 to 1980, to calibrate the public perception about me and my perceived capabilities!

I was returning to my home cadre after 14 years of deputation with the governments of India and J&K. When an officer returns after such a long break, he is quite often made to wait for a posting and may remain attached with PHQ for pay and allowances purposes for some time. So it was a very pleasant surprise when I got my posting orders as IGP Chambal even before I set foot back in MP. I was happy to be returning to a familiar terrain with familiar people and political leaders who also knew me well. Digvijay Singh was the CM, and a thorough professional police officer, S.C. Tripathi, was the DGP. The fact was that the dacoity menace was rearing its head again and it was perhaps thought that I would bring a possible solution.

As IGP, I had four districts: Bhind, where the Paan Singh encounter happened when I was SP in 1981, followed by the surrenders of Malkhan Singh, Phoolan Devi and many others as a consequence of this; Morena and Sheopur, formerly a sub-division of Morena not elected to a district; and Datia. My range had interstate borders with Rajasthan and UP.

My long absence from the cadre had almost made me a stranger, just a name in the civil list. Much had changed in MP during the years I had been away. The post of DIG in the field was abolished and upgraded to the rank of IGP. The DIGs were all staff officers concentrated at the PHQ.

Very soon, I also realized that the quality of policing had deteriorated. My juniors in the district were much younger than me, often with a gap of 16 to 20 years between us. It was clear that I could not function merely as their first-level supervisor but had to play the role of mentor too. The level of corruption in the police had also increased considerably. The freshers and youngsters were trapped in the quagmire of corruption. But for me, the most stupendous and formidable challenge was the fact that some notable politicians and middle-level policemen were in regular contact with the dacoits. They were taking money from them, and the relationship, based on caste considerations, made the problem even more complex.

The fabric and texture of the problem had also undergone a change. While murders were still rampant, dacoities had reduced, and kidnapping for ransom was the most preferred activity. As the saying prevalent in rural Rajasthan goes, '*Chith bhi meri, path bhi meri, aur goti mere baap ki*! (Heads I win, tails you lose, and anyway the coin belongs to my father!)'

There were only two main gangs operating in the districts of Bhind and Morena. They were led by Raju Kushwah and

Ramesh Kushwah, both of whom hailed from Bhind. Their area of operations extended beyond the Chambal into the UP districts of Agra, Etawah and Jalaun, and Dholpur District in Rajasthan. Neither of them had more than eight to 10 hardcore members, in addition to a few casual members. They were well armed, but none had weapons superior to what we in the police force had. Both gangs were known to be vicious, brutal and relentless.

Kushwahs are Thakurs, but low in the Thakur pecking order; in some Indian states, they are classified as Other Backward Classes (OBCs). Communities in the Chambal take great pride in there being an active and operating gang from their community, and provide logistics and support to nurture and strengthen them in every manner needed. For their vastly superior knowledge of the lay of the land, dacoit gangs belonging to the Gujar (cattle owners) and Gadaria (cattle grazers, shepherds) communities are the hardest to track. Every gang, irrespective of the caste of its leader, tries to ensure that they include at least one or two members of these communities. In modern-day diplomatic parlance, this would be seen as a 'strategic alliance'!

The Mother-in-Law's Plea

On any given day, a large number of people throng the residences of the SP and IG in the morning. While most come with grievances regarding police work, some come for recommendations for arms licences, some to exchange pleasantries and establish a bond, and in my case, some of the old familiar people of Bhind came along to see how much I had changed from my days as a youngster when I was SP Bhind. They would comment on my balding head and some, relating my lack of a paunch to a sadly depleted state of health, would leave with assurances of bringing me home-made ghee and pulses cultivated in their fields on their next visit.

I often also had visitors who came to share information on criminal activities in my area. Such people would usually come before me with their faces covered and look around the room and adjoining areas furtively to ensure that no one was within hearing range. After being reassured, they would unmask themselves and reveal some information. I was required to respond suitably. And if the response was to their satisfaction, they would embrace me in glee, an act that invariably made me reel, acutely aware of the state of their dental hygiene!

It was on one such morning, after 20 or 30 people had been attended to, that I noticed an elderly woman in a distressed state of mind, wailing loudly and inconsolably, making her way to my office. Her words were incoherent but she kept repeating them and I eventually deciphered, '*Saheb, saheb, mujh par daya karo saheb, meri beti ko bachalo saheb, mujh par daya karo.* (Sir, have mercy on me, rescue my daughter, sir, please have mercy on me.)'

What did she want? I told my office staff to calm her down, offer her something to eat and a cup of tea, and when she was composed, to bring her to me. It was clear that she wanted to convey something exclusively to me, so I instructed my staff not to ask her why she wanted to talk to me.

When my steno brought her in, she was less agitated but still weeping and had a vacant expression on her face. I told him to ensure no calls and no disturbances, and he left the room, closing the door behind him. The woman fell at my feet, sobbing loudly. Between sobs she repeated, over and over, '*Saheb, meri beti ko vidhwa mat banao!* (Saheb! Please, please don't make a widow of my daughter!)' The sad truth is that I did leave a trail of widows—of dreaded dacoits and of informers too—in my first innings in Chambal. She revealed that she was Raju Kushwah's mother-in-law and had come with a proposition.

Yes, she had come to offer her help. She would persuade him to surrender, failing which she would help us trap him. All she wanted was the assurance that if he was arrested, he would not be killed. Under no circumstances must her daughter be made a widow.

The Profile of a Police Informer

My informer for action against Raju Kushwah's gang was unusual in many ways. Informers are usually those who have reasons to eliminate a dacoit leader or gang. Close relatives almost never fit this bill! The reasons are usually related to revenge: land disputes and violation of the honour of a woman family member are the most common reasons for a person to turn against a gang, however fearsome it may be. Inducements like cash rewards, grant of land and, more importantly, a liberal sanction of arms licences for self-defence are the carrots normally dangled before a potential informer.

In the Chambal, no informer would ever want to assist the police in merely arresting a dacoit! The aim of an informer is to have the entire gang physically eliminated, in particular its leader. Some are even prepared to kill the gang members themselves and only want to have the appearance of a police 'encounter'.

Informers often test officers who are new to the district in different ways. As SP Bhind, I faced numerous occasions when in the dead of a severely wintry night, I would be woken by an informer with what would be presented as absolutely genuine, accurate information. This is the start of the test! After conveying the input, the informer closely scrutinizes every activity of yours.

Have you taken the input seriously or are you making excuses to put him off?

In the process of listening to him, are you simultaneously calling up the right people to mobilize the resources required to launch a meaningful operation?

Does he perceive in your behaviour even a minuscule amount of hesitation or lack of trust and faith?

After all the preparations are completed and you commence on the operation, he mentally makes note of the time consumed in the process.

It is already decided how far travel to the spot will be in vehicles, and from which point the foot march will begin. The march is usually 10–15 km, at the end of which the informer will show telltale signs of cooking and people having camped there, and then in a clumsy apologetic tone, bemoan that the whole gang was there only a few hours ago, and obliquely convey to you that it is your fault because your preparations to launch the operation took too long and the gang had left.

The most basic truth about the informer is that you will never be taken to the intended target on the first contact. A century on debut in anti-dacoity operations is impossible! Unlike in cricket, it is more customary to fail on debut.

Working with the Mother-in-Law

The informer I had to work with did not fall into any classical category of informers.

I had left Chambal in 1982 and when I returned in 1999, the image that people who mattered had of me was that in anti-dacoity operations, I would go the distance. To that extent, my reputation remained the same as I had left the place with. Having worked in the SPG and having access to 10 Janpath gave me, in this Congress-ruled state in the Indian context, a certain standing! In addition was the unwarranted reputation of being a 'killer', which provoked the heartrending plea '*Saheb, meri beti ko vidhwa mat banao*!'

She belonged to a district outside my jurisdiction and since she had chosen to come to me, I did not consider it prudent to make a field inquiry about her and only verified some facts in the Raju Kushwah gang history sheet. It was well known that Raju Kushwah more often than not stayed away from his gang as he was a compulsive and incorrigible womanizer. It was arranged between me and the informer that she would update me of his whereabouts. I was to never seek her out but wait until she got in touch.

She did keep us informed.

A few months later, in December 1999, I received a wireless message from the Bhind control room that I should contact my residence in Gwalior immediately. I was in the interior of Bhind, travelling within my jurisdiction incognito with one gunman and my PA in a non-police vehicle, a practice I had the habit of following. I was not far from the Bhind District headquarters, so I informed the control room that I would shortly be reaching the SP's office. I was informed that both the SP and Addl SP were away on tour in the district. When I got there, I sat in the SP's chair and mused briefly on the days, nearly two decades previously, when I had sat in this same chair and schemed and plotted to end the overground support system of the various dacoit gangs operating in the area.

The call to my residence was put through immediately and my telephone orderly informed me that the elderly lady was there and that she had some very important information. Without giving details, she conveyed to me that her information pertained to Bhind town. I told my orderly to send her to the office of the SP Bhind in my official car without any delay. I also inquired about the whereabouts of the SP and Addl SP, and sent word requesting them to meet me urgently at Bhind. I wanted to meet the lady first and make decisions on the spot, so I drove towards her location and met her en route.

She told me that Raju Kushwah was going to spend the night at a house in Bhind town, and that she was prepared to guide the police there. I took her along with me to chalk out the course of action. By this time, it was around 11 o'clock at night. I shared the information with the officers and decided that it would be best for all if they also met her and understood the layout of the place she was talking about. As the details of the action plan were being finalized, the lady reminded me, with accompanying emotion and drama, of the condition that Raju was not to be killed. My officers reluctantly agreed. I told them that it was my solemn commitment to her, which we were all duty-bound to honour. In any case, the house in which Raju was holed up was in a thickly-populated area in the heart of the town, and a shoot-out would have collateral damage, which we had to avoid at all costs.

Now this lady insisted, against all reason, that she had to be physically present throughout the operation. Such was the extent of her lack of trust in the police!

I tried to convince her that her presence in Bhind during the operation would compromise her identity and consequently her security and well-being later. But she remained adamant, arguing that her sole purpose was to ensure that the dacoit should be arrested alive and that he was welcome to do whatever he wanted later, harm her or even kill her if he wished. She repeated that her sole concern was that her daughter should not become a widow.

I left for Gwalior, instructing the SP to inform me as soon as Raju Kushwah was caught. I did not want to remain in Bhind during the operation because once our plan succeeded, the public and media would give the entire credit to me because of my track record. I wanted the SP and his officers and men to handle the situation themselves and succeed.

Around 4.00 a.m., I got the call that I was waiting for. Yes, Raju Kushwah had been taken alive. But he had injured himself by jumping from the first floor, shouting as he jumped: '*Neta-ji, bachao*! *Bachao*!'

These words spread like wildfire, and the local media churned out all kinds of juicy 'didn't we already tell you this' type of stories, alluding to a certain MLA who hailed from the district and was perceived as the rallying point for all Thakur elements in the Chambal.

I told the SP to immediately send the lady back before news of the arrest spread. Even though it was early in the morning, I called up the DGP and gave him the glad tidings. By 5.30 a.m., the affable and courteous home minister phoned with his congratulations. (Tragically, he was one of those who were killed in the Naxalite ambush in Dantewada District of Bastar in May 2013, when he was the Pradesh Congress chief.)

The home minister, accompanied by the state DGP, reached Bhind by 8.00 a.m. by helicopter to felicitate the Bhind police. They handed over the reward of ₹2 lakh on Raju's head to me. The elderly woman requested for just ₹20,000 to undertake some urgent repairs in her Shivpuri house. The balance amount was put in fixed deposits in the names of her two minor granddaughters, to be claimed by them on attaining the age of majority.

In a few months' time, Raju was released on parole. He tortured his wife as the provider of information leading to his arrest. He eventually killed her and was sentenced to life for doing so. Sadly, his mother-in-law had a heart attack and died soon after her daughter's death. Perhaps she felt validated that her beloved daughter never had to face the life of a widow, shunned by society and stripped of every comfort.

Another One Bites the Dust

The arrest of Raju Kushwah turned out to be a major turning point.

I had requested my DGP not to associate me or any officers working under me in the special interrogation team being set up, as I wanted the entire muck to come out in an unbiased and dispassionate manner. A team under the direct supervision of the then Addl DGP (CID) was set up. The interrogation team was headed by a senior officer of SP rank who, at the time, had impeccable integrity and credentials. During his interrogation, Raju revealed much about the dacoit–police–politician connection.

The other major gang, that of Ramesh Kushwah, became inert for a long period of time. Unless a gang commits crimes, it becomes difficult to plot their movements and understand their mindset in order to take any coercive action. Inactivity usually signifies a period of planning some big catch in terms of kidnapping. The closest I came face to face with Ramesh Kushwah was when I learnt that a boy of the Tomar Thakur caste was trying to contact him to garner support for the local college student elections in the Ambah Tehsil of Morena District.

I ascertained the credentials of the boy from the college principal and learnt that he was studious by nature and that he was doing his master's in Hindi Literature. I requested the principal to visit my residence in Gwalior along with the boy and asked the local police station to arrange a vehicle for this purpose.

After a few days, they came to see me. The boy admitted that Ramesh Kushwah was a distant relative and that he had contacted him. I reminded the boy of his excellent academic achievements, and how an adverse police record could jeopardize the future career in academics about which he was very serious. He offered to become my informer. I shot down the offer and asked the principal to persuade him to change his college.

The boy shifted to the college in Porsa Tehsil about 15 km away. However, he insisted on keeping in touch with me and one day, he invited me to his home in Ambah, which I accepted. A visit by an IGP can never remain secret. When Ramesh came to know of it, he was devastated. How could a close relative of his possibly be the friend of the IGP? Someone of lower rank, yes—but such a senior person?

Ramesh had become an absconder after committing a double murder in a fit of rage. If he had good legal counsel, he could have surrendered. But such is the lucrative nature of dacoity in the area that an absence of active dacoit gangs would impact the livelihood and well-being of a whole army of harbourers and logistics suppliers! It is, very clearly, an economic activity.

Over time, it was clear that Ramesh's psyche was transforming. He would indulge in kidnappings but would soon release his victims without taking any ransom. We, the policemen of the Chambal, were accustomed to dacoits running away from death. And we were now being confronted by a dacoit gang leader who was running away from life! He once kidnapped the aged parents of his fiercest enemy because of some land dispute. Aged people and children are the most difficult for a dacoit gang to care for. After a few weeks, the news filtered out that the elderly couple had been released. I made it a point to meet them and debrief them. I was dumbfounded when they told me that Ramesh had taken them on a pilgrimage to Mathura and Varanasi at his own cost! All my efforts to nab him proved futile. A few years later I learnt that he had been killed—by his own gang members, because they saw him as a weak leader. It was only through the extensive forensic investigation of his skeletal remains that his identity could be established!

Around 10 years later, I met the student whom I had befriended. He was doing his doctorate in Hindi Literature at the Central Hindi University where I had gone to attend a seminar on left-wing extremism. I was gratified to learn that he had already visited Finland and Germany on student exchange programmes. Surely he had come up well, a credit to his hard work and professionalism.

Bidding Adieu

Tekanpur, a small village about 25 km from Gwalior, lies in an area of dense forest sliced through by the Gwalior–Jhansi Road. Passengers on this road suffered frequent road hold-ups, even in state-owned buses. This was the place K.F. Rustamji, founder of the BSF, chose for the BSF Academy.

The institution is a unique organization among the uniformed forces, one in which every rank receives induction training under one roof, fostering closer understanding and camaraderie across the ranks. Over the years, other institutions have been housed there, including India's only tear smoke manufacturing unit, and our first national dog-training school. The erstwhile hunting lodge of the Scindia family houses the office and the senior officers' mess.

In November 2000, when I received an invitation for a passing-out parade at the BSF Academy, I noticed that the chief guest was E.M. Rammohan, DG BSF. I had come to know Mr Rammohan during my days with the SPG and ITBP, and had a lot of respect and admiration for him. I decided to attend so that I could meet him too.

I reached there early in the morning and attended the 7.30 a.m. parade in full uniform. Spotting me after the parade, the DG waved out and asked in his booming voice what I was doing in the state and why I was not joining the BSF. He then walked towards me with his usual swagger and repeated the question in a conversational tone: 'Would you be willing to join the BSF?'

'Sir, my two-year "cooling off" period in the state after my last deputation has not ended yet.'

'Oh, don't bother about these things! Are you willing to join? Tell me! Is that YES or is it NO?'

'YES, sir!'

'But you will not get Delhi!' he added, asking if I would be okay with Kashmir.

I told him that I had done it before and was willing to do it again. When I said I wanted Srinagar, he refused, explaining that he had a special assignment lined up for me in Jammu.

He was to retire on the 30th of the month and was keen that I join the BSF before that because he wanted to issue the orders of my posting to Jammu.

I had no idea what the assignment waiting for me was about. Srinagar was considered more difficult, but as IGP Security for two years, I had cultivated more contacts and friends in the valley than in Jammu, and this gave me access to information that would be useful in the BSF's fight against militancy.

I duly received my orders of transfer on deputation to the BSF on 24 November. The state government's clearance also came on the same day. I had been away from the state for 14 years and technically could not leave again before 'cooling off' for two years; I had barely completed 20 months. I later learnt that my two-year stint in J&K had been conveniently accepted as the 'cooling off' required, displaying the essential ingenuity of our glorious babudom!

'My People': A Short Aside

Gwalior being conveniently connected to Delhi by train, I chose this mode of travel. The Taj Express leaves Gwalior at 4.50 p.m. and arrives at Delhi's Nizamuddin Railway Station at 11.30 p.m.

What was the Taj Express doing in Gwalior?

As per the Indian Railways naming protocol, 'Taj Express' indicates a fast-moving, air-conditioned chair-car train catering to tourists on a day trip to Agra, which it was. During Rajiv Gandhi's prime ministership, Madhavrao Scindia, member of parliament from Gwalior, was the railways minister, and it was he who extended the train's destination to Gwalior, about 100 km from Agra, with whistle-stops at Dholpur and Morena, all of which also have archaeological sites and natural vistas that tourists could now enjoy.

One day, I was having lunch with my friend Najeeb Jung at Rail Bhavan, which in those days served the best food of any government establishment in Delhi—yes, better even than the PMO. It had both class as well as taste! Mr Jung was the collector of Raipur when I was SP there in 1982–83 and a good friend. He was now PS to Madhavrao Scindia and we met regularly over lunch at Rail Bhavan. That day, we were sitting in his office when

Maharaj peeped into the room, and on seeing me, said, 'Hi, Vijay, what are you doing here?'

I murmured my reasons, and he gestured to us to follow him back to his chamber, as he wanted to show us something. There lay a bundle of Hindi newspapers on his table. I could see that they were the day's newspapers from Gwalior and Morena. He picked one up and, in visible distress, showed us the headlines that read, in translation: 'The Taj Express has been extended to Gwalior. Very soon it will also be renamed Scindia Express!'

'Why can't they appreciate that what I have done is for the good of the people of Gwalior?'

Both of us tried to pacify him, reasoning that such idle talk should not bother him. But he cut us short, saying, 'It is my people who are saying all this!'

The significance of the term 'my people' was not lost on either of us. He deeply loved the people of Gwalior; they were his people as much as it was his place.

Full Circle

On the 26th evening, I boarded the Taj Express for Nizamuddin. As the train pulled out, my mind took me back to another rail journey, way back in March 1973, when I was travelling from Bhopal to Delhi for my UPSC interview. Soon after the train left Gwalior Station, around 5.00 in the evening, the attendant entered the compartment and pulled down the window shutters and bolted the doors. When I enquired, he explained that we would soon be entering the dacoit-infested Chambal area and this was done for the safety of passengers as the dacoits sometimes stopped the trains and tried to board and loot them.

At another turning point of my life, making a journey on the same route and around the same time of day, I was reminded of Julius Caesar's 'Veni, Vidi, Vici (I came, I saw, I conquered)'!

As the train hurtled along, I walked to the corridor and smiled at myself in the mirror above the washbasin, thinking, 'Isn't that what I did in Chambal, even though in a limited way?'

11

A FENCING DUEL WITH PAKISTAN

I was received with appropriate ceremony at Nizamuddin Railway Station, and accommodated in a lavish suite at the Tigri BSF officers' mess. On the 27th morning, I went to the BSF Headquarters in the CGO Complex on Lodhi Road and after completing the formalities, was ushered into the DG's chamber. The DG, E. Rammohan, signed my order of posting as IG BSF Jammu Frontier and handed it to me with the order for me to take charge the next day. This is when he told me that I was being detailed to undertake a fencing duel with Pakistan in Jammu. It was a real surprise.

I first heard the term 'border fencing' while I was in the SPG, when I overheard a conversation between then PM Rajiv Gandhi and Home Minister Buta Singh during a car journey, sometime in 1988. They were in the rear seat and I was seated next to the driver. The context was the rising militancy in Punjab. The idea was to effectively fence the Punjab border with Pakistan to check the to-and-fro movement of militants across the border. By then, Pakistan's complicity in aiding and fuelling the militancy in Punjab had become evident. When informed by Buta Singh that the financial burden for the project in Punjab was about ₹150 crore, the PM responded, 'What is a few hundred crores if we can restore peace and normalcy in Punjab? The economy of the state and the hard-working nature of the people are such that this investment will generate ample dividends very soon.' Buta Singh, himself a Punjabi, could not have disagreed!

Our Border Security Force

I was with the BSF from November 2000 to June 2004, and it is one of the best organizations I have had the privilege to be a part of. It is an organization with an excellent command structure and chain of control. In keeping with the farsightedness of its founder, Director General K.F. Rustamji, it has its own Air Wing, Water Wing, Engineering Wing and, most importantly, its own Intelligence Wing. I must say that anything I may have achieved there was entirely due to the excellent people and the team spirit with which we worked.

The Need for a Fence

After the Indo-Pak War of 1971, Bangladesh was liberated and a dismembered Pakistan wanted revenge. Subsequent to the surrender, when 90,000 troops laid down their arms, India's military superiority was clear. So, Pakistan launched a proxy war that was started by fuelling militancy in Punjab. This was entirely curbed once the border in that area was made secure with fencing and floodlights, as the routes via air, sea and other land borders did not have local support, and the infiltrators were invariably trapped.

Pakistan then launched militancy in J&K in 1990 and this intensified, with more than 20,000 lives lost in five years. The BSF alone sacrificed 200 to 400 men each year. Since the Kashmir border is inaccessible for several months of the year due to snow, the international border in Jammu was the most vulnerable.

Work was entrusted to the Central Public Works Department (CPWD), which had successfully completed the task in Gujarat, Rajasthan and Punjab, and had the relevant experience to fence the border between Jammu and the section of Punjab that lies in Pakistan. Work commenced on 2 July 1995. But at that point,

Pakistan started opening fire. This had not happened in Gujarat, Rajasthan or Punjab. It happened here on the orders of General Musharraf, the then president of Pakistan. Work was suspended on 7 July 1995.

General Musharraf declared that the state of J&K was disputed, and therefore no border fencing was permissible. He cited international conventions that did not permit any defence installation within a certain distance from the border. L.K. Advani, then home minister and later deputy prime minister, objected strongly: How could they claim that Jammu was disputed?

The debate continued but with firing on the border, it was no longer possible for civilian labour to do the fencing. It could not be done by the CPWD.

The matter remained under consideration with the government until it was approved in July 2000 and the BSF—a force specializing in border management and with almost no technical knowledge—was entrusted with this task. Someone was required to lead the project, and by God's grace, I was picked for the job and started work in November 2000.

En Garde

I had seven battalions looking after the international border of about 189 km between Pakistan and Jammu. This was the length to be fenced. Another great thing about Jammu is the large number of rivers flowing from India into Pakistan, and this also had to be taken care of because infiltration could take place through the riverbeds, even when the river was in high flow.

Anticipating that the work would start soon, the CPWD had already done the procurement, and it was only the physical act of erecting the fence that remained for us to do, which the Pakistanis were refusing to allow.

Some of my commandants were also sceptical that we would accomplish this successfully. In a way they were right, because the entire job would have to be done by our men alone: the digging, erecting—all the physical tasks involved. We would not get any additional personnel. We had to clear and level the ground, collect material at the work site, dig pits for four different types of pickets, lay the concrete flooring or plinth, fix barbed wire and spikes, fill the expansion joints, paint the pickets to prevent rust, lay concertina coils, and so on. During the daytime, we would work on erecting the fence, and at night, we would have to continue patrolling. It would be a huge toll on our resources and a task outside the normal duties that our men, soldiers without mechanical or engineering skills, were trained for.

However, the men rose to the challenge with such enthusiasm and patriotism, understanding that the fence would be a force multiplier and taking pride in their role in it.

There were some historical relics that made our task easier, and these were the border outposts. This was the result of the annexation of J&K by Maharaja Ranjit Singh of Punjab in 1819, who gifted it to one of his chieftains, whose descendants were the maharajas of Kashmir.

These outposts were a historical confirmation of the border. However, we had to construct the fence at the required distance from the actual line and also face firing while we did so.

The length, 189 km, was daunting, but not when broken down into smaller units. So, I started step by step, unit by unit, assigning short patches of 1 or 2 km to each battalion. First, the alignment would be drawn based on the border outposts and after that the line on which the picket would be erected, at the required distance. The first task was to dig around the border alignment to a depth of 10 to 12 feet, scoop out the earth, and create barriers on both sides so that when bullets came, they would be absorbed in that mud wall.

We decided to follow the strategy of excavating and building a mud wall during the night, and putting up the fence during the day. The idea was that the mud wall would provide protection to the men who were deployed to build the fence. In this manner, the fencing of this difficult frontier was completed. As a bonus, a ditch and mud wall, about 100 km long, were constructed, and these could prove to be very useful for the army in times of war.

On 14 January 2000, the auspicious day of Makar Sankranti, we started work on the first pillar, and began working step by step, day by day, kilometre by kilometre. My target was to complete about 20 km by the end of the financial year, 31 March 2000. Resources were available, the team was enthusiastic, and the target was easily doable. But the Pakistanis were not going to let us do it in peace.

To build the fence, we needed earth-moving and digging equipment varying in size and function, from road rollers to bulldozers and excavators. As soon as we deployed these machines, the Pakistanis unleashed heavy firing on us. They would specially target the lights at night, in order to paralyse the ongoing work in the darkness.

The excavator has a lever that has to be raised and come down for the shovel, the excavating part of the equipment, to dig out soil. The Pakis would target the junction between the two arms. Once that got damaged, the equipment was ruined and nothing could be done; that excavator had to be replaced. We reacted by encasing it in bulletproof material. That protected the joint—but then they started firing at the driver's cabin.

One head constable driving an excavator was hit in his leg by a bullet and had to be hospitalized. Once he was discharged from the hospital and ready for duty, he requested that he be given the same job again. His request was granted, but unfortunately, he was shot at again and injured in almost the same way he had been earlier.

Meanwhile, we had been working on converting the driver's cabin into a bulletproof cabin. Anyone who has travelled in a bulletproof cabin knows that they are in a sealed space and cannot survive without air conditioning. We installed ACs in the cabins.

Now, working in a government set-up, there was a reason why I could get these big changes made so quickly that we hardly lost any time despite the substantial damage inflicted. As per protocol, I was reporting the incidents to my DG. Fortunately, my DG in the BSF was Gurbachan Jagat, who had been my DG in my previous stint in J&K also, and we had an excellent rapport—he knew my style of work. One day he told me, 'I think that instead of conveying each incident to me, it would be better if you report directly to the home secretary.' That is not the normal protocol; there is a hierarchy of reporting that we follow, and we don't have direct contact with the home secretary. But I had no problem with this and spoke to the home secretary, Mr Gopalaswamy at the time; he was previously chief secretary, Gujarat, and later chief election commissioner. He would give me an immediate response and directions. When I called to inform him that the excavator had been hit and that I didn't know what to do, he said, 'Raman, just give me 10 minutes. Call my PS in 10 minutes.'

When I called the PS after 10 minutes, I received the number to call. This happened to be the number of the head of Bharat Earth Movers Limited, a Bengaluru based company. And he was absolutely shocked to hear that his prized high-tech machines had sustained bullet injuries! Within 24 hours, his team of engineers arrived in Jammu to inspect the damage and arrange for the replacement that was required. We were back in action seamlessly—and that was frustrating for the Pakis!

Inspecting the fencing of the Line of Control between India and Pakistan at Jammu, as it came up

Success depends on the police officer's ability to adapt himself as quickly as the situation demands.

An International Landmark in a Conflict Zone

When one hears news of action taken by Pakistan against India on the border, rest assured, whether it is the Line of Control or the international border, we are not sitting quiet. Whatever they do, we are giving it back to them in full measure. That is what I saw, that is what I faced. There would hardly be a day when there was no firing on the fence.

In March, as expected, my transfer orders came. We had covered some ground, and even done a part of the lighting. There is a place called Chicken's Neck in an area called Akhnoor in J&K, where the Chenab River flows, and we had lit this up. It could be seen clearly from the sky; pilots who crossed it on the flight path would tell me that it looked like Marine Drive in Bombay! In fact, the phrase entered common parlance and the air traffic control (ATC) from Karachi would ask the pilot, '*Kya aap ne Marine Drive cross kiya?* (Have you crossed Marine Drive yet?)' We had created an international landmark in a conflict zone! We had erected the fencing at a cost lower than the estimated project costs. However, I was still short of the target I had set myself and suggested to my DG that he let me continue.

My DG responded saying it was time to give someone else a chance to carry it forward. He explained that to start with, there was a unanimous view that under the prevailing conditions the fencing could not be done. And that is why Mr Rammohan, who knew my background, had called me in. Now, however, the present DG said, 'Look, you have proved that it can be done. Now let the next chap come and tell me that he can't do it!'

12

MY TRYST WITH INDIA'S OSAMA

In 2002, I returned to Delhi as IG BSF Personnel, also a crucial post in the BSF, as it deals with human resource management of personnel across all ranks. It was an important and enjoyable task, and while I was doing it, I realized that my contacts in J&K during my IGP Security stint had not forgotten me! These were people who had received protection in my time. And they stayed in touch, calling quite frequently.

One of them, whom I knew quite well, I had met during my previous stint in J&K when I was sitting and talking with the governor of the state in his office. He had entered and the governor had introduced us, but we already knew each other, as I had been responsible for his security too. He was someone whom I knew I could trust. In 2003, when we had ensured that the Indian tricolour was hoisted at Lal Chowk in Srinagar at the height of militancy, he was one of those who had shouted pro-India slogans and proudly waved the Indian national flag.

The governor had said to me, 'Please look after him.'

The governor of J&K requesting the state's IGP Security to look after someone: I knew what that meant. Deploy security personnel, give him a safe car, make sure he stays safe—and don't ask questions.

Raising the Indian tricolour with pride on Independence Day, at Lal Chowk, Srinagar

I had said, 'Sir, no problem.'

In time, we had become friendly. And now, when I had left J&K and was in Delhi, he was calling me to say, 'Can you come back?'

One day he said, 'Sir, *Ghazi Baba shehar mein hai.* (Ghazi Baba is in town.)'

And that became a refrain.

I would say, what can I do? You need to report this to the right quarters! You can give my name if you like but this should be conveyed to the IGP Srinagar, not to me! They will make inquiries and take action. Then two or three days later, I would get the call again.

'What can I do?'

'No sir, you have to come. Please come back. You're the only one who can do this. We know you will take care of it.'

It had now been three years since the attack on the Indian Parliament masterminded by the terrorist Shabaz Khan, better known as Ghazi Baba. A Pakistani national hailing from Bahawalpur, his name was Rana Tahir Nadeem. The name Ghazi is a title of victory, signifying one who has achieved a military mission successfully without being conquered. He had indeed remained in hiding, and the people who were calling me, local Kashmiris, were determined that he should not get away with it. I suppose my Paan Singh reputation gave them the sense that I would see to it.

As it so happened, the incumbent IG BSF in Srinagar had developed a medical condition and was requesting a move to a place with better medical facilities, where he did not have to live surrounded by snow. Well, I was IG Personnel, and when the DG instructed me to issue his posting orders to his hometown, I did so. Then a few days later, the DG mused to me, 'Now who shall I send there in his place?'

I instinctively replied—and I must admit that Veena was quite annoyed with me about this!—'Sir, with your permission, I can go.'

IPS officers who go on deputation to the BSF are required to do so only on one frontier. I had done mine in Jammu, and as per these norms, I was not required to do any more. I could have completed my five-year tenure in Delhi itself.

My DG Gurbachan Jagat, an excellent officer whom I had worked with as IG J&K, reassured me, 'There is no need to take up this difficult and dangerous assignment. You have given enough and more. It's time for you to spend time with your family.'

No decision was made, but he retired, and the new DG was Ajay Raj Sharma, previously the commissioner of police, Delhi. Mr Sharma was from the UP cadre, and he was posted in Agra when I was SP Bhind, so we knew each other well. It was during his tenure as commissioner of police there that the attack on the Indian Parliament took place. This naturally gave him a very strong urge to bring the Ghazi Baba story to a satisfactory conclusion.

I said to him, 'Sir, if you want Ghazi Baba, send me there. I can get him.'

At that point, this was just a wild claim. I was depending on somebody's assurance. Could I really do it? I had never used this informer for such a task before. We had a relationship of trust and faith and confidence, that was about it. And here I was, using it as the basis for a tall claim to my DG!

But Mr Sharma looked at me and asked simply, 'How long will it take you?'

'Well, sir,' I reminded him, 'we have both worked in the dacoit areas. There's never a statute or time limit to these things! We have to put in effort, make his life miserable. It all depends on how long his lifeline is—on his fate, on our fate!'

I got posted as IG BSF J&K in mid-2003, and took up my residence in the quarters allotted in Srinagar. Within two or three days, my informer arrived to see me. We discussed the matter and made plans, and I realized that we could easily set up a joint operation. Before doing so, however, I wanted to do a recce of the place. I had no intention of barging in with guns blazing—I wanted to know what to expect and go in only when I was fully prepared. My informer agreed to this, and we set out in a camouflage vehicle.

When I say 'camouflage', what I mean is that we were not travelling with a pilot and spare in front with eight or 10 vehicles following. I was in a non-BSF vehicle. The number plate was changed, there was no red light, no siren. All of us were wearing civvies. For the boys, this was new—they had never seen an IG of the BSF enter a militancy-affected area in plain clothes without security staff. We were carrying weapons, of course, but these were well concealed.

That day, we drove around the place without making our presence felt. There were a few BSF battalions located in the area because the BSF was in charge of Srinagar. However, I didn't want anyone in my unit to know what we were planning.

Back at home that night, I sat down to sketch the locality and plan how we would proceed. Gazing at what I had drawn, I realized that something was missing. What was it? I could not put my finger on it and eventually decided that I had to go back. I called my informer, explained my requirement, and he reluctantly agreed, warning me that if they saw us snooping around a second time, they were likely to suspect something.

We set out once more after a few days in a Tata Sumo, with the PSO next to my driver, Harinder, and the informer sitting to my right on the back seat. Arriving in the area, he directed us towards a small alley. All of a sudden, he yelled: 'Janaab! There he is! That is Ghazi Baba!'

I did have an idea of what Ghazi Baba looked like from news reports. In 2001, when the Parliament House attack took place, I was posted as IG BSF Jammu; I happened to be on a tour to Rajouri at the time and remember my DG asking me if I'd heard the news. A week or so later, I was visiting one of the units and, sitting for a while in the recreation room for the constabulary, I leafed through some magazines. One of them was a Hindi *India Today* that carried a photograph of Ghazi Baba with a woman, playing with a child. It also mentioned that the girl was his third wife and she belonged to Tral. Yes, this was the same man, we clearly had Ghazi Baba right in front of us!

I tapped Harinder's shoulder, saying, '*Roko*! Stop the car!'

I had my hand on the door handle and was opening the door, ready to leap out when my informer grabbed my forearm in a tight grip and shouted urgently, 'Hurry! Drive fast! *Jaldi, jaldi*, we must leave immediately!' There was panic in his voice, and Harinder was absolutely clear in his mind whose orders he should follow! Without the slightest hesitation, he stepped on the accelerator, driving like a madman, and got us back home in about 20 minutes instead of the usual thirty.

My informer was still sitting with my arm in a tight grip, and my arm was turning blue. It was August, not yet winter; the weather was still pleasant. We arrived at my home. Seating my informer on a chair in the living room, I walked through my bedroom into the attached bathroom and poured warm water on my arm to restore the circulation.

Till then, I had not uttered a word to him, nor had he given any explanation for his hysterical reaction. By the time I came back to the living room, my orderly, who knew that I liked my Kashmiri guests to be served kebabs (though I myself did not eat kebabs), had served him a plate. He stood up from his meal and gave me a hug.

'Janaab, there's one thing I forgot to tell you. I'm so sorry, that was a mistake,' he said.

'What?' I asked.

'When Ghazi Baba comes out into the open, it is to make a phone call to Pakistan. We know which PCO he makes his calls from. We also know that whenever he goes out on his own, he wears a belt of explosives. Always. Whether he is armed or not, under his Pathan suit, there are always explosives. When I saw you telling the driver to stop, I knew that you were going to jump out and run to catch him. And the rest of us would also follow to help you. And I knew what was going to happen next. You did not know about the explosives, but I did—that is the reason why I stopped you.'

Initially I didn't know whether to believe him. But then I realized that here was a young man whom I had known five or six years ago. He had retained contact with me and kept insisting that I come back to Kashmir to help solve an important national problem. And he had made all the arrangements I asked for. Look at the man's fidelity. Look at the man's sincerity. Look at the man's loyalty. He knew me well and could anticipate my reactions, and he had stopped me from consequences that would have been fatal to all of us. I felt satisfied with his explanation.

Making the final changes to the layout map I had prepared, I knew that we were ready. I knew exactly what was where, what the possibilities were, and what we would have to do if we needed to launch an operation. And I had full confidence that my team would rise to the occasion.

Entering the Lair of a Terrorist

On the night of 29 August 2003, at about 9.30 or 10.00 p.m., I received information from my commandant of Battalion 60 that Narendra Nath Dhar Dubey, the second-in-command (2IC) who was now in charge, had asked for me. He wanted to see me, I was told, because he had received information about where Ghazi Baba was.

So far, I had not told anyone I was working with why I was back in J&K. Quite often, in the forces it is more practical to keep certain things secret even from your immediate subordinates. It's better that way, because you never know who will talk where and how information will leak. Nobody knew that my posting had a specific purpose—nobody except my DG and ADG. On arrival,

I had not discussed the matter of Ghazi Baba with any of my subordinates or inquired about his whereabouts or anything of that sort. I trusted my informer, and that was enough. Nobody knew what information the informer was bringing. So, when Mr Dubey phoned me, I said okay, I'm coming. And I wondered whether what he was going to show me would match what I had already seen.

What had happened was that a man had been apprehended. Prime Minister Atal Bihari Vajpayee was visiting J&K, and my BSF personnel were patrolling every small bylane of downtown Srinagar. A patrol party had halted a man walking, moving a bicycle along with his right hand, to question him. Instead of stopping and answering them, he panicked and tried to escape. They overpowered him, and a search revealed a belt of grenades wrapped around his body, a pouch of prime grenades and magazines, and a bag on his bicycle carrier that held an AK-47 rifle. His left knee was fitted with a wireless set and a pistol was strapped to his right leg. There was no indication why he was so heavily armed.

For one hour, he did not give a single clue as to who he was, so they changed their tactics. Eventually, it came out that he was a Pakistani. He led the interrogating team to his house and showed them his secret chamber. From it, they recovered a huge armoury of pistols, hand grenades, rocket bombs, as well as a map of New Delhi, ₹65,000 in cash, and a scanner machine to make fake ID cards. This man was the deputy chief of Jaish-e-Mohammed, second in command to Ghazi Baba. He revealed some of Ghazi Baba's routine and his call sign, but he did not know where Ghazi Baba's safe house was and neither did Ghazi Baba know where his hideout was. This was tactical planning by the Inter-Services Intelligence (ISI) so that if one of them was caught, the other's location would remain unknown.

Vijay Raman inspects the recovered weapons;
photo courtesy N.N.D. Dubey

Two days later, after interrogating the owner of the house, my officers located the carpenter who had made the secret chamber. With some persuasion, the carpenter led them to the location of another safe house in the Noor Bagh area, which he told us he had equipped with similar secret chambers. This confirmed what I had seen, and I was now sure that the place he was talking about was the same one my informer had taken us to.

There is sometimes a competitive wariness that arises in the forces. BSF personnel sometimes feel that IPS officers are not as well trained and experienced as they are, that they are unaware of the basics of tactic and strategy, and that when it comes to border management and taking on militants, they are far more professional. Well, all that was of no consequence! I was only interested in knowing whether what this person was saying was true or not, and I realized that it was true.

Suggesting that we wait until sunrise to begin our assault on Ghazi Baba's den, I left the arrangements—manpower, firearms, transport, and so on—in the able hands of 2IC N.N.D. Dubey, returned to my office and waited. At about 3.30 a.m., my phone rang. An attack had been made; a number of our men were injured and were now in hospital.

I called up the GOC core commander, Lieutenant General Nirbhay Sharma, and informed him that some of my boys were injured and were being sent to the military hospital. He assured me that they would be taken good care of. I left to visit the hospital to meet the injured boys and, satisfied that they were being given the best treatment possible, I proceeded to the site.

The End of a Menace

The building was surrounded and a huge crowd was watching. The DIG was there, and I requested him to get a local person to make an announcement, asking for all civilians to come out. The announcement was made, the doors opened and people began walking out. We could see elderly people, women, children, infants.

One of them was a young woman with a child, and I recognized her. I had seen her when I was IG BSF Personnel in Delhi, on a visit to Tral, a small place with two BSF battalions. I had been sitting in the commandant's room, a small temporary settlement, when he pointed out a young girl walking outside carrying an infant child and said, 'That is Ghazi Baba's third wife, with his child. They live here.' And now the same woman was here. Ghazi Baba was certainly inside.

The civilians had all come out. There was firing coming from inside, but we had not stopped firing either.

I received a message that GOC Nirbhay Sharma wanted to speak to me, so I went to a nearby battalion to place my call. 'Vijay, do you need any assistance? Do you need additional manpower? Anything that I can do?' he asked. I reassured him that we were handling things. Then he wanted to know why we had not blown up the building.

In a case like this, where a wanted terrorist is known to be holed up, it is not considered necessary to wait—the building can be blown up. But we could not do this because two of our men were lying injured on the terrace.

I explained my reason. He immediately offered to send a helicopter to airlift the boys.

I said, 'Sir, this is a very highly populated place and the local police have just arrived. We don't know who else lives here. If there is even one militant somewhere and he takes a pot shot, a chance shot at our helicopter, the news in Pakistan will be that they have gunned down an Indian Army helicopter! I would like to avoid that. Let us wait and get the fellow.'

He then asked, 'Who, Vijay? Whom are you after?'

I told him, adding that my information was absolutely gospel.

And then he said something to me that I can never forget: 'Vijay, since the Parliament attack, a large number of security agencies have killed a large number of Ghazi Babas! So, tread carefully, dear boy.'

Those words stuck in my mind, and in the years to come, I would repeat them often. GOC Sharma went on to serve as a member of the UPSC and later the governor of Arunachal Pradesh. One day, I was attending a UPSC meeting and mentioned to others there what GOC Sharma had said to me that day. He stopped me with, '*Bas karo, bhaiyya!* (Come on, man, stop it!) I think we've all heard that one once too often!'

But this was truly one of the best pieces of advice I have ever received.

India's Osama Slain

N.N.D. Dubey had taken a full burst of bullets to his chest, from which he never fully recovered, even after multiple surgeries, and eventually took premature retirement as he was left partially disabled. I campaigned very earnestly for him to receive the Ashoka Chakra for this encounter, a gallantry medal given to army personnel for action during peacetime, but somehow could not manage it; he only received the Kirti Chakra.

His adventure had begun in the early hours of that day. After apprehending the deputy chief and finding the carpenter, the team had not slept for three days and decided to get some rest. At 3.00 a.m., they left for Shah Manzil where the troops were waiting, along with the carpenter. It was night and completely silent, so they could not use a vehicle. They walked to Noor Bagh and surrounded the house. As they stood there watching it, the top-floor light came on and then went off. There was no indication why. Nothing else was seen.

Silently, Dubey and his boys entered the house along with the carpenter. They passed a room on the ground floor where some women and children were sleeping. As they climbed the stairs, a woman with a baby in her arms was climbing down. She was later identified as Ghazi Baba's wife, and a laminated photo of her in army camouflage, holding an AK-47 and wearing an Afghan cap, was found in his wallet!

They searched the first floor and found nothing. There was nothing on the second floor. And then they reached the top floor. It was dark. They entered a bedroom that was about 10 ft x 12 ft. There was nobody in it, no indication of occupancy. There were nine of them in the room, plus the carpenter. The rest were still climbing the stairs. There was nothing to be found, and they grilled the carpenter once again. He pointed at a large mirror fitted into the wall. There was a tray at the bottom of the mirror with perfume, lotion and deodorant bottles. It looked like an ordinary dressing mirror.

The moment the carpenter indicated the mirror, one of Dubey's officers hit it hard—and they were immediately met with a burst of gunfire.

Until that moment, Ghazi Baba had remained inactive. He had seen the men coming. He was sitting in a chamber behind the mirror. And—in those days when such things were rare and mostly unknown—he had fitted close-circuit TV cameras with a night vision device on top of the mirror. Later, in a media briefing, I displayed the beard, turbans, disguises, American jackets, photo albums and other incriminating items that were discovered in the hideout, live on TV.

Right from the beginning, even as they entered the building, Ghazi Baba had been watching. They were not aware of this. He probably did not open fire because he did not know that the carpenter was in their custody. He probably thought that they would search the house, find nothing and leave, and he could go back to his life and activities as before.

The volley of bullets from Ghazi Baba and the two others who were with him did their damage. One hit my jawan Balveer Singh Shekhawat. He was subsequently awarded the Shaurya Chakra. Five were injured and left the room. Now there were only three—C.P. Trivedi, M.R. Binuchandran and Dubey.

Ghazi Baba's deputy, Tariq Bhai, was firing. He threw a grenade and jumped from the balcony. In his attempt to escape, he was killed by the forces deployed on the ground floor.

Dubey moved to fire 15 rounds from his AK-47. That was when he realized that he could not move his right hand because it had been hit by a burst of bullets. Then a bullet was shot into his stomach, he received another in his right leg, another in his left shoulder, and a pellet in his finger. Dubey was put into a Gypsy and taken to the hospital, where seven bullets were extracted from his body.

There were three escape routes. One was through the stairs they climbed, the second was the balcony. The third was an iron staircase Ghazi Baba had designed for his escape. It was only after the entire building was demolished in the operation that the staircase was exposed. But as long as Trivedi and Binuchandran were in the building, there was no way we could blow it up. My mind was fixated on how to get my officers down.

One of the constables standing with me that evening happened to be a Keralite like me. He said, 'Sir, we have so many battalions around, why don't we collect mattresses from them and stack up a hundred mattresses against the wall? Then we can tell the officers on the roof to come to the edge and jump on to the mattresses.' Yes—a great idea! But I had to take credit for the idea myself because if I had said, 'Wow, this constable has had a great idea—go quickly and bring all the mattresses you can find,' the DIGs and commandants would have scoffed. How can a constable have a good idea? Unfortunately, this is the way our forces work.

I gave the order, and while the men were enthusiastically arranging for the soft landing, I got one of the injured boys on the wireless.

As fate would have it, one of the boys stranded on top of the building, a deputy commandant rank officer, was also a Keralite. I spoke to Binu in Malayalam, telling him we knew they were injured but were arranging a soft fall for them and asked whether they would be able to roll to the side of the terrace and jump or slip over the edge to where the mattresses were being laid out. 'We'll be there to hold you,' I reassured him. And we were: the ambulances were waiting, doctors were waiting, and they were rushed to the hospital where others who had been injured were also being treated.

Then, once the boys were taken to safety, there was nothing to stop the forces from bombarding the building. India's Osama was gone.

'Are You Sure You Got the Right One?'

Two bodies were recovered from the building. However, what GOC Nirbhay Sharma had told me was still ringing in my ears and I did not want to commit to the media until I was completely certain! The one person who could conclusively identify the body as that of Ghazi Baba was the *India Today* photographer. I sent people to locate him.

In the debris of the building, it was also discovered that the frame of the entrance door had a rotating door with a CCTV, so that everything happening outside could be seen.

The bodies were brought first to the BSF control room and then, as the public were assembling to see them, I gave permission for them to be taken to the ground. Yes, I could see that it was Ghazi Baba all right—the photographer would confirm this later—but now he was clean-shaven, not bearded as when I had seen him a few days before. The other body remained unidentified until a few days later.

For now, we could finally announce with authority that yes, we had slain the criminal. Congratulatory messages poured in. The governor himself came to my office and very graciously got Home Minister L.K. Advani on the phone who congratulated me. He then got the PM Atal Bihari Vajpayee on the phone and he too said warm words of praise for the BSF and my team. Later, I had occasion to meet the PM at my DG's residence on the Raising Day of the BSF, and he knew who I was. We had never met before, but he talked about the achievements in Srinagar and that was a gratifying moment indeed. As I addressed the press and basked in all the praise, the message that I repeatedly tried to convey was that this was not my victory—it was the success of the team and I felt so grateful to each one of them. A number of gallantry medals were given for this encounter.

Shaking hands with Atal Bihari Vajpayee

Tracking Ghazi Baba, I had also seen that he used to change his call sign regularly. During the period in which this encounter took place, his call sign was Victor-2. After the encounter, the message being conveyed between the militant stations was, 'Victor-2 *Allah ko pyaare ho gaye.* (Victor-2 is no more.)'

The tone and tenor of those messages, the manner in which the voice conveying the message was breaking, were very emotional rather than the abusive, aggressive language usually used. From these messages I did feel confident that I had got my target. When the photographer was brought to me, he too identified the body. Since he had seen Ghazi Baba with a beard, we had kept an artificial beard ready at hand so that there would be no doubt.

At the site of the encounter, with the corpses of Ghazi Baba and a gang member, and the items confiscated from their lair

To the surprise and disbelief of the local police, the job was done. I had fulfilled my promise to my DG; I had fulfilled my promise to my informer; my mission was accomplished, and it was time for me to leave.

This brought my three stints in J&K, all very rewarding and fruitful, to a close. There was much nostalgia and many friends and well-wishers remained in touch. I had interacted with the spectrum of the BSF, both officers and men. Just as in MP I was identified with the Paan Singh encounter, here I came to be known through two major events: initiating the border fencing in Jammu, and the annihilation of Ghazi Baba in Srinagar. I could now go back to my cadre.

> It's the policeman who must create terror in the terrorist.

During this intense and difficult period, Sheru, the family's beloved dog, would be waiting when Vijay returned home. They would spend quality time together while the helpers waited, leading him away after they had finished bonding. Sheru was a big support in the evenings when he was on his own and Veena and Vikram were away in Delhi

13

THE DARKEST DAY OF MY LIFE

MP is a good cadre, with good people—a good place to work in. In 2004, I was posted to Bhopal as ADG MP Police. After about five years, a vacancy came up for Special DG CRPF in Delhi, and I opted for it. The CRPF was the third of the paramilitary forces I would be serving in.

It was at this time that the Naxal problem was assuming great proportions. They were wreaking havoc, and central government intervention was called for in a large number of states. The government had created a common grid and wanted a senior officer to be their first commander, and I was picked for the post. My headquarters were at Raipur to begin with, and subsequently at Kolkata. It was from here that I retired after two years, in 2011.

As Special DG Anti-Naxal Operations in the CRPF, I was heading a unified command. However, different states have their different ethos and work practices, and these need to be streamlined accordingly. In Maharashtra, the Naxal population was concentrated in the Gadchiroli area; they were in parts of MP; and the most highly infested was Chhattisgarh. Orissa, Jharkhand and West Bengal were all badly infested. Each had different types of governments with their own priorities, and sometimes the cooperation required from local police was lacking. Amongst all these states, I must admit that Maharashtra was the most effective and I got the best results in Gadchiroli. We had the best cooperation, and they also had a crack force called 'C 60', very specialized. It's a great force.

The Root of the Matter

When I visited villages in this area as SP Raipur, I was shocked and distressed to learn that many people here had still not received compensation for their land that were acquired by the government more than 50 years previously.

In these areas, the tribal people live in the forest areas and live off the forest. For them, the land is precious—very, very dear. Over the years, I have begun to understand the fundamental problem of how Naxalism emerged, dating back to the mid-1950s, when our giant public sector steel plants were coming up: in Bhilai, Rourkela, Durgapur, Bokaro and other places. The Tatas also built one in Jamshedpur. For all of these, land close to the mines had to be acquired, and these were tribal lands.

The public sector undertakings (PSU) belong to the central government. But the Government of India doesn't deal directly; it must go through the state, and it is the local government representatives and collector who acquire land for a PSU. They earmark the land and payment is made through them. So, whatever went amiss took place locally. It was at the grassroots level that somebody did not play their role properly, efficiently, effectively and sincerely. The government representatives unfortunately—and this has happened all over the country at every level—did not actually represent the nobility of the government. They were people with their own defects and personal inadequacies, and these are what left their mark.

The tribal areas are also very sensitive because they have their own social norms that are different from the mainstream, with traditions that people from cultures prevailing in other parts of India are unlikely to understand. I had experienced this during my MP Darshan as a trainee in 1977. It was fascinating to visit the tribal villages, never imagining that one day in the distant future, it would be my duty to confront the Naxal menace in this region. We travelled on forest roads as far as possible and then walked, trekking through the forest for hours. I remember one visit to a village on top of a hill. It was evening, and most of the villagers had gone to the fields to drink sulfi. This is a local intoxicant that has some food value, and the custom is that it should be taken only before sunrise or after sunset. They returned by about 8.00 p.m. On hearing that some officials had arrived, they rushed to meet us, quickly lighting a bonfire in the centre and seating us around it. Most of the men of the village assembled there, and through an interpreter we spoke to them of various things and became aware of their innocence and lack of worldly knowledge. We had carried our own provisions, as nothing that we were used to eating was available in the village. After a late-night dinner, we retired for the day on bamboo cots kindly provided to us. We got a good sense of how the tribals lived, their livestock, their food, the way they hunted, and their system of medicine.

To preserve their culture and protect them from exploitation, their areas were restricted by the government. Though the arrangement was set up for their protection, over time and as the world around them progressed, it also isolated them completely. With no outside agency given any access so that there would be no interference, even government agencies did not connect with them. I remember that there was only one All India Radio station in that area, and it had such a weak transmission system that whatever was being broadcast could not be heard even 20 km away. The government even lacked a system by which they could communicate with these people.

It is not surprising that the government was unable to protect tribal land from being forcibly taken over by upper castes. The area has rich forest diversity and some forest produce is of great commercial value. While the government is committed, on paper, to preserving the forests and honouring its residents, in reality there has been a lot of smuggling of forest produce. The wily buyers have exploited the innocent tribals, ensuring that they remain indebted and impoverished.

When the Naxals entered, they easily filled the vacuum that the government should have responsibly occupied. They provided medical and other services, even essential items for daily living—and with this local governance, they were able to unobtrusively replace the position the Indian government should have held. And that is how what they said soon became the law. The philosophy was imported, but these people were ripe to grasp and take it. I saw this in Bhilai and there is nothing to stop us from believing that there may have been a similar situation in Bokaro, Durgapur and Rourkela too. These are the most badly impacted states, where Naxalism thrives.

A Day of Tragedy

It was the worst day of my life, and remembering 6 April 2010 would always bring me sorrow. That was the day on which my brave CRPF men were killed in the course of their duties.

An inquiry was conducted by a one-member committee consisting of the retired IPS officer E.N. Rammohan, and he submitted his report in 15 days.

When I reflect on that time, my most persistent thought is whether the policy of flooding that area with force was really the best solution. The media even gave a name to this: Operation Green Hunt. Was another solution possible? A large number of BSF, CRPF and ITBP battalions, a large number of people who knew nothing about the terrain, who knew nothing about the problem—were pumped in, in large numbers. We had senior police officers who were sent to the area as advisers because they had dealt with militancy in Punjab by flooding it with paramilitary forces. However, the situation here was so very different! Punjab was more urbanized; this area was backward. And its people had been oppressed and marginalized for decades. We flooded the area with people, weapons, a huge number of landmines; too many casualties took place. I don't know whether that was the right policy. I do believe that the more we try to deal with their issues with military options, the more the movement will spread, the more it will become stronger. I know that this view is shared by Mr Rammohan and many others like us. We have to understand that this is an issue of social justice. Here, too, people have been oppressed by upper castes.

Many years have passed, but the Naxal attacks on the paramilitary forces and the encounters by the latter have continued. There have been surrenders, things have improved somewhat. We can only hope for the best.

> When adversity strikes, remain brave. Accept the circumstances, and continue to do your best.

14

A LAST HURRAH

I retired from active service in 2011 and we settled in Pune, giving us the opportunity to be near our close and extended family members, and some dear friends who were also living there. Veena and I both took up volunteer work, Veena at an NGO and I at Bhandarkar Oriental Research Institute, where I was involved in streamlining the administration.

I now had plenty of time for reflection! Looking around me, I could see the huge changes that had taken place in the challenges faced by the police. When I first started my career, I worked in the Chambal, and my task was to capture dacoits and bring law and order to a very unstable region. In those days, many parts of India faced thugs, dacoits, ransom demands and revenge killing. In the cities, our job was to catch pickpockets, black marketeers, gamblers, conmen and distillers of illicit hooch. At the other end of the spectrum were the murderers and rapists.

While caste crimes and honour killing remain prevalent in rural India even today, globalization and technology have brought more urban offences such as cybercrime into the interiors. Terrorism too has changed the world—not just policing but even the security practices of daily life. In many other ways as well, the modus operandi has been changing. From country-made pistols and 12-bore guns, we have moved more to chemical, nuclear and drone attacks, and laser guns. There are fewer pickpockets, more snatchers of chains and mobile phones. While we had more burglaries in the past, today robberies are increasingly seen as 'insider' jobs. Online fraud, money laundering, narcotics—these are the challenges of modern law-keeping. One of the biggest changes is the greater attention given to crimes against women, which in the past were often condoned, as they were ingrained in society and tradition.

Just as I started getting used to a quiet life, a phone call changed things. It was a day in November 2015. The High Court of Madhya Pradesh had ordered for an SIT to function as a watchdog committee of the court and also to supervise the Special Task Force (STF) investigating the Vyapam examination scam, and I had been selected to lead the police investigation.

Vyapam, the Madhya Pradesh Professional Examination Board (MPPEB), is best known by its Hindi acronym, where 'vyakahrik' means professional, 'pariksha' is examination, and 'mandal' is board. Headed by a senior government official, it was set up in the early 1970s to prevent public entrance examination malpractices in regions where students would enter exam halls with knives, cheating, copying, and using various malpractices to get marks higher than they deserved, to qualify to enter professional institutions. Vyapam streamlined the process of conducting examinations, announcing results, making selection lists, arranging counselling, and giving college admission certificates, but over time things went horribly wrong. Preying on the ambitious parents who push their children to enter professional institutions they are not capable of getting admission into, touts hired students who had already passed the examination to impersonate children who would not be able to get admission on their own merit.

The SIT was headed by a retired High Court judge, Justice Chandresh Bhushan. C.L.M. Reddy was appointed as Member, Technical. I had retired as Special DG of the CRPF, having served in senior positions in the SPG, BSF and CRPF, and as IG J&K. These were all connected with what I had been recruited into the force for, trained for, and had been groomed for. This appointment was different, and I recognized it as a singular honour. It was a call from the higher judiciary. The attributes sought were probity, sincerity, concession, dedication to work, and integrity. I took it as the highest compliment.

It was a pleasure and an honour for me to work along with Justice Bhushan and C.L.M. Reddy, professionals of the highest order. After a few months of the inquiry, however, the investigation was handed over to another government body.

I returned to Pune and continued with the routine Veena and I had settled into. We were fortunate to come across the Chinmaya Study Circle, which was not far from our home. This gave me a wonderful opportunity to reflect in a spiritual way on the actions I had taken during my policing career.

I have never been a person who performed mindless rituals, but I always had a strong spiritual streak and connection to the divine. We began to get immersed in the teachings of Vedanta, which were beautifully shared with us through reading, discussion, and a summing up by Swami Siddheshananda of the Chinmaya Mission. We both looked forward to the weekly Wednesday classes and for me, the teachings gave a context to the events of my life. If I ever spoke about the decisions made and incidents that had taken place during the course of my duties, Swami-ji would put them into perspective.

During the pandemic, classes continued on Zoom and then resumed in person. Unfortunately, my health came in the way of my attendance. The teachings gave me the strength to cope with the knowledge of my uncertain future. I kept in mind the words of Swami Chinmayananda: 'We should seek the Lord's Grace to keep us on the path of virtue, courage and wisdom, and the belief that service to our country is service to the Lord of Lords.'

I hope and pray I did not disappoint the Lord.

With BSF jawans at the battalion bada khana. Vijay Raman was always adored and respected by his team as someone who cared deeply about them. He was always recognized as a people's man, a forces man; one who would always say, after every achievement, 'I may be the leader, but they are the ones who did it.'

Vijay's other family! Gathered in Delhi to celebrate the birth of Vijay and Veena's grandson, Shaurya

EPILOGUE

A MEMORABLE INTRODUCTION

M.D. Sharma remained my boss for the first seven years of my career. For me, it was a very fulfilling process of education and understanding all aspects of policing. Many years later, long after my trysts with Paan Singh and Ghazi Baba were over, I happened to be in Delhi and was invited to attend a small private celebration at the Delhi Gymkhana Club. It was a select gathering of senior police officers and when M.D. Sharma saw me, he was very happy, as I was to see him.

As he spoke to the crowd, he asked me to come up, so that he could introduce me. And here is what he said, in summary:

> Here's the man who was my favourite probationer. I've had so many probationers—but none, none like him.
>
> This is the boy who terminated Paan Singh and, recently in J&K, he got Ghazi Baba too.
>
> But before all this, I must tell you, this boy started his foray into encounters as a probationer, arresting seven dacoits by firing just two 12-bore bullets. Would you call that a police encounter with dacoits? He fired two bullets, and he brought the gang back to the police station tied to the bullock carts they were transported in so that they could not run away.
>
> And he has not changed since then. The quality of the person, the integrity of the person, the clear knowledge that here is someone whom no temptation can lure! These are the very best qualities of this officer.

These words of regard and affection will always remain with me because they put into context all my doubts regarding legality, illegality, morality, immorality, propriety, non-propriety, and what a policeman should do in situations of uncertainty and conflict.

A life well lived

THE GENTLEMAN BEHIND THE COP

An afterword by
Veena Raman

Vijay saw himself as an introvert, and this was sometimes mistaken for the arrogance of a successful person. But it was his nature. He wrote about it in this letter to me when he was young. And he did not change!

> Ever since I left school, I have developed a strange liking for loneliness.
>
> This is not to suggest that I am not friendly or not interested in people! I am certainly interested in people, and would always like to be of assistance and useful to others. But if and when I am faced with any problem, dilemma or setback, I have never found it possible to unburden myself before anybody to seek solace and consolation which I believe is the role that friends should play. Even with a lifelong association I doubt whether you also may be able to understand me perfectly.

Reading the many letters he had sent me over the years brought me a little comfort after he passed away. He was mature even as a young man, and stuck to his values right till the end. Sometimes, he wrote on particular themes—once on the quote 'happiness is being married to your best friend':

> Veena, for a man to have a successful and satisfying career, a lot depends on the atmosphere that prevails in his home,

> and the rapport between him and his wife. Being brilliant or smart or intelligent are only some of the criteria for success. What is far more important is a stable personal life which affords peace and tranquillity of mind.

In one of his letters, he mentioned the selections for the women's World Cup hockey tournament to be held in Jaipur in early 1979, and expressed his feeling of guilt that he had come in the way of my hockey ambitions. He assured me that I was free to take my own decisions in the matter, and that he would welcome them no matter what they were.

In the 1970s, such sentiments were extremely rare and young people of today may not understand how unusually mature and liberal the person making them would have been!

Soon after we were married, I learnt one day that Major Dhyan Chand, one of the greatest hockey players of all time, who took India to two Olympic gold medals in the 1960s, had been invited to a district sports meet in Dabra, where we were living. I asked Vijay if I could go along, and he was absolutely fine with it, though we both knew that I would be the only woman there. In fact, it turned out to be a topic of gossip among our neighbours: how shameless I was to sit and laugh and talk amongst men. But for me, that was nothing compared to the two hours of very fulfilling conversation I had with my supreme hockey guru, as well as the faith and support of my husband.

As a young man, he had written to me of the debt we all have to our parents, and the physical impossibility of ever repaying it. Sure enough, when his parents grew older, he was the ideal son, focused on their comfort, physically present with them whenever it was possible. His father had been extremely strict with him when he was young, grooming him as a role model for his younger brothers, and when he died, Vijay was distraught, appreciative of the upbringing that had given him the discipline and high standards by which he lived his life.

Looking back, I can see that it was in 2010 that Vijay's body had begun preparing for the next phase, when he suffered a stroke.

Vijay had been highly successful in everything he did, and the Dantewada attack was the biggest personal challenge of his life. Friends, family and support staff were encouraging and supportive, and helped him deal with the situation and overcome the grief of loss as well as his disappointment with himself.

I was in Delhi and he was in Kolkata, the headquarters of the CRPF Naxal operations. His left side was paralysed. His DG, Vikram Srivastav, a good friend who had worked with him in the SPG, was extremely helpful and took care of all the logistics. He arranged for Vijay to be brought back to Delhi. K. Vijaykumar, who took over as DG from him, was also very supportive. As he healed with regular physiotherapy, our nine-month-old grandson Shaurya's smile and antics, and seeing him grow, were like a tonic that helped him bounce back.

Vijay's last years were peaceful and happy. His illness was difficult for us, but we never let him see our fear or grief. After we lost him, it gave me comfort to continue working on his book till it was complete, reliving the memories of our life together, and knowing that his valour, his dedication to truth and justice, and his achievements would live on in the minds of those who read about them.

ACKNOWLEDGEMENTS

I am grateful to those without whose support Vijay's memoirs could not have been completed.

Saaz Aggarwal, for understanding and accurately compiling and presenting Vijay's life.

Dr Ram Datar, for helping me record a series of interviews with Vijay. They were an invaluable resource.

Our daughter-in-law Divya and son Vikram, for their meticulous manuscript reviews.

N.N.D. Dubey, for sharing his memories.

Preeti Gill, for being a sounding board and guiding me throughout the journey.

Sonali Singh, Devika Nadiq and many friends and family members, whose support was crucial. Thank you.

Last but not least, I am grateful to Dibakar Ghosh of Rupa Publications and his team for their excellent cooperation. Vijay was a hero to all who knew him, but he considered himself an ordinary person, and I'm grateful to them for enshrining his characteristic reaction, 'Did I really do all this?'

—Veena Raman

विख्यात धावक

डाकू पानसिंह

ഗാസി ബാബയെ വധിച്ച സംഘത്തെ നയിച്ചത് മലയാളി ഐ.ജി.

WORLD RECORD

GUINNESS BOOK OF RECORDS

दैनिक जा

का मास्टरमाइंड गाजी बाबा ढेर

ष बदलने में माहिर था गाजी बाबा

The Statesman

the slain: Jaish ■ Parliament accused to identify body: minister

pa shot in Srinagar...

RESIDENT'S | SPECIAL | PRESIDENT'S | MERITORIUS | 50TH

Statesman
Sunday 31 August 2003
Ghazi Baba shot in Srinaga
After tackling
jay Raman comes to Naxa
VIJAY RAMAN
R.K. KAISTHA
PRIME MINISTER
New Delhi
July 23, 1983
ar Shri Vijay Raman,
Congratulations on your undertaking the "Circumnavigation of the World" by car. It is indeed gratifying to know that the Guinness Book of Records have recognized your claim for the World Record for this event.
You have done us proud.
With regards.
Yours sincerely,
(P.V. Narasimha Rao)
ARGEST SELLING
CYCLE
IGHT
STRATEGY